THE
PERFECT FATHER

The True Story of Chris Watts,
His All-American Family, and a Shocking Murder

JOHN GLATT

St. Martin's Paperbacks

Published in the United States by St. Martin's Paperbacks, an imprint of St. Martin's Publishing Group.

THE PERFECT FATHER

For information, address St. Martin's Publishing Group, 120 Broadway, New York, NY 10271.

www.stmartins.com

Library of Congress Catalog Card Number: 2020009570

ISBN: 978-1-250-78268-7

Our books may be purchased in bulk for promotional, educational, or business use. Please contact your local bookseller or the Macmillan Corporate and Premium Sales Department at 1-800-221-7945, ext. 5442, or by email at MacmillanSpecialMarkets@macmillan.com.

Printed in the United States of America

St. Martin's Press hardcover edition published 2020
St. Martin's Paperbacks edition published 2021

10 9 8 7 6 5 4 3 2 1

For my wife, Gail Freund,
for her invaluable help and encouragement

CONTENTS

PART TWO

PART THREE

ACKNOWLEDGMENTS

This is my twenty-second true-crime book and perhaps the most disturbing. There are so many unanswered questions as to why Chris Watts, a seemingly perfect father, would annihilate his entire family. Nobody who knew him saw it coming.

"He was a great father," Shanann's father, Frank Rzucek, told investigators. "Husbandwise the same way."

So what could have been going on in Chris Watts's mind to make him do the unthinkable? So far he has not undergone a single psychiatric examination and neither the prosecutors nor his public defenders have ever requested one. Perhaps if he had undergone a mental evaluation some of these questions might have been answered.

There are so many victims of this senseless crime who may never know what really happened in those early morning hours of August 13, 2018, which Chris has said he will carry to the grave. As he languishes behind bars for the rest of his life, with photographs of Shanann, Bella, and Celeste posted to the walls of his cell, who knows what he is thinking.

And although he still writes letters to Shanann and the girls, which his parents read out over their graves, so far he has shown no remorse.

Among the victims hardest hit are Chris's family. His parents, Ronnie and Cindy Watts, and his older sister, Jamie, are still trying to accept what he did. I would like to thank the Watts family for talking to me at length about the Chris they knew and their daily battle to survive the consequences of his actions. For the record, I want to make it clear that they do not benefit financially from my book.

Unfortunately, the Rzucek family did not wish to co-operate with the book and I respect this. Their lives have been shattered by the killings, and my heart goes out to them as they try to heal.

This book took eighteen months to write and I would like to thank everyone who helped me both on and off the record. I would like to especially thank Jeanna Dietz, who hired Shanann in North Carolina as a nanny and then became close to both her and Chris after they moved to Colorado to be near her. As Chris and Shanann lived in her house while their own was being built, she had a unique perspective on their relationship.

I would also like to thank Matt Francis, who took the insecure teenage Shanann under his wing in his theater class at Pinecrest High School, and gave her the confidence to become successful in business.

Other thanks goes to Dr. Michael Stone, Tyler Alore, Jamie Baxley, Trent Bolte, Colby Cruse, Joe Duty, Byron Falls, Bill Ferrie, Stacy Fowler, Mike and Coleen Hendrickson, Morgan Lankford, Claire Littlejohn, Tori Schneider, Madeline St. Armour, Nathaniel Trinastich, Don Watt, and Briana Wilson.

As always, much gratitude to Charles Spicer and Sarah Grill of St. Martin's Press for all their help, always steering me in the right direction. Thanks also to my agent, Jane Dystel, of Dystel, Goderich and Bourret Literary Management, who is always there with help, encouragement, and support.

I'd also like to thank Emily Freund, Debbie, Douglas and Taylor Baldwin, Lenny Millen, Annette Witheridge, Ian and Helen Kimmet, Jo Greenspan, Galli Curci, Chris Frost, Danny, Cari, and Allie Tractenberg, Ty Stube, Fred Taraba, Martin Gould, David Bunde, and Berns Rothschild.

THE PERFECT FATHER

PROLOGUE

Nickole Atkinson's alarm went off at 7:45 A.M. Half-asleep, she checked her cell phone for messages from Shanann Watts. A few hours earlier they had returned from a grueling weekend business trip to Scottsdale, Arizona. Bad weather had delayed their flight by more than three hours. At fifteen weeks pregnant, Shanann had been in pain and discomfort throughout.

Just before 2:00 A.M. Nickole had finally dropped Shanann off at her home at 2825 Saratoga Trail in Frederick, Colorado, waiting to leave until she was safely inside.

"Normally when we come back from these [business trips], she harasses me," explained thirty-seven-year-old Nickole. "Like, 'Come on. Let's call people. Let's get things goin'. Let's work business.'"

So it was odd that there was nothing from her team leader, especially as they had an important business lunch that day. Nickole put the lack of messages down to thirty-four-year-old Shanann's morning sickness and went back to sleep.

But after an hour passed and still no word, Nickole instinctively knew something was wrong.

Shanann had not been her usual upbeat self all weekend. The helicopter mom of two beautiful little girls, Bella, four, and Celeste, three, had been seriously depressed. Her boundless energy and optimism were replaced by a big black cloud. During the trip, she had tearfully confided that her husband, Chris, was acting strange. After six years of happy marriage she no longer knew him. Shockingly, he had informed her that he no longer wanted their new baby.

"He wasn't being the loving Chris that he normally was," said Nickole. "He wasn't touching or hugging her . . . and he wasn't being attentive to the girls."

On Saturday night Shanann had received a bank alert charge of $68 for a salmon dinner and was immediately suspicious. Chris had told her that he'd gone to a baseball game with some workmates and then dined alone. Shanann thought the price was unusually high for just one person and wondered if he was cheating. She told Nickole she would confront him about it when she got home.

All through the morning, Nickole texted and called Shanann without any response. That was unusual. Shanann lived on Facebook, promoting Thrive, the lifestyle supplement that had changed her life. The charismatic social media maven had a legion of online followers and was known for her catchphrase "I'm super-excited."

She projected the image of the perfect family with her handsome husband, Chris, and their two young daughters as costars. Shanann had even broken the news of her pregnancy to Chris in a Facebook video entitled "Oops . . . We Did It *Again*."

So it was strangely out of character for her not to have posted anything on Facebook that morning or texted anyone on her team.

Nickole also knew that Shanann had a 9:00 A.M. prenatal doctor's appointment and had been looking forward to hearing her baby's heartbeat for the first time. So after calling the doctor's office and finding Shanann had not kept the appointment, Nickole knew something was very wrong.

Finally, around midday, she drove over to Shanann's house.

Nickole hadn't wanted to bother Shanann's husband, Chris Watts, as he worked out in the oil fields. But after ringing their doorbell and getting no answer, then seeing Shanann's white Lexus in the garage, Nickole called him.

"I'm worried about Shanann," she told Chris. "Her car is here but she's not at home. Do you know where she's at?"

Chris seemed unconcerned. He said Shanann had taken their girls to a friend's house on a playdate, although he did not know which one.

Suddenly, he informed Nickole that he and Shanann were separating and selling their house.

"[Chris], your personal stuff is none of my business," Nickole told him. "That's not my concern right now. But where is your wife?"

Chris said he was too busy to talk and hung up.

Nickole wasn't the only one worried. Shanann's mother, Sandi Rzucek, and several friends had also been trying in vain to reach Shanann all morning. They, too, had spoken to Chris and were shocked by his apparent lack of concern. It just didn't add up.

Outside the house Nickole held a conference call with Sandi and several friends, to decide how to proceed.

"I'm like, 'What do I do? [Chris] said she's with a friend,'" Nickole recalled. "And they [told me], 'Call the cops!'"

PART ONE

I
A STAR PUPIL

Christopher Lee Watts was born in Fayetteville, North Carolina, on May 16, 1985, the second child of Ronnie and Cindy Watts. His sister, Jamie, was six and a half years older and helped raise him. Ronnie worked as a parts manager for a Ford dealership, while Cindy was a secretary and notary.

From an early age, Chris idolized his father, who was quiet and reserved.

"Ronnie and Chris were so close," said Cindy. "They did everything together."

Chris loved sports, and his father would take him to basketball games in the winter and football and baseball games in the summer.

They also shared a love of NASCAR and went to more than two hundred races together, including the Daytona 500. Ronnie also taught his son car mechanics, which Chris discovered a natural talent for.

Unlike his gregarious older sister, Jamie, who took after her mother, Chris was shy and withdrawn like his dad. When he started school, he was an average student but shone at sports, winning many trophies, which his parents still proudly display in their living room. His father would always come to watch him compete in school sports, cheering him on from the sidelines.

Chris was also close to his maternal grandmother, Gertrude Schottner McLeod. She would quiz him on state capitals while they waited outside Pine Forest Middle School to pick up Jamie.

"He knew all the capitals of the United States and was learning the capitals of Europe," said Cindy. "It was just something they did to pass the time."

At fourteen, Chris followed his parents and sister to Pine Forest High School, where he became even more withdrawn. He kept to himself and was uncomfortable around his schoolmates, who largely ignored him.

"He didn't go out with friends," said his sister, Jamie. "I was more of a social butterfly, and he was quiet and interested in mechanics and cars. He was just a focused person."

Chris enrolled in the Automotive Technology class taught by Joe Duty and soon became one of his star pupils. Duty was something of a mentor to Chris, believing he was destined for great things.

"It's hard to find a more perfect kid," said Duty. "He was in the top ten percent of students I ever had. He was very quiet [and] introverted, but he was always completely polite and courteous."

The gangly, tall teenager with braces and a bowl cut impressed his teacher with his encyclopedic knowledge of NASCAR stats and trivia. He was obsessed with the sport and would spend hours in his bedroom reading about it.

"He had a photographic memory," recalled Duty, "and he could recite anything you wanted to know about NASCAR from memory . . . right off the top of his head. And I was very impressed with that."

Duty was also struck by how isolated Chris was and never saw him speak to a girl, let alone have a girlfriend. Ironically, many girls at the school had crushes on the handsome teenager, who was too "awkward and shy" to do anything about it.

"That was one thing I always wondered about," Duty recalled. "Many times I would look at him and think, 'What's going on in his head?' It was like the wheels were spinning but he was by himself."

One girl Chris did become close to in high school was Brandi Smith, who remembers him being "smart and gentle."

She said, "Most of our conversations that I recall were about music and things like that. I was a bit of an outcast and he kinda just seemed to understand me."

Lance Alfonso played football with Chris and remembers him being almost too easygoing.

"I've never seen him get angry at anybody," he recalled. "[He] wouldn't hurt a fly."

In the 2002 Pine Forest High School yearbook, Chris appears in a group shot of Academy of Applied Technology students. He is also in a Patriot's Day photo spread, taken on the first anniversary of the World Trade Center 9/11 attacks.

On another yearbook page entitled "Life in the Fast Lane," Chris was asked whether American cars were better than foreign ones.

"American sports cars," says Chris, "because Fords are made in America."

Joe Duty remembers Chris driving a Ford Mustang his father had bought him and helped him fix up.

Unlike his older sister, Chris never rebelled as a teenager or caused any trouble. But as he grew up, Jamie often wondered if something was wrong with Chris, as he was so obsessive and controlled.

"I really thought he was autistic," said Jamie, "like he was on the spectrum. He had to get things in order . . . from the way he would eat to the way he had to say his prayers at night. It was his mannerisms. It was hard to hold a conversation with him unless we were talking about cars."

On March 18, 2003, Joe Duty brought seventeen-year-old Chris Watts and another student to Winston-Salem, to compete in a North Carolina Statewide Automotive Competition. They had spent months training for the prestigious competition.

The Fayetteville Observer had featured Chris in a story headlined "Auto Tech Students Compete for Garage Glory."

"When Pine Forest High School senior Chris Watts . . . lifts the hood of a Toyota Matrix next week," read the article, "[he] will find an assortment of problems. Their teacher, Joe Duty, can only stand on the sidelines and watch. If he gives any help, the team will be disqualified."

Alongside the article was a photograph of Chris working on a car engine, and he was also interviewed.

"When I was a kid, I watched car shows and went to races," he told the reporter, adding that his dream car would be a '69 Boss 429 Mustang.

"It's not just a paper test," Duty said. "They get to compete. They have to perform. It tells you whether you can do the job."

But unfortunately, at the competition the Pine Forest team placed a disappointing third out of the four teams competing.

At the end of May 2003, Chris Watts graduated from Pine Forest High School. The yearbook has a color picture of him wearing a tuxedo and black bow tie, an enigmatic knowing look in his eyes. A female admirer had to invite him to the prom, as he was too shy to ask.

Before graduation, Joe Duty gave his star pupil a pep talk. Chris had just been awarded a $1,000 scholarship to the NASCAR Technical Institute in Mooresville, North Carolina, and his auto teacher was convinced that he would go far.

"He had everything going for him," said Duty. "I told him, 'Chris, if ever I had a student who was going to be tremendously successful, it's you.' I was sure that one day I was going to read about him [being] a crew chief of a NASCAR team."

In the summer of 2003, eighteen-year-old Chris Watts left home for the NASCAR Technical Institute in Mooresville, North Carolina. Lying 120 miles west of Fayetteville, the Charlotte suburb was his first taste of city life.

"We paid his rent until he got on his feet," said his mother, "because he had to go to school five days a week. We would help him out with his groceries, pay his car insurance and all of this stuff."

To supplement his income, Chris found a part-time job at a Ford dealership in Mooresville, renting an apartment with another NASCAR student named Richard Hodges.

"He was straight as an arrow," recalled Hodges. "He was very dedicated to his work . . . and wasn't the kind of guy that went out and partied."

While most of his classmates were out every night drinking, Chris studied in his bedroom. He dreamed of a career in NASCAR and devoted himself to achieving it.

"He was pretty reserved," said Hodges, "and not the kind of guy who's just going to walk up and introduce himself and try and make friends."

Around the same time that Chris left home, his sister, Jamie, got married and also moved out. Now studying and working a part-time job, Chris rarely came home. Ronnie, who had once been so close to his son, seemed to fall apart.

"I never came back," Chris later explained, "and I think that hit [my dad] pretty hard. He was used to me being around. He's my hero. He's my best friend."

To feel better, Ronnie Watts secretly began snorting cocaine and became addicted. He was soon spending so much money getting high that Cindy thought he was having an affair.

"At first I thought, 'Okay, maybe something's wrong,'" said Cindy. "'Do you have another family or something, because we're supposed to have money in the bank.'"

Finally Ronnie confessed he was hooked on cocaine because he was so depressed after Chris had left.

"It shocked me . . . because I trust him," said Cindy. "I put Ronnie on a pedestal because I thought he does no wrong. And I realized that with Chris leaving, maybe this was an outlet and he couldn't cope. Ronnie doesn't tell you how he feels."

Finally Cindy told her children what was going on at an emotional family meeting.

"You could see it in his face and eyes," said Chris. "He was losing a lot of weight. His nose was bleeding all the time."

Chris staged an intervention and Ronnie agreed to give cocaine up.

"He just quit," said Cindy. "He stopped right there and then."

In 2006, Chris graduated from the NASCAR Institute with honors. He found a full-time job at the Mooresville Ford dealership as a service technician, making good money. But the twenty-year-old still dreamed of a career in NASCAR, sending off a stream of job applications. He only got one interview, which went nowhere, and his dreams of joining a NASCAR race team were shattered.

Over the next few years Chris worked at the far-less-glamorous Ford dealership, buying himself a hot-rod Mustang and saving for the future. It was a big disappointment for him although he never complained and bottled up his frustrations.

"He was making good money," said his mother. "He bought a toolbox and started buying tools. He enjoyed it and was doing well."

He also found his first steady girlfriend, who was on the rebound after a messy divorce. But he never once brought her home to meet his family and it soon ended badly.

"I was helping her get through her divorce," Chris later explained. "And then she went off with someone else. I'm like, 'Oh, nice to know.'"

Then his cousin Nicole Canady suggested he send a Facebook friend request to her work colleague Shanann Rzucek, who was coming out of a bad marriage. He plucked up his courage and did so, but it would be months before he got a reply.

2

"VERY INSECURE"

Shanann Cathryn Rzucek was named after Sha Na Na, the popular sixties rock-and-roll doo-wop group who played Woodstock. She was born on January 10, 1984, in Passaic, New Jersey, to Frank and Sandi Rzucek. Almost two years later her brother, Frankie, arrived to complete the family.

Shanann always stood out with her vibrant personality and intelligence. But she was a sickly child who constantly needed medical attention.

"When she was a baby," explained her father, "we took her to all kinds of doctors because she always had migraines. Brain surgeons . . . to find out why she was having these problems. She took those real strong pills and used to get shots for it."

When Shanann was still little, Frank moved the family to Clifton, New Jersey, where she attended Number 11 Elementary School in the Lakeview section. Growing up, she and her young brother formed a strong bond.

"[We were] pretty close," said Frankie. "She would tell me things she wouldn't tell [our] parents."

Shanann was insecure and often bullied at school, so Frankie became her protector, getting into numerous fights on her behalf.

"They'd poke her on the school bus," said Frankie. "I'm like, 'Leave her the hell alone!'"

Years later Shanann would describe her miserable time at school: "I had people who picked on me and said mean things. I wasn't the popular kid in the group."

Around 1999, Frank Rzucek moved the family to Aberdeen, North Carolina, where job prospects were better. He started his own home-improvement business, and Sandi worked in a hair salon, dreaming of opening her own one day.

At fourteen, Shanann began her freshman year at Pinecrest High School, in Southern Pines. Founded in 1969 as a progressive school, Pinecrest boasted team teaching, closed-circuit-television instruction, and a fully equipped media center. It specialized in arts and drama, and the school's Pinecrest Players competed in regional theater competitions every fall with original productions.

Soon after enrolling at Pinecrest, Shanann Rzucek joined Matt Francis's theater class. The charismatic twenty-five-year-old drama teacher instilled his passion for drama in his students. His class would change Shanann's life, giving her confidence and a new set of friends.

"Shanann was a very insecure young lady who didn't have a lot of friends when I met her," Francis remembered. "She did not have a good self-image of herself, but she was brave enough to sign up for beginning acting."

The ninth-grade theater class had almost forty pupils, and the shy teenager soon had to prove herself in a group situation.

"Right away Shanann realized we were about ensemble," explained Francis. "She was with a group of people that were much more outgoing than she was. But she also realized that they cared about her . . . so I think she started to really thrive."

Shanann soon became close with Colby Cruse and Claire Littlejohn, who were also in the theater class.

"We became friends all throughout high school," said Colby. "She was one of the sweetest girls you could ever encounter. She got involved with the acting, and she also did some of the tech crew and stuff like that."

Shanann started with improvisation and acting, but Francis soon realized that her real talent lay behind the scenes, organizing the props and stage scenery. Over the many hours they spent working together on various productions, Shanann and her drama teacher became close.

"He connected with her on a mentor level," recalled Claire Littlejohn, "whereas I was more of a friendly classmate."

After school, Shanann was often in Francis's office, opening up about her "horrible" home life. She told him that her parents were going through a bitter divorce, although they never were divorced and are still together after thirty-eight years of marriage.

"[She told me] she didn't get a lot of attention from her dad that I know she wanted," recalled Francis. "I think there was a lot of hurt and frustration in the divorce. I mean it was pretty fresh."

Colby Cruse also knew about Shanann's problems at home: "She did overcome some challenges in her life. There were some struggles. I don't want to say that she didn't really have a good father figure, and Frank did the best he could. She spent a lot of time at my house. I'll put it to you that way."

During high school, Shanann had a tight group of

friends that played softball together and socialized outside school.

"She was the mother hen of the group," said Colby. "The responsible one."

But Shanann was often absent from school with various medical problems, which she was secretive about.

By her sophomore year Shanann had become a key part of the theater class. The Pinecrest Players were now working on *Little Shop of Horrors,* and Shanann ran everything backstage.

"She was a rock for me," said Matt Francis. "She became a stage manager and a production person and was always there to help with the tech crew, but she'd also work amazingly with the actors. She loved that role."

Shanann viewed the theater group as a safe haven, often working late painting the sets. She made regular runs to Back Yard Burgers to feed her crew, and everyone would sit around to eat.

"We had so many stupid moments," recalled Francis. "I remember laughing a lot with them in the middle of chaos."

One time Colby Cruse spilled water over her white slacks and was embarrassed. So Shanann took the initiative to break that awkward moment.

"Shanann put water on her crotch," said Francis, "and then everyone else in the class spilled drinks over themselves, so Colby didn't have to feel singled out. It was pretty awesome."

In her junior year, Shanann stage-managed a production of *Godspell,* as well as helping with the Pinecrest High School yearbook and volunteering for many clubs.

Over the summer vacation, Shanann found a part-time job at Vito's Pizzeria in Pinehurst, where she became close friends with Morgan Lankford, who was two years ahead of her in high school.

"We were hostesses," Morgan recalled. "We answered the phones and to-go orders and cut pizzas."

Morgan had seen Shanann in school, where she seemed shy and withdrawn. But at Vito's she opened up and they started socializing.

"We went midnight bowling," recalled Morgan. "She spent the night with me a few times . . . and we would talk and get our nails done together."

Shanann was now spending so much time in Matt Francis's office pouring out her problems at home that the school principal intervened, sending her to a more qualified guidance counselor. But she kept going to Francis, whom she viewed as her confidant.

"She just trusted me," he explained, "and could tell that I really did care. She didn't trust the guidance counselors, so I just listened a lot."

In 2002, the Pinecrest Players won a state award for an original play called *Maximum Capacity.* Soon afterward Matt Francis left Pinecrest High School to get married. Eighteen-year-old Shanann wrote him a heartfelt letter saying she would never forget him. "You have been like a father figure to me," she told him, "even more than my own father."

In her senior year, Shanann started dating a fellow Pinecrest High School student named Leonard King. It was a whirlwind romance.

They were already engaged and planning their future when Shanann graduated.

For her graduation message she quoted Muhammad Ali: "Friendship is the hardest thing in the world to explain. It's not something you learn in school. But if you haven't learned the meaning of friendship, you really haven't learned anything."

Soon after graduation Shanann married Leonard King. Some of her friends worried that she was too young and needed to see more of life before settling down.

"She was adamant about starting her life and having a family," said Cruse. "They got married so quickly and she was young and very ambitious."

Shanann started college while her new husband joined the army, as a means to go to law school. They also each took out large life insurance policies through USAA.

But Shanann soon dropped out of college, getting a job selling pagers and cell phones. Within a couple of years the marriage had gone bad.

"I never completed college," said Shanann many years later. "I started into a bad relationship [and] quit college to take care of him so he can go to [law school]."

Then in 2006, Shanann became manager of a cell phone store in Fayetteville, North Carolina, owned by Lebanese-born entrepreneur Hisham Bedwan. For the next few years Shanann worked for Bedwan, eventually becoming the bookkeeper for his new company the Dirty South, a custom car fittings and wheels company with stores in Fayetteville and Charlotte. It had a wealthy clientele of rappers, sports players, and car enthusiasts.

She worked long hours managing both stores, which were 130 miles apart, and had the use of a custom-fitted Cadillac Escalade.

Later Leonard King would say that after Shanann started managing the Dirty South she stopped coming home at night, refusing to tell him where she had been. They went to several marriage counseling sessions, but Shanann had little interest in saving the marriage.

In 2007 they divorced and Shanann moved to Charlotte, where she enrolled for a psychology course at Queens University. She would later describe the tough time she had during their breakup: "I went through a real awful divorce, and that relationship took a lot from me. It literally took everything. I had to start . . . financially all over."

And finding herself alone as a single divorcée at just twenty-three brought back all her childhood insecurities.

"All the doubts," said Shanann, "all the fears, everything that I had in me came flooding back into my life. I wasn't happy."

That fall, Shanann decided to build a house and began looking around Charlotte for suitable land.

"My goal was to buy a house . . . that I could resell one day," she later explained. "I was tired of paying someone else's mortgage."

On November 30, 2009, Shanann King signed a $309,000 mortgage to build a luxurious brick mansion overlooking Lake Wylie, in the swanky Charlotte suburb of Belmont. Over the next few months she supervised the building of 1000 Peninsula Drive.

"I was twenty-five years old when I built my first house," said Shanann in May 2018. "That was the biggest accomplishment . . . I have ever done because I did it by myself. I did it by working my tail off."

The four-thousand-square-foot, twelve-room mansion had four bedrooms and four bathrooms. Set in its own grounds, it had a balcony with sweeping views of the lake, a sunroom, and a custom-made kitchen. Shanann bought top-of-the-line furniture.

Her brother, Frankie, would later estimate she was earning almost half a million dollars a year during this period.

"She was very wealthy," he said. "She was doing very

good [and] she was very business savvy. She was pretty but she could talk the talk and walk the walk."

Soon after moving into 1000 Peninsula Drive, Shanann became ill. Her hair started falling out and she lost twenty pounds in a month, going from a size six to a size one.

"I was feeling extremely terrible," she later recalled, "to the point where I did not want to get out of bed for days."

She finally "dragged" herself to a doctor, who did a barrage of tests to find out what was wrong, and why her entire life had been dogged by illness.

In May 2010, Shanann was diagnosed with lupus, an incurable autoimmune disease, in which the body's immune system attacks its own organs and tissues. It is difficult to identify as the signs and symptoms mimic those of other illnesses.

"When they diagnosed me with lupus . . . I was lost," said Shanann. "I had no idea what in the world lupus was."

She immediately googled *lupus,* reading that there was no cure and it could be fatal.

"I was freaking out. I was overreacting. I had all these things going on in me and I had no idea."

She then contacted the Lupus Foundation of North Carolina, who provided support and treatment information. And over the next two months she sought second opinions from a host of rheumatologists, who all confirmed she had lupus as well as fibromyalgia.

She was prescribed heavy medication that gave her flu-like symptoms, and her weight ballooned to almost 170 pounds.

"I completely lost it," she remembered. "I wasn't feeling good. I was in a dark place. I was really sad, emotional . . . and I didn't know where to turn."

Shanann then quit the Dirty South, telling Hisham Bedwan that she could no longer manage his stores.

"I just said, 'I'm done,'" she recalled. "'I can't do this anymore. You don't understand what's going on in my life.'"

Then in late July 2010, when Shanann was at her lowest point, she received a second Facebook message from Chris Watts. This time, she replied.

3

COURTING

Two weeks later, Shanann and Chris went on their first date, to the classy EpiCentre theater in Charlotte, where they serve cocktails and gourmet meals during the movie. Chris arrived in a T-shirt, army camo shorts, and DC shoes, while Shanann had dressed up for the occasion.

"I didn't really know what I was walking into," Chris recalled. "There was a doorman . . . dressed in a suit, and I was like . . . 'This isn't good.'"

There was little chemistry between them, and Chris was too nervous to even eat.

"She was just chowing down," he said. "She's like, 'You're just like a bird.'"

A few days later, Chris invited Shanann to a Kid Rock concert, and she agreed to give him another chance.

"I was persistent trying to pursue her," said Chris. "I liked her."

When he arrived for their second date, Chris was so anxious he forgot his ID and had to run back to his car to collect it. It was a sweltering day, and by the time he got back to Shanann at the turnstiles, he was soaking wet. But the concert went well and she agreed to see him again.

Not until a trip to Myrtle Beach in late August did Chris finally win her heart. After a day at the beach Shanann had a lupus flare-up on the drive back to Charlotte.

"He let me lay on him," Shanann fondly remembered, "and fall asleep for three and a half hours on his lap while he had to pee."

That was the moment Shanann decided that Chris Watts was the man of her dreams.

During their courtship, Shanann went back to working part-time at the Dirty South to help pay off her mortgage and living expenses. She had also started a photography business, specializing in weddings and child portraits.

"She dabbled in photography," said her friend Amanda Aikman. "[She] was so artistically creative and talented, and she did an entire-day photo shoot with [my daughter] Madison."

Shanann also branched out to advertise her services on-line as a nanny and soon found a customer.

"We hired her to be our nanny off a website," said Jeanna Dietz. "We interviewed her and she really loved children."

Jeanna, a nurse who was expecting her second child with her husband, Charlie, paid Shanann to look after her eighteen-month-old son, Ely, several times a week. Before long, Shanann had bonded with her new employers.

"She was a wonderful nanny to my little boy," said Jeanna. "During the end of my pregnancy I ended up home quite a bit [while] Shanann was still there as my nanny. We [got] to know each other really well."

Shanann was often in great discomfort and pain from the lupus, as well as the side effects from all her medication. But few people even realized that she was sick.

"I always put on a fake smile," she said, "and let people see what they want to see. People always want to see you happy."

Shanann was now becoming increasingly dependent on Chris Watts, who was always there at her beck and call.

He seemed to enjoy organizing her complex regime of medications, dutifully sorting them all out in an eight-day flip-top pillbox.

"I dragged him to a colonoscopy," said Shanann. "I dragged him to a rheumatology appointment [and] to my spinal tap, which was awful. And I ended up falling in love with him."

That fall, Chris moved into 1000 Peninsula Drive and started sharing expenses. He had saved $11,000 working at the Ford dealership, which he duly gave Shanann to look after. She began introducing Chris to all her friends, who were impressed by his slavish devotion.

On November 25, 2010, Shanann went public with her new relationship, posting a photograph of her and Chris on Instagram with the caption "My baby!"

A few days later they had a cookout, inviting both sets of parents and Chris's sister, Jamie. It was not a success; a harbinger of things to come.

"We went over to dinner at their house," recalled Cindy Watts, "on the insistence of Chris. Her dad and brother were very, very nice, but Sandi was very outspoken. I just didn't feel comfortable around her."

Cindy also wondered how her son's first girlfriend she had ever met could afford to live in such luxury without a full-time job.

"Shanann's house was unbelievable," said Cindy. "She had the best of everything. How could she afford that?"

Jamie also questioned Shanann's expensive lifestyle and whether she was living beyond her means.

"I mean, for a twenty-six-year-old that's a pretty nice house," explained Jamie. "Was it really on the up-and-up? There were just so many questions that we couldn't pretend we didn't want to ask."

Shanann's parents were only too well aware of these suspicions, leading to tension at that first family meeting.

"They were floored when they saw her house," said Sandi. "Shanann was a hard worker and wanted to eventually sell and make a profit. Comes from a family of contractors."

After the cookout, Shanann and Chris took their fathers and Jamie on a tour of the house, leaving their mothers alone on the back porch.

"It was just me and Chris's mom," remembered Sandi. "She leaned over to me and said, 'Shanann was married before?' I said, 'Yes, just like your daughter [Jamie] was.'"

According to Sandi, Cindy then told her that she didn't think Shanann loved Chris.

"I knew she was going to be a thorn in the marriage," said Sandi. "So every time we had cookouts, his mom and sister were quite distant, we weren't [accepted]. They made that known."

Jamie, who was now pregnant with her second child, said they wanted the relationship to work out for Chris's sake.

"We met her and we weren't sure," said Jamie, "but we would do anything to make him happy . . . because he was happy."

Shanann and Chris celebrated their first Christmas together at her parents' house in Aberdeen. It was the first year that Chris had not spent the holidays with his family, and they missed him. He and Shanann posed for a series of romantic photographs that she later posted on Instagram. But she was in pain throughout the holidays.

"My lupus was flaring," she wrote under one of the photos. "You can see it in my face."

They also rang in 2011 together with Shanann's parents

and brother, Frankie, posting several photographs on Instagram.

"Our first New Years together!" read her caption.

In late February 2011, Jeanna and Charlie Dietz moved to Broomfield, Colorado, just a few weeks after their daughter, Eva, was born. Over the last few months Shanann had grown close to the Dietzes and had become part of their family, although they still hadn't met Chris.

Shanann drove them to the airport, already making plans to visit them in Colorado.

"Going to miss you guys a lot," she told them on Instagram. "Chris promised me a visit out to Colorado."

Over the next few months, Shanann was in daily contact with Jeanna Dietz, who kept telling her how good the fresh Colorado mountain air would be for her lupus. The trained nurse knew all about Shanann's medical condition and often advised her on treatments.

"We were constantly texting and talking," said Jeanna, "and I brought up the idea that they should move to Colorado."

4

THE ENGAGEMENT

Shanann and Chris fell into an easy routine at 1000 Peninsula Drive. Early every morning Chris drove off in his 2006 Ford Mustang to his job at Mooresville Ford, while Shanann worked part-time at the Dirty South and ran her photographic business.

Shanann was dominant in the relationship, while Chris was happy to just go along with everything she wanted. She had a fiery temper, while Chris never displayed any emotion and was like a blank canvas. With her strong personality and his apparent lack of one, they seemed the perfect fit.

At the beginning of August they rented a house in Ocean Isle Beach, North Carolina, and Shanann's parents joined them there. Chris had now summoned up the courage to propose to Shanann on the beach and had bought an engagement ring. But first he gallantly asked Frank Rzucek for his daughter's hand in marriage.

Frank immediately gave his blessing, and the Rzuceks were delighted to welcome Chris into their family.

"They were so in love," said Sandi. "They were a great team."

That Thanksgiving the newly engaged couple flew to Colorado to spend a week with Jeanna and Charlie Dietz in their new home in Broomfield. It was the first time the Dietzes had ever met Chris Watts, and they were impressed by how devoted he seemed to be to Shanann.

"He was very doting," recalled Jeanna. "Attentive, kind but shy and introverted. He loved my kids."

Charlie Dietz was renovating their new house, and Chris immediately volunteered to help.

"Chris was a doer," said Jeanna. "They were supposed to be on vacation, but he got on his hands and knees and helped my husband put in hardwood floors throughout the downstairs of our house."

During their visit, Shanann and Chris decided to move to Colorado, as it would be good for her lupus and fibromyalgia. So they called a local Realtor, who took them on a tour of available property.

Chris would move to Colorado first and stay with the Dietzes, while Shanann remained in Charlotte to sell her house before joining him. When he told his mother they were moving to Colorado, she was horrified.

"Colorado was Shanann's idea," said Cindy Watts. "Why did she want to leave and take him all the way to Colorado?"

Shanann and her mother were now busy organizing her engagement party. They asked Chris's sister, Jamie, to mail out the invitations and order strictly gluten-free food. It was a disaster. Later Sandi claimed that the food Jamie ordered contained gluten so Shanann couldn't eat anything, and most of the eighty invitations did not go out. Jamie denied it.

"I sent out the invitations," she said. "I may have missed one or two people, but everybody was there."

At the engagement party, tempers flared. Shanann and her future mother-in-law had a huge fight after Cindy accused Shanann of turning Chris against his family.

"I didn't want to be there," said Cindy, "but we went and we were cordial and polite. Things like that happen in families."

After the party, apparently at Shanann's instigation, Chris broke off all relations with his family. He stopped taking their calls and told them to leave him alone.

"He wouldn't even talk to us anymore," said Cindy. "Shanann was very controlling, and he was in love and there was no talking to him. And it frightened me for him."

In desperation, Jamie reached out to her brother to try to repair their relationship.

"I was trying to open doors," she explained, "so we could mend the fence to be able to go [to the wedding]. But I couldn't get a response."

Years later, Chris Watts speculated on why he had turned his back on them: "I blew up at my family, to a point where I said [that] I didn't need them anymore because I have Shanann. I cussed my mom out. I don't know if . . . Shanann coached me to do it or if it was just rage like I'd never seen before."

In early April 2012, Chris quit his job at Mooresville Ford and came to Broomfield, Colorado. He moved in with Jeanna and Charlie Dietz, soon finding a job at the Longmont Ford dealership, through his reputation as a master mechanic.

"Chris lived with us for six months before Shanann was able to move," said Jeanna. "She was still back in North Carolina selling her house and tying things up."

Working long hours at Longmont Ford, Chris started saving for their new life.

"He was just putting money in the bank," said Jeanna, "so he wasn't around a ton. He's very soft-spoken and kind and helpful."

Jeanna was much impressed by how well Chris bonded with her baby daughter, Eva, thinking he would one day be an excellent father.

"He became kind of a third parent to her," said Jeanna. "She wanted him when she was sad or when she was sleepy."

Back in North Carolina, Shanann remained in constant contact with Chris, pushing him to take an online communications course back at the Central Piedmont Community College in Charlotte. She also wanted to make sure that he wasn't being unfaithful while he was away from her.

"Shanann wanted him to work towards a degree," said Jeanna. "She had him doing those classes while he was here as a single guy."

On April 22, Charlie Dietz videoed Chris in the kitchen delivering a nine-minute talk as part of his coursework, entitled "Relationship, Deterioration and Repair." He needed an audience so he asked the Dietzes to invite a few of their friends over.

Wearing a short-sleeved black shirt, jeans, and looking slightly overweight from Jeanna's home-cooked meals, Chris read from notes on his laptop, accompanied by a PowerPoint presentation.

Nervously palming his fist and rocking back and forth, Chris first tackled how a relationship deteriorates. Just a few months into his first real one, his speech would prove eerily prescient.

"The relationship begins to fall apart, crumble, or fail," he told his audience. "You have weakening bonds. You get bored with an everyday routine. Even at the job you might meet a new person, and it could strengthen into something else and weaken the bond you have with [your] partner."

He then moved on to "interpersonal deterioration" and growing apart from your spouse. "You have more awkward silences at dinner. You disclose less of your feelings and show less affection towards each other."

Watts told his audience that everyone in a relationship must eventually ask if he or she has the desire or moral obligation to stay in a relationship or if it is a necessity. "According to my research, sometimes the necessity can be children. Sometimes when . . . your relationship starts to deteriorate, a child could help repair it."

He then described two different types of deterioration—sudden or gradual. "Sudden would be . . . infidelity. If someone is not faithful to their partner. Gradual would be if you met someone at work . . . and as it goes on, you see that, 'okay, maybe this relationship has more potential than the relationship I have with my partner.' And that would gradually push the old relationship out and push the new relationship in."

Through his research, he told his audience, it was the "more attractive one" that usually leaves.

"Repair is not an option, and they want to get away and start anew."

Chris ended his presentation by saying, "I'd like to say that relationships are hard, but they're worth it in the end. And as the Swedish proverb says, 'A double joy is a shared joy, and a double sorrow is not a shared sorrow.' Thank you."

Then to the applause of his small kitchen audience, Chris gave a satisfied smile.

Later, when the talk was posted on YouTube, Shanann commented, "Great job Christopher! Good information!"

In early August, Shanann finally sold 1000 Peninsula Drive for $349,900—almost $41,000 more than she had paid for it three years earlier. It was bought by asset manager Byron Falls, who said she was so desperate to sell that she left all the furniture behind.

Soon afterward, Shanann moved to Broomfield, to start a new life with her fiancé. She moved into the Dietzes' basement with Chris while they looked for a house of their own to buy.

Shanann found a sales job at Longmont Ford, where Chris worked. She had a natural gift for salesmanship and was soon selling more cars than anyone else there.

"She was a great salesperson," said Tyler Alore, who also worked at the dealership. "She sold a bunch of cars. She was very friendly."

Tyler's father, Greg Alore, who managed the Longmont

Ford dealership, soon noticed how Chris always handed his wage envelope to Shanann.

"He was very passive," said Greg, "and she was very aggressive with him. Bossy. Do this. Do that. Telling him what to do. Dominating the relationship."

But Chris never complained or appeared resentful, apparently happy with the arrangement.

"Shanann usually made all the decisions," he later explained. "Because I'm more of the go-with-the-flow type."

Soon after starting work there, Shanann befriended some of their coworkers as Chris cheerfully tagged along.

One of these friends was Jeremy Lindstrom, who had just moved to Colorado from California with his wife and children. "Chris was just an easygoing dude," he reflected.

They also became close friends with David Colon, who reconditioned cars at the Ford dealership.

When Colon bought a house in Frederick, Colorado, Chris and Shanann helped him move in. They liked the small but growing town deep in the Rocky Mountains and started looking at property there.

It was an exciting time for Chris and Shanann. For the next year, they both worked long hours at Longmont Ford, but spent most nights and weekends with the Dietz family. They became like one big family, spending all the holidays and birthdays together and cooking elaborate Italian meals.

"Shanann's and my big passion was cooking," said Jeanna. "We would always have these fun nights where Shanann and I would tear up the kitchen cooking, and the boys would have to clean it up."

Every Monday night, Jeanna and Shanann watched *The Bachelor,* while their husbands played computer games. The Dietzes often had friends over, and it soon became painfully obvious how uncomfortable Chris was in any social situation.

"You almost felt sorry for him in a public setting," said Jeanna. "Just a total introvert. Shy. Almost awkward socially [but] very kind and soft."

Shanann would try to get him more involved with company.

"She just did all the talking and introducing," explained Jeanna, "and usually put him up to some task, which he was happy to do so that he could be doing something. He wasn't one to initiate a conversation. Just very shy."

On October 1, Shanann started a countdown on Instagram to her wedding. Over the next month she would give daily updates of her progress, describing everything from bridesmaids' gifts to wedding-card holders, and posting photos from her bridal shower with their new pet dachshund, Dieter.

Then on October 17, Chris signed a $392,709 mortgage for 2825 Saratoga Trail in Frederick, which was still being built. It was part of a new development on the Wyndham Hill Estate.

"Not even married yet," Shanann posted on Instagram, "and at 12:30 pm Christopher Watts will be signing his life away to build our new home in Colorado! ☺ Super STOKED!"

Two days later, "Shanann & Christopher's Wedding Website" appeared online, and the soon-to-be bride invited everyone to check it out. Guests were informed that the couple had dedicated their wedding to the Lupus Foundation, where people should donate in lieu of gifts.

But Shanann made it clear that the Watts family would not be welcome at the wedding, and Chris had agreed.

Each day Shanann posted a romantic photograph of her and Chris, who had already bought her a $10,000 wedding ring. She carefully posed all the photographs, and Chris went along with it. He never complained.

"Chris worshipped the ground she walked on," said Jeanna, "and very heavily doted on her. He did whatever she asked and then some but seemed very happy in that role."

The Dietzes often discussed Chris's subservience in the relationship, although they agreed they were a perfect match.

"My husband and I would joke because it's not our dynamic," said Jeanna. "He wouldn't be happy if I was telling him what to do. But Chris not only seemed happy, but he seemed to thrive in that role of having the domineering spouse and loved it. And so they always had the perfect dynamic. It worked for them."

That Halloween, Shanann and Chris were back in North Carolina, making the final preparations for their wedding. On Thursday, November 1, they took out a wedding license at the Mecklenburg County Registrar of Deeds in Charlotte. The following night they held a rehearsal dinner, and the Dietz family flew in from Colorado to attend. Shanann had appointed Jeanna her maid of honor; her son, Ely, ring bearer; and her baby daughter, Eva, a flower girl.

On Saturday, November 3, 2012, Shanann married Chris Watts in a fairy-tale wedding ceremony at the DoubleTree Hilton Hotel in Charlotte. The bride wore a Cinderella wedding gown with a beaded corset bodice, a long white veil, and a tiara. She carried a bouquet of peonies and even had rhinestone-encrusted high heels with the words I DO engraved on them. The dashing groom wore evening dress.

At the reception the Pittsburgh Steelers–themed wedding cake was in honor of their favorite football team.

Shanann had invited many family friends from New Jersey, but few were able to make it because of Hurricane Sandy, which had struck a few days earlier. The only member of Chris's family to attend the wedding was his grandmother, with whom he proudly took the dance floor instead of his mother.

"I was crying," remembered Frankie Rzucek. "Thanking God for him being in my sister's life."

For once, Chris seemed to lose all his inhibitions as he performed a raunchy dance made famous by Channing Tatum in the movie *Magic Mike,* about a male stripper.

"It was unbelievable," said Frankie. "He tried to do this Magic Mike dance and he's so awkward, but he did it all for her and goofballed that . . . made us all love him more."

The next day, Chris and Shanann left for a short honeymoon in Myrtle Beach, South Carolina. They had planned to go to Cancún but could not afford it. Later, Shanann posted romantic pictures of them on the beach on Instagram, thanking everyone who came to the wedding.

"Chris and I had an amazing time," she wrote, "and we will never forget it! Thank you to all of our friends and families who love and support us! We had a wonderful time! Love you guys!"

A few days later Chris and Shanann returned to Colorado and moved back in with the Dietzes until their new house was finished. Full of optimism and hope for the future, they started married life together.

"They were very happy," said Jeanna Dietz. "They were newlyweds and it was wonderful."

That winter, Shanann tried to get pregnant. She had been warned by doctors that she might not be able to conceive because of her lupus, but she and Chris desperately wanted a baby. She downloaded an ovulation app for her iPhone to monitor her cycle and started taking fertility drugs.

"She didn't think she could get pregnant because of the lupus," said Chris. "We had been trying for a while and nothing was happening."

So as a consolation, Shanann ordered a $7,500 super-charger for Chris's 2006 Mustang, to improve its engine performance in the mile-high state. She planned to give it to him as a birthday present.

"And that weekend," he said later, "we conceived Bella."

6

2825 SARATOGA TRAIL

At the end of April 2013, Shanann and Chris finally moved into 2825 Saratoga Trail in Frederick, Colorado. The idyllic small town, just outside the Denver metro area, is perched up in the Rocky Mountains. Lying in the heart of Weld County, Frederick's grassy plains are littered with drilling rigs and oil wells. With an official logo of a gas lamp set against a mountain-range background, the town motto is Built on What Matters.

When the Wattses arrived in 2013, the population was only around eight thousand, but growing fast. Their upscale Wyndham Hill community was a key part of the town's ambitious expansion program. It boasted a clubhouse, parks, a playground, and a swimming pool, advertising itself as "a home for every dream."

Their brand-new 4,177-square-foot yellow two-story house with brown trim had five bedrooms and hardwood flooring. Its gourmet kitchen had a double oven and granite countertops, and the huge basement had a nine-foot ceiling. The monthly mortgage was $2,800, and the deeds were registered in Chris's name.

On May 16, Chris Watts celebrated his twenty-eighth birthday, and Shanann surprised him with the Mustang supercharger, which had just arrived. She had secretly stayed late at Longmont Ford the night before, placing the gift-wrapped charger by his toolbox.

"Shanann would do anything for Chris," said Tyler Alore. "It was Chris's birthday and he had wanted this part for his Mustang. She had got it for him and set it up on his toolbox under a wrap and everything. So when he showed up for work, it was right there."

In early July, Shanann Watts, who was now three months pregnant, started a new job working nights at the Pediatric Call Center at Children's Hospital in Aurora. Jeanna Dietz got her the position, in the same pediatric emergency triage unit where she worked. It paid $18 an hour plus extra for weekends and holidays. Chris remained at Longmont Ford but was starting to suffer from carpal tunnel syndrome from the repetitive mechanical work he did.

On July 9, Shanann posted an Instagram photograph of her holding a baby's dress with the caption "Bella Marie Watts coming this Christmas 2013. So excited."

Shanann had chosen the name because *bella* was the Italian word for "beautiful," and Marie was her mother's middle name.

A few days later, Chris called his parents with the news that Shanann was pregnant and made peace with them. It had been more than two years since they had spoken, and suddenly Chris was acting as if nothing had happened.

"She found out she was pregnant and allowed us back into her life," explained Cindy Watts. "I said, 'Okay, I'm throwing up the white flag and I will say nothing more. If this is what Chris wants, I will shut my mouth.'"

Shanann meticulously chronicled her pregnancy on Instagram, posting numerous photographs of her holding her expanding stomach. She went on a shopping spree, buying dozens of baby dresses, toys, and even a bikini for her unborn daughter.

When she and Chris went to a Bruno Mars concert, he photographed her in the parking lot.

"My baby bump at Bruno Mars!" she wrote. "Lil Beemer at her first concert!"

Soon afterward, Shanann proudly posted a photograph of Bella's new closet, with dozens of dresses and outfits hanging immaculately from two rails, as well as a row of children's videos and books.

Jeanna Dietz remembers Shanann buying baby clothes years earlier in preparation for motherhood: "Before she and I had even met, she had clothes for her firstborn. So she was always very prepared."

Over the next few weeks, Shanann posted photos of her top-of-the-line new crib and its luxurious canopy cover with Bella's name engraved on it. In another photo Bella's now-finished closet was bursting with dresses.

Shanann and Chris were now running up their credit card debt. They seemed oblivious of the financial hole they were digging themselves into. Shanann held the family purse strings, and Chris seemed content to let her buy anything that took her fancy.

"Shanann was living way above her means," said Ronnie Watts. "She wanted the best of everything."

Several weeks later, Shanann and Chris took a Lamaze class to prepare for childbirth.

"This time last year, Chris and I were getting ready for our wedding," she posted on Instagram. "Tonight we start our first Childbirth preparation class! Could not be any happier!!!!"

That Halloween, Shanann wore a cardboard oven out-fit with the door open, showing her pregnant tummy with a bun painted on it. Chris gamely dressed up as a baker with the words THE BUN MAKER!! on his chef's apron.

On November 3, the couple's first wedding anniversary, Shanann threw a baby shower, posting a photo of her and Chris passionately kissing.

"She was so happy to be pregnant," said Jeanna Dietz.

Shanann and Chris had recently become friends with Jeremy and Jennifer Lindstrom, who had just moved into their neighborhood. They would often visit the Wattses' house and wondered if Shanann might have OCD, as everything was so organized. They also noticed how Chris did all the cleaning.

"She's very meticulous with everything," Jeremy explained. "She's got labels and storage containers in the walk-in pantry. Everything's in a certain place."

On one occasion, Jeremy arrived to take Chris to the airport, but Shanann made him finish cleaning first.

"Everything had to be clean," said Jeremy, "and he couldn't . . . go to the airport until he was done cleaning up the basement. She's very controlling in that way. So we always thought, 'Man, he's got to be a really good dude. She's found the right guy . . . with the right personality.'"

7

BELLA MARIE

On Monday, December 16, 2013, Shanann's water broke right after she came off a night shift. Chris rushed her to the hospital, where she went into labor for sixteen and a half hours.

Bella Marie Watts was born the following day at the Good Samaritan Hospital in Lafayette, Colorado. Chris was in the delivery room with Jeanna Dietz to witness the birth of his daughter.

A few hours later, Shanann posted a photograph of Chris holding their new baby and staring proudly at her.

"The love he has for Bella is wonderful," she wrote.

On Christmas Eve Shanann had him dress up in a full Santa Claus outfit and pose next to their Christmas tree with Bella's presents.

A week later, she posted a New Year's message to all her friends and family, noticeably omitting any of Chris's: "2013 has been an amazing year! I am truly blessed with our baby girl Bella, my amazing husband and father Chris Lee Watts. Chris and I built and purchased our first home together! So much to be thankful for this year."

Then she announced that they were already planning a baby brother or sister for Bella.

* * *

The first week of January, Ronnie and Cindy Watts flew to Denver to meet their new granddaughter. It was the first time they had seen their son since his engagement, and they wanted to establish a good relationship with Shanann.

"We didn't want to rock the boat," explained Cindy. "We noticed things when we were there, but we were afraid to talk to him because we were just back where we were able to see him and [our granddaughter]."

Chris's parents instantly bonded with Bella and would from then on visit Colorado twice a year. Although Shanann continued posting online photo after photo of her and Chris's seemingly idyllic marriage, her mother-in-law saw a disturbingly different side of their relationship.

"Chris always seemed anxious," she said. "And when she needed something, he would run. He wouldn't walk, he would run. It was very odd. He just seemed nervous."

On January 10, Shanann celebrated her thirtieth birthday, posting photographs of her in-laws holding three-week-old Bella.

"I tried to like her," said Cindy. "I tried to love her, and at times I did love her. But then it just started all over again, because she always found something wrong with us."

Chris appeared to relish fatherhood, changing Bella's nappies, giving her a bottle, and reading to her every night before putting her to sleep. He loved fussing over his beautiful new daughter and seemed like the perfect father.

In turn, Shanann packed Bella's nursery with clothes and toys and, above her crib, lovingly painted a chandelier on the wall.

In May, Chris left Longmont Ford to work as an oilfield contractor for Covenant Testing Technologies in Greeley, Colorado. Shanann had found him a job that paid more money.

Chris went into oil fields testing wells and doing general maintenance. His carpal tunnel soon cleared up.

That spring, Shanann's lupus flared up while she worked nights at Children's Hospital. She also worked part-time at Children's Place in Colorado Springs, as well as doing direct sales for custom-jewelry and instant-coffee companies.

"She's business-minded," explained Chris. "So it all just fell into place. She could use all the business IQ she has from running those . . . various auto-custom shops."

In early July, Frankie Rzucek arrived in Frederick for an extended stay. He wanted to meet his now six-month-old niece and was considering relocating to Colorado. While he looked for work, Frankie often stayed at home to look after the baby.

"I was happy to help with Bella," he said, "and [Shanann] was a new mom. Everything was superclean and superprepared. We were having so much fun."

During his stay, Frankie closely observed his sister's relationship with Chris and was surprised at how subservient he was. One time Shanann even asked him to tell Chris to insult her, just to get some emotion out of him.

"Shanann said, 'Can you tell him to call me an asshole?'" Frankie recalled. "'Tell him to call me a bitch or something.' He was just one of those yes-men [and] he was in love with her. He was obsessed."

In mid-August, when Frankie couldn't find a job, he flew back to his parents' house in Aberdeen.

That summer Lauren Arnold, an old friend of Shanann's from Pinecrest High School, had moved to Aurora, Colorado, after her husband was stationed there by the army. Soon after they arrived, Shanann invited them for dinner. It was the first time Lauren had met Chris.

"He was really nice," she recalled. "He was quiet but he got along with my [husband] really well."

All Shanann's friends liked Chris. He might have been difficult to talk to, but he was always willing to lend a hand.

"If you needed help with your car," said Jeremy Lindstrom, "he'd help you. If you needed help moving furniture, he'd be over there in a heartbeat."

Another friend from Longmont Ford, Dave Colon, thought Chris and Shanann had the perfect relationship and considered him a great father.

"I was honestly surprised because of their personalities," he said. "Chris is very noncombative, nonconfrontational [and] he's perfect for her because she likes to run things."

The week before Christmas, Shanann and Chris signed a lease on a new 2015 Ford Explorer, with payments of $588 a month. This was on top of their monthly $2,800 mortgage for the house and growing expenses. They were now hemorrhaging in debt, and it would soon be catching up with them.

8

"YOU ARE AN AMAZING HUSBAND AND FATHER"

On January 10, 2015, Shanann turned thirty-one and announced she was pregnant on Instagram.

"Twelve and counting!" she wrote next to a photograph of her standing by her front door, proudly showing off her new baby bump.

Chris was hired as an operator by the Anadarko Petroleum Corporation, one of Colorado's largest oil and gas drillers. The job paid $61,500 a year. He worked out of Anadarko's Platteville, Colorado, office but was mainly out in the field, maintaining the scores of oil sites dotting the area.

Bella was now fifteen months old and walking. She was quite a handful, and at the beginning of March her mother posted a photo on Instagram of her trying to eat a tampon. Another picture showed a smiling Chris holding his little daughter by the waist.

A couple of days later, Shanann went online to announce that their new baby was a girl and would be named Celeste.

"Not too much longer till we meet our Princess Celeste!" she wrote.

A few weeks later, Frank and Sandi Rzucek moved into Shanann and Chris's basement, leaving their son behind in Aberdeen to take care of their house.

"We lived with them for fifteen months," Sandi later told Dr. Phil. "I closed up my [hair] salon and moved to Colorado to help my daughter [through her pregnancy]."

Later Chris would describe living with his in-laws as "stressful" because Shanann and her mother would often argue.

"When they first got here, they didn't have a job," said Chris, "and so they were around all the time."

Frank soon found work in construction and Sandi in a local hair salon, relieving a lot of the pressure on Shanann, who worked nights and was home all day. It took Chris some time to get used to living with his in-laws and the dogs they had brought with them, leading to tension between him and Shanann.

"Her mom would tell her how to raise [Bella]," he said, "and it was a clash every day. Every time I got home, I didn't know if Shanann was pissed or if she was okay. So it was like walking on eggshells."

On May 16, Chris Watts turned thirty and Shanann marked the occasion with a photograph of her and Bella posing with him.

"Happy Birthday to my best friend, my husband and father of our princess [and] soon to be princess," she gushed. "I hope you have a fantastic day! You are an amazing husband and father to our little girl! We are truly blessed to have you in our life! Love you baby and Happy Birthday #dirtythirty."

The first week of June, Shanann and Chris filed for Chapter 7 bankruptcy. They now owed almost $450,000, including $70,000 on credit cards, medical bills, and student loans. In their Chapter 7 filing for protection, Shanann and Chris had less than $10 in their two savings accounts and only $860 in their checking account. Most of their debt came from credit card purchases from a string of retail stores, including Macy's, Sears, Nordstrom, and Toys "R" Us.

The bankruptcy filing showed their combined 2014 income was $90,000, a sharp drop from the $147,256 the previous year. Mortgage and car payments ate up most of their $4,910 joint monthly income.

"The Watts are expecting another child," noted their filing, "and Mrs. Watts will work fewer hours."

On Friday, July 17, Shanann gave birth to Celeste Cathryn Watts at Avista Hospital in Denver, Colorado. Once again Chris was in the delivery room to see his new baby being born.

Celeste was sickly and diagnosed with eosinophilic esophagitis (EoE), an allergic swallowing disorder. For her first year of life, she had to be put on steroids to help her breathe.

In August 2015, a federal judge agreed to discharge most of their debt if they each completed an online credit course. They took the course and passed, earning a Financial Management Course Certificate. Two months later, their bankruptcy was discharged.

Shanann told few friends that they had filed for bankruptcy, but did discuss it with her mother.

"She did speak to us about bankruptcy," said Sandi Rzucek. "A lot of debt. With all the medical bills."

And Shanann also told her old school friend Lauren Arnold.

"She kind of presented it like, 'Oh, it's going to help us in the long run,'" recalled Arnold. "But she never seemed stressed-out about the finances. She just mentioned that they got behind on things and they argued about it sometimes."

Later Chris would claim that it had taken him by

surprise, as Shanann handled the finances. He now felt more pressure in the marriage, especially with another baby on the way. But, as usual, he bottled it all up.

"Bankruptcy was something I never thought was going to happen," he said, "and a lot of it was from the wedding, because we just put it all on credit cards."

He never mentioned their financial problems to his parents.

"I had no idea they were bankrupt," said Ronnie Watts. "He was making decent money but she wanted the profile . . . the best of everything."

9

THRIVE

In mid-January 2016, Shanann signed on as a promoter for the lifestyle supplement Thrive. It would transform Shanann's life, giving her a new set of friends, a lucrative new job, and a powerful social media outlet for the attention she craved.

The Thrive Premium Lifestyle regimen consists of capsules, a drink mix, and a DFT (Derma Fusion Technology) patch, worn anywhere on the body to deliver a formula directly into the body. Its parent company, Le-Vel, was founded in 2013 and now claims more than $1 billion in annual direct sales.

Later Shanann would admit she was going through a rough period when she started on Thrive.

"I was broke," she said, "working full-time at the hospital, and had a part-time job. So I was working about sixty hours a week and still a stay-at-home mom. I worked all night, took care of them during the day."

So Shanann bought her first round of Thrive and persuaded her out-of-shape 245-pound husband to take it with her.

"Day one," she said, "Chris started with me [and] definitely noticed a change right away. He took the capsules and the shake and the DFT, and he was like, 'Shanann, I feel like I can run a marathon.'"

Shanann then started recruiting her friends and family. Within five days she had enrolled two new customers and sold $800 worth of Thrive, earning her a VIP 800 award.

"HUGE Congratulations to Shanann Watts for smashing her VIP 800!" posted her team leader, Amanda Aikman, on Facebook. "This GAL is on Fire sharing the Thrive Experience. WAY to GO Shanann!!!!"

A week later, Shanann had achieved VIP 1600 status, recruiting another two customers and making more sales. She was now a convert and started preaching the benefits of Thrive with an evangelical fervor.

Later Shanann would describe her "huge aha moment" when she woke up one morning at five thirty and reached for her Thrive shake.

"I did two loads of laundry before seven o'clock," she enthused. "I had the kitchen rearranged. I was cleaning out cabinets. I made homemade pancakes. I just wanted to enjoy my kids that day."

Soon Shanann had her parents on Thrive, posting a photograph of her and Sandi both proudly displaying their DFT arm patches.

"Thriving with momma!" Shanann proclaimed.

She now started posting on Facebook to a growing number of followers about her personal transformation, claiming she was no longer in pain and had stopped taking her lupus medication.

"I was literally dancing around the living room," she said, "having fun with [Bella] while CeCe was taking her nap. I felt amazing. I had no aches. I had no discomforts. I really, really felt . . . that feeling of bliss."

By her fourth week, Shanann had progressed to 4K VIP status, earning over $1,000 in commissions as well as a free iPod.

"This Girl is on FIIRRRRRRE!" posted Aikman.

"She's a dynamo and feeling fantastic. She is running circles around her babies and living the life she deserves."

Shanann began contacting all her old high school friends back in North Carolina, trying to sign them up. It was the first time many had heard from her in years.

"She would . . . call and text," said Colby Cruse. "Mostly it was about pushing for Thrive. She wanted me to get on board [but] that was just not my cup of tea."

Shanann was more successful with Morgan Lankford.

"She got me on my first month of Thrive," recalled Morgan. "She sent it to me and it helped. She was really good at promoting it."

Shanann also signed up Lauren Arnold, who didn't stay the course due to the high price.

"I think she had everybody on it," said Arnold. "I gave it a shot [but] I didn't stick with it. I could see where it was beneficial with her because she had lupus. [It] seemed to help her mentally and physically."

Shanann also enlisted Chris as a Thrive promoter, having him recruit his Anadarko workmates. Shy and withdrawn, Chris was not a natural salesman, so Shanann wrote all his Facebook posts and he grudgingly went along with it.

By April, Shanann had advanced to a 12K VIP to qualify for Le-Vel's VIP Auto Club, earning $800 a month toward a new car. She chose a white Lexus and persuaded Chris to trade in his beloved Ford Mustang. His father was appalled.

"He loved his Mustang," said Ronnie, "and they ended up trading that in."

Chris Watts had now been working for Anadarko for sixteen months. He was good at his job, where he was known as the Rain Man, because of his photographic memory. His workmates didn't quite know what to make of him as he rarely spoke, but looked up to him to solve any work problems they encountered.

In April, Luke Epple became his new boss and soon considered Chris a reliably solid part of his new team.

"He's a little quiet and reserved," said Epple, "so sometimes I've got to pry conversation out of him. But he's a good employee."

Each morning, Watts began his workday at Anadarko's Platteville office, where his team met to receive their assignments for the day. Chris was closest to another field coordinator, Troy McCoy, who had originally trained him.

While they worked in the oil fields, Chris's sole topic of conversation was Bella and Celeste and how well they were doing.

"He would just light up," said McCoy. "They were the center of his world."

Meanwhile, Shanann was busy establishing herself in the online Thrive community, and her natural gift of salesmanship was paying off. She started hosting phone-in events to sell the product, and her growing success gave her a new independence and self-affirmation. Naturally empathetic and caring, she believed she was on a mission to improve people's lives.

Over the first few months she made a string of new friends whom she eagerly adopted as her surrogate family.

"I love this girl so much," wrote Addy Molony on Facebook. "There isn't a more genuine, caring soul than Shanann Watts. I'm so happy this company has connected us in friendship. You're pretty intense, girlfriend. . . . And I Love it!"

On May 31, Shanann marked her four-month Thrive anniversary with a heartfelt Facebook posting:

"My name is Shanann Watts and this is my 4 month Thrive Experience! I am a 32 year old mother of two girls

(10 mo and 2 yr old) and married to the love of my life, Chris."

She credited Chris with inspiring her to stay the course with Thrive: "My only motivation to keep going was my husband Chris, who on his first day of Thrive was a revived person. He beamed with euphoric joy, energy and the mental clarity that Thrivers all speak of. I wanted to feel as good as him."

DADDY'S THRIVIN'

That summer of 2016, Shanann preached the Thrive gospel on Facebook. She posted numerous photographs of her, Chris, and their daughters extolling the product. But something about the succession of grinning pictures of Chris, drinking protein shakes or flashing his DFT patches, was hollow.

Later he would admit that he "hated" being out there in social media and only did it to help his wife's business. But as Shanann called all the shots in their marriage, he never complained and went along with her wishes.

"[Shanann] would be like, 'Take a picture with your patch,'" he explained, "so I would send her pictures and then she'd make a post about them."

On July 17, Shanann threw a party for Celeste's first birthday, and her mother invited Nickole Atkinson, who worked with her in a hair salon.

Nickole immediately hit it off with Shanann, as they had children the same age. Shanann turned her on to Thrive, and she was soon an integral part of Shanann's Thrive team.

"She got me doing Thrive with her," said Nickole. "It gives you mental clarity. You actually stop craving stuff . . . like ice cream. I don't crave ice cream anymore. I don't drink coffee."

Meanwhile, Chris was busy teaching Bella to swim. He became a familiar sight in the neighborhood, pushing his daughters' wagon to the Wyndham Hill Estate swimming pool.

"He seemed like a very doting dad," said Coleen Hendrickson, who lived two doors away. "I would see Shanann walk by and I'd just say hi and how cute her little girls looked."

When Nate Trinastich moved in next door to the Watts family, Shanann came straight over to welcome him to the neighborhood.

"Shanann was always really friendly," he remembered. "The girls were always running around laughing, having a great time. Chris was really quiet. He was kind of stand-offish."

The first week of August, twenty-nine-year-old Anthony Brown started work at Anadarko.

"Chris actually trained me," said Brown. "He took me under his wing."

Watts drove him around his team's oil field routes, giving him valuable professional tips and showing him how to troubleshoot the tanks and wells.

"He knew everything," said Brown. "He would show me the routine day-to-day on my route."

On the six-year anniversary of Chris and Shanann's awkward first date, she celebrated by posting a photo of the happy couple at the Wyndham Hill swimming pool sporting their DFT patches.

Lauren Arnold, a frequent visitor to 2825 Saratoga Trail, thought they were a devoted couple.

"People that don't know her would say that maybe it's a front," said Arnold. "That she's trying to portray her perfect marriage. But that's how it was."

Undoubtedly, Shanann felt she was in a blissfully happy marriage, although Chris disliked being constantly thrust into the Thrive spotlight. But he never wanted to rock the boat and assert himself, so the seeds of resentment silently grew.

Over the next few weeks, Shanann posted a stream of photographs of her picture-perfect family on Facebook. Many of them showed the girls playing together in all their different outfits.

"How they love each other," commented their grandfather Frank Rzucek.

She also photographed Chris in a muscle T-shirt, mowing his front lawn with Bella and CeCe strapped to his back.

"Daddy's Thrivin'," Shanann wrote. "Got tired of chasing them so he attached them."

That August, Shanann and Chris enrolled Bella, now two, at the Primrose School of Erie at Vista Ridge. Every morning at 8:00 A.M. Shanann would drop Bella off at the private preschool, then collect her at five in the afternoon. It meant Shanann could concentrate on her growing Thrive business.

And during the drop-offs and pickups she chatted to the school's director, Amanda Thayer, about the benefits of Thrive. It would take Shanann nine months to persuade Amanda to join her team.

11

#TEAMROCKSTARS

By September, Shanann had progressed to 40K VIP Brand Promoter, taking her to a new level in the company. She now had scores of customers and promoters underneath her and was thinking of quitting Children's Hospital and going full-time.

"One of the biggest accomplishments I've ever done!!" she wrote. "Next stop 200K."

On behalf of her team, Addy Molony congratulated Shanann on "working her butt off."

Molony wrote, "There is no more deserving leader!! Shan, you make us so proud . . . your dedication is abundant and it's paying off."

Shanann went to great lengths to present herself and Chris as a team, adopting the hashtag #TeamRockStars. She did all the work on his behalf, posting on social media and staging elaborate Thrive photo opportunities.

Under her supervision he reluctantly achieved 12K VIP Status, earning his Le-Vel car bonus. She instructed him never to tell anyone that she was behind his success.

"She put me underneath her," he later explained. "If I wanted to talk to somebody at the mall or the pool about [Thrive], I just stumble all over my words. I'm not a salesman."

But on Facebook, Shanann applauded her husband's sales prowess.

"So excited for my husband Chris for earning his car bonus!!!" she wrote. "So proud of you honey!"

Both Bella and Celeste were constantly ill, and Shanann was regularly taking them for medical treatment. She described one such scenario to her Facebook followers:

"Up all night long back and forth to each bedroom," she wrote, "trying to help them to breathe better, sooth their cough and comfort them. Hate them feeling so bad and miserable."

Four days later, Shanann took Celeste to the hospital at 4:00 A.M. for an eye procedure for a blocked tear duct. Then she had to go to the dentist after "busting her mouth."

Soon afterward Bella was admitted to Children's Hospital with pneumonia. Her mother posted videos of her at the hospital in a surgical mask after having chest X-rays.

"Bella and Celeste were back and forth to doctors," said Sandi Rzucek. "I told Shanann that they had asthma and that she needed to fire [the] doctors."

Chris often took time off work for his daughters' doctor's appointments, telling his boss, Luke Epple, about their health issues and the problems they were causing.

"Both of his kids have been pretty sick over the past couple of years," said Epple. "So he would talk a little bit about the stress that that puts on him and his wife."

In late September 2016, Shanann began posting live Facebook videos. She boosted her presence on social media with the videos, regularly proselytizing about Thrive.

Once shy and insecure, she was a natural in front of the camera, and her business increased exponentially.

Once Shanann went live on Facebook, there was no stopping her. She even invented her own catchphrases such as "I'm super-excited."

Her old drama teacher, Matt Francis, became a fan, impressed with how far she had come from the shy teenager he had first met.

"I would encourage her," he said, "and say, 'I think it's awesome what you're doing.'"

Francis, now back in touch with Shanann, followed her Facebook broadcasts avidly.

"She turned her self-loathing into a [positive]," he said. "She flipped the switch and said, 'I'm going to put my life out there and encourage others. Period.'"

Shanann secretly recorded Chris in the kitchen singing the *Mickey Mouse Clubhouse* song "Hot Dog!" with Bella and Celeste looking on. He was wearing his favorite METAL UP YOUR ASS Metallica T-shirt and had recently got a giant shoulder-to-shoulder Metallica tattoo on his back as a tribute to his favorite band.

Unaware of being videoed, he even did a little dance at the end. Shanann titled it "Best daddy EVER!" with the hashtag "#HesGoingToKillMe."

Through their constant promotion of Thrive, Shanann and Chris had earned an all-expenses-paid getaway to New Orleans. It would be their first real vacation together, and she would finally get to meet her new Thrive friends in person. The highlight of the New Orleans trip would be a fancy masquerade ball, so Shanann took Chris shopping for a suit to wear.

The night before they left, Shanann posted a picture of her nightstand, showing the books she was now reading.

There was a copy of Dale Carnegie's *How to Win Friends & Influence People* and of *The Four Year Career, Young Living Edition,* by Richard B. Brooke, with a framed photograph of her and Chris.

On Wednesday, October 5, Shanann and Chris flew out of Denver Airport, posting a photograph of themselves on the plane showing off their Thrive patches. They had a stopover in Houston, where Shanann met fellow team member Chrissy McMullan for the first time and excitedly posted photographs from the terminal.

After checking into the Hyatt in New Orleans, they went out to explore the French Quarter with Cristina Meacham, an old friend of Shanann's from North Carolina who now lived in Hawaii. They ate a Cajun dinner at the Café Soulé, posting a group shot on Facebook.

The next night Shanann and Chris attended the masquerade ball. Shanann wore a purple sequined gown with a side-slit to the thigh and a graphic decorative mask. Chris wore his new suit and tie and a Phantom of the Opera mask.

Chris appeared to be enjoying himself, posing with the others for a series of Thrive photo opportunities for Facebook. Although he disliked being in the limelight, he buried his true feelings, even posing for a goofy picture in a bunny hat before boarding the flight home.

With the holidays approaching, Shanann increased her presence on Facebook. Besides holding Thrive promotions for her customers, she now chronicled almost every aspect of her and Chris's apparently idyllic family life.

Much of it was hard sell as she introduced creative incentives to recruit new customers. She even invested her own money to buy competition prizes.

In another Facebook Live she described how Chris became a cleaning machine after taking a new Thrive product: "Chris literally cleaned the house while I was out running errands. And then he lifted weights for an hour."

12

"HE COMPLETES ME"

By mid-November 2016, Shanann was ready for the holidays. She had already taken Bella and CeCe to see Santa in a local mall and trimmed her two Christmas trees in the living room. Her friend Addy Molony challenged her to share everything she was grateful for every day for two weeks. Shanann had no hesitation with her number one.

"My husband Chris," she wrote. "He is my biggest supporter! He's an amazing father to our beautiful girls and the BEST husband EVER!"

Then, becoming emotional, she wrote how he was growing as a person: "My husband is very shy. So we blend very well as individuals because I'm very outgoing and very vocal, whereas he's shy and behind the scenes, so to speak. And he's grown a lot in the last couple of months."

By Thanksgiving, Shanann was counting the days until her and Chris's next Thrive vacation, to Punta Cana. Chris's parents were coming to babysit Bella and Celeste. Shanann and Chris had never before been abroad, so they applied for passports. They had wanted to honeymoon in Cancún, she said, but had not been able to afford it.

"Chris and I have not been able to travel the world

together like we wanted to," she said. "We should have been on a couple of vacations by now . . . and we haven't been able to."

Chris had already requested time off work, and she was getting her body back into "bikini shape" for the beach.

"I love being able to travel with my husband," she said, "and with my kids when we are ready to go. And to take them places and go to Disney. Those are the memories you are creating with your family."

On November 27, Shanann posted one of her last "gratitudisms" from Addy Molony's challenge.

"I'm grateful for my in-laws!" she wrote. "It was a rough start 6 years ago, but today we are closer than ever. I am blessed to have supportive, motivating and encouraging in-laws. They are amazing grandparents and amazing 2nd parents for me."

A few days later they were buying Christmas presents in Toys "R" Us when Chris bought himself something special. Shanann thought it so hilarious that she went on Facebook to tell everyone. For the next few minutes she teased her viewers about what it could possibly be— before revealing it was a fart blaster.

Then, with a big smirk, she started demonstrating the toy, pulling the trigger to make fart sounds.

"This is what Chris wanted?" she asked, pulling the trigger again. "Seriously Dude!"

The first week of December, Celeste ate two small cashew nuts and had a severe allergic reaction. She was sick all over her mother and broke out in hives. Shanann rushed her to Children's Hospital, where she vomited three more times.

"Extremely scary," posted Shanann from the hospital.

"Chris came from work, which I'm grateful for. They gave her epi pen, Zofran and prednisone."

The doctors kept CeCe under observation for nine hours, before diagnosing a severe allergy to nuts, which had caused an anaphylactic reaction.

Later that night Shanann thanked all for their support.

"Officially home and SHOWERED!!" she wrote. "Thanks everyone for prayers and thoughts today. The scariest thing we have had to deal with."

Shanann was now broadcasting longer and longer Facebook Lives from her home office. She would usually begin with her current Thrive promotion, before recounting her daily life as a wife and mother. A recurring theme was her love for Chris.

"I couldn't have asked God for a better man in my life," she said in one Live, "because he's so supportive. He takes care of me. He's probably the best father I could have asked for, for my children. And I couldn't have asked for a better man. But he completes me. I know that's a cliché but it's the truth. He completes me."

On December 17, Bella turned three years old and Shanann threw her a Princess Sofia party and invited all Bella's friends.

"Happy Birthday my beautiful princess," Shanann posted. "These 3 years you have taught us so much! Your love is pure and innocent! You're an amazing big sister and a wonderful daughter! Love you so much!"

But the very next day, Bella had to be rushed to Children's Hospital.

"Bella has an ear infection," posted Shanann. "Celeste is throwing up I'm hoping from congestion and not another virus. I have a DFT Ultra and Reg DFT to keep me healthy and strong for my sick kiddoes."

She later announced that both girls had been diagnosed with a croup infection of the upper airways, which blocks breathing and causes a loud barking cough.

On Christmas morning Chris Watts once again dressed up in a full Santa Claus outfit to give Bella and Celeste their Christmas presents. Shanann was delighted with a present he had bought her—a T-shirt with the words WIFE, MOM, BOSS.

13

PUNTA CANA

On January 1, 2017, Shanann welcomed the New Year with a live broadcast from her Lexus with Chris driving. Wearing a Pittsburgh Steelers vest, she told her followers about her new vision board, to help her and her family attain their goals for 2017.

Endorsed by Oprah Winfrey, a vision board is a collage of images, pictures, and statements of dreams and desires. The idea is to visualize goals and then attain them.

"It's truly an incredible thing to do," she explained, "when you see your goals everyday, you see your dreams [and] what you want to accomplish. I think it really sets forth a guide for the year."

She planned to have two vision boards in her office, as well as others throughout the house.

"I think the more you see what you want to accomplish," she said, "whether it's tiny or big. It really keeps in the mindset and you will work towards it. It's truly inspiring."

Shanann said her first vision board a decade earlier had helped build her first home.

"And I did that at twenty-five years old," she said. "So I think it's very important to sit down, look at what your past year's been . . . what you loved and what you want to bring into 2017—just things that empower yourself."

Since joining the Thrive program, Chris Watts had toned up his body and got into shape. He was now eating healthy food, had joined a gym, and went running every morning before work.

"He would drink water like crazy," said his workmate Anthony Brown. "Two or three gallons a day."

Chris would occasionally join his workmates for after-work drinks at the Georgia Boys BBQ in Frederick.

"They usually came in as a big group for lunch," remembered bartender Bill Ferrie. "The oil industry do a lot of business right here in this restaurant and I recognized his face."

Kodi Roberts, who also worked with Chris, said he was quiet during those get-togethers.

"He keeps most of his personal life to himself," Roberts said. "That's just who he is. When the kids [were] sick, he [said] something. A new car, he [said] something. He's quiet but friendly."

Shanann's Facebook Lives were becoming more personal, focusing on Chris and their children. She would become emotional as she described her perfect marriage.

"Chris and I have an amazing relationship," she said in late January, relaxing outside on her deck in sunglasses. "We get each other. I'm definitely the dominant one in the relationship. He's very sweet. He's very calm. I'm the high-strung one."

But there were hints that not all was perfect in the Watts household. Their neighbor Nathaniel Trinastich and his wife sometimes heard Chris and Shanann screaming at each other late at night during raging arguments. But whenever he saw them together, they seemed loving and affectionate.

At the end of January, Ronnie and Cindy Watts arrived in Frederick for two weeks to take care of their grand-daughters while Chris and Shanann were in Punta Cana. Shanann posted videos of Cindy, now affectionately known as MeMe, arriving at Denver Airport to be welcomed by Bella and Celeste.

Shanann took her mother-in-law for a manicure and pedicure, posting a photograph of it on Facebook. Then she signed Ronnie up as a Thrive promoter.

"She tried to pump everybody full of Thrive," said Cindy. "She got my husband on it and I took it and it made me so jittery. We did it for Chris."

A couple of days later Shanann posted a photograph of her father-in-law proudly displaying his new DFT patch on his upper arm.

"A huge shout out goes out to Ronnie Watts for hitting 4K VIP and 4K rank," Shanann wrote. "You are on fire."

On Tuesday, January 31, Chris and Shanann flew to Punta Cana, with a stopover in Charlotte, North Carolina. While waiting for their connecting flight, Shanann posted a playful photograph of Chris with his teeth bared, pretending to bite her face-filter-app bunny ears.

They landed in the Dominican Republic at 1:30 A.M., welcomed by three merengue players. Chris did a little dance for the camera before he and Shanann took the bus to the Hard Rock Hotel & Casino.

The next morning, Shanann gave her Facebook followers a tour of their hotel room, pointing out the Jacuzzi and a fully stocked bar.

"This place is absolutely gorgeous," she gushed. "Like paradise."

Back in Colorado, their two sets of parents were not getting on. Cindy and Ronnie stayed upstairs with Bella and Celeste, while Frank and Sandi remained in the basement. Shanann's mother later complained that they had not been allowed to see their granddaughters.

"[Cindy] brought them upstairs and stayed upstairs," Sandi said. "She wouldn't let us hold them or anything. I found that very odd."

Finally, according to Sandi, she asked Chris's mother for an explanation, and a screaming argument in front of the girls ensued.

"I texted Shanann over and over again," said Sandi, "and she said, 'Relax, Mom. I'll take care of it when we get home.' I never spoke to Chris's mom again. I had enough."

A few weeks later, Frank and Sandi Rzucek moved back to Aberdeen, North Carolina, taking their dogs with them. Frankie had been living in their house since they had moved to Colorado and was not doing well.

Shanann told a friend back in North Carolina that her younger brother was having "some issues" and couldn't pay the bills.

"It was real quick," the friend said. "[Shanann] told me they didn't want to lose their house. But I know it did bother her. I think it hurt her feelings."

14

"FAT BURNING MACHINE"

In February, Shanann invited Primrose School director Amanda Thayer and her husband, Nick, to their house. They brought along their daughter, Amalie, who immediately bonded with Bella and Celeste. Chris and Nick also got along well and started running together every morning.

From then on the two families became close, meeting up at weekends. Shanann soon turned them on to Thrive, and Amanda became a promoter. She thought Shanann was absolutely smitten with Chris.

"She just talked about how much she loved him," said Amanda, "and how he was her rock."

Nick was also impressed by what a loving family the Wattses appeared to be.

"It was always fun and laughing," he recalled. "They just seemed like a happy couple."

The two couples would often go out to eat together or hang out at the Wattses' house playing board games.

"Had a great time with our friends last night playing Uno!" Shanann posted after one evening. "The men cheated !!!"

That Easter, Shanann booked a session with a professional photography studio in Denver for a series of family photographs. The Wattses posed with a life-size Easter bunny, and Shanann uploaded all the photos to social media over the Easter holiday.

She also started posting inspirational daily love notes purportedly from Chris, scribbled in black marker on Thrive Lifestyle Mix sachets. One read, "Strive For Greatness— I'm so Lucky to Have You $ 80K 200K." Another said, "DETERMINED! STRIVE FOR GREATNESS. 80K 200K. NO LIMITS."

"I love my note my husband writes every day!" she told her followers.

But some wondered if she was writing the notes herself.

Shanann posted a photograph of her and Chris setting off for a "date night" at Benihana.

"Looking fabulous!" commented Amanda Aikman. "Has Chris lost weight? Y'all have that Thriver's glow!"

"Thank you," replied Shanann. "Chris is down over 40 lbs. He's 194 again. Wearing a shirt that I bought him 7 years ago. He feels amazing."

Although Shanann wrote all of her husband's Thrive Facebook postings, she kept up the pretense that it was him. He was now a 12K VIP promoter, and at the beginning of April, she posted a photo of him working on his iPhone in a muscle T-shirt.

"Love watching him work his business," she wrote, "and help his friends start their Thrive Experience!"

At the beginning of April, Shanann quit Children's Hospital to devote herself full-time to Thrive. She proudly posted the news on Facebook with a photo of her Pediatric identity card.

"Officially retired from Children's Hospital!!" she wrote. "Turned in my computer and badge! I'm really excited and looking forward to working from wherever my girls are."

That week Cindy and Ronnie flew in from North Carolina to spend a few days with their granddaughters. Once again there was tension between Shanann and her in-laws, who were struggling financially.

"It was a strain to go up there twice a year," said Chris's mother. "We spent money on the kids, which went on our credit cards. So it was difficult and she didn't seem to understand that. Nothing we did seemed like it ever satisfied her."

And although Cindy never saw her son argue with Shanann, Cindy suspected that all was not right in the marriage.

"I've never seen her scream at Chris," she said, "but I'm sure there was something in private, because she always had that angry look on her face, like she was disgusted with him. And he tried to please and please and please."

A week later a gas-leak explosion destroyed a house in Firestone, Colorado, killing two men and injuring a woman. It was just yards away from an aging Anadarko oil well and eight miles from the Wattses' house.

In the wake of the tragedy, Anadarko shut down three thousand oil wells to investigate the cause of the explosion. Chris and his team put down their tools while every well was examined for gas leakages.

"We shut down all our wells," said Anthony Brown. "Our team had meetings because they were . . . checking procedures for safety."

During the hiatus, Brown became closer to Chris Watts.

"There wasn't a lot for us to do except wait for instructions," explained Brown, "and we would talk . . . and just hang out. [Chris] was big into sports and we talked about DraftKings and 'Did you see this on the Rockies' game?'"

Twice a month their Anadarko team had poker nights. Chris was always invited, but never went.

"We're always looking for regulars . . . to get a game going," said Brown. "Chris said he was going to come a few times, but he never did, so we stopped asking him."

On May 16, 2017, Chris Watts turned thirty-two, and Shanann gave him a Metallica T-shirt and tickets for their upcoming show in Denver. He was ecstatic. She had bought the tickets when the tour had first been announced and managed to keep it a secret.

"I need a gold 🏆 for buying Chris' birthday present over 3 mo ago," she said. "That's huge for me. I think this birthday gift is up there with the Roush supercharger I bought him 4 years ago."

Then Shanann streamed him live opening his birthday present, wrapped in a large Thrive box, as his excited daughters looked on.

"Oh, you've got to be kidding me," said Chris, as he pulled out a black Metallica Colorado T-shirt and a pair of concert tickets. "Are you serious?"

Then he gave Shanann a big kiss. It was perhaps the only genuine display of emotion he ever showed online.

"Oh my goodness," he said breathlessly. "Hell, yeah!"

"You deserve it bro," commented Frankie Rzucek under the video. "Such a great man."

On June 5, Celeste started at the Primrose School, nine months after Bella, who was now in pre-K1. It would be expensive, costing $25,000 a year for both girls and prove even more of a drain on their finances, although Shanann justified it by saying she would be more productive without their distractions.

"Both girls are in school first time together," she posted. "Chris and I have accomplished so much today since we dropped the kids off."

A week later, Shanann and Chris took their seats for the Metallica show at the Broncos' stadium in Denver.

"We are wearing Metallica's favorite DFT!" posted Shanann. "Black Label!"

Chris, wearing his new Metallica T-shirt, looked ecstatic in the video Shanann later posted on Facebook.

"Birthday boy is happy," she wrote, as he pumped his fists in the air to "Creeping Death." Further into the show, Shanann filmed him blissfully rocking back and forth holding his cell phone, a strange smile on his face.

Shanann posted a photograph of Chris proudly displaying his new twin DUO patches, directly underneath a massive Metallica back tattoo he had recently gotten. The new product guaranteed double the energy of the regular patch.

"FAT BURNING MACHINE!!!" Shanann wrote beneath it.

Over the next few months, Chris lost another twenty pounds, turning his basement into a gym with weights and an elliptical machine. He was now fanatical about his daily runs and workouts.

"He was on a lot of Thrive," said his mother. "He had the DUO patch on . . . that is a double patch that you wear for losing weight."

Shanann was now posting videos of her husband doing push-ups with Bella and Celeste on his back.

"Girls really giving daddy a workout," she commented on one. "Probably his 50th push up #DaddyHulk."

On Thursday, June 22, Shanann flew to Toronto for her third Le-Vel lifestyle getaway. Although she had earned an all-expenses-paid trip for two, Chris stayed home to look after the girls. Shanann gleefully told her Facebook followers that he would wash all the carpets while she was gone.

"Missing Chris on this one," she wrote. "It's OK, he will be with me on the next one in the fall."

The first night Shanann attended a thrift-shop-themed party, wearing a carnivalesque outfit with long white tassel earrings, a tight-fitting top with bell sleeves, and stiletto shoes. She went on Facebook Live during the festivities.

"One of the perks of coming to a lifestyle getaway is it is strictly like fun vacation, no training," she said. "Nothing to do but mingling."

The next night she went to a surprise VIP party in the ballroom at the Fairmont Hotel, where it was announced that the next lifestyle getaway would be in October to Puerto Vallarta.

"Oh how I can't wait," she posted. "Chris we are going to have so much fun!!!"

On Monday, July 17, Celeste turned two and her parents threw her a birthday party. They invited all their friends, including Nickole Atkinson and her one-year-old daughter, Madison.

"Happy Birthday my sweet Celeste!" posted Shanann, alongside pictures of Chris and the girls at the party. "I can't believe you are 2 already! These last two years have shined so bright! You are silly, energetic, fearless, happy, loving and have an amazing personality! Couldn't thank God enough for placing you into our family!"

Two days later, Bella was admitted to Children's Hospital with trouble breathing. She was diagnosed with viral pneumonitis, inflammation of the lungs, and hypoxia and treated with deep suction, steroids, and oxygen.

"She's a tough little girl," wrote her mother on Facebook. "Between Celeste's hospital visit last week for difficulty breathing I'm going to know all the RT's, nurses and doctors over here!"

The next day Shanann announced both girls were being treated with a nebulizer for asthma and viral pneumonitis. She posted pictures of them hooked up to the breathing masks.

Every morning after a grueling five-mile run with Nick Thayer, Chris Watts drove his Anadarko truck to the company's Platteville office. He'd walk into the break room around six fifteen and join his other team members as they waited for their assignments.

Recently a young woman named Nikki Kessinger, who worked in health and safety, had been assigned to the Anadarko office. Each morning she walked through the break room and into the cafeteria to put her lunch in the fridge. She always turned heads.

"Nikki [was] a brunette with a good body," recalled Anthony Brown. "Chris would be on his laptop, and when she'd walk by, he'd look up . . . and stare at her awkwardly."

Most days someone would comment on what she was wearing and make locker-room talk.

"She knows she's attractive," said Brown, "and she was just trying to get attention. We talked about her, and [Chris] would smirk. He kept quiet."

Later, Kessinger would tell detectives that although she did notice Chris Watts, they never exchanged words.

"I'll go in the cafeteria," she said. "Him and his whole team are sitting in there. I don't talk to them. I just walk out."

But according to police records, at 11:00 P.M. on August 3, 2017, she searched the internet for Chris Watts. A month later, she googled Shanann Watts.

15

"A VERY ACTIVE FATHER"

That August, the Anadarko team had a competition to see who could lose the most weight in three months.

Said Anthony Brown, "[Chris] is like, 'I can't lose any more weight than I already have."

Chris tried to sell Brown the Thrive DUO patch to help him win the competition. Brown refused, calling it a "pyramid scheme."

Brown recalled, "And he's like, 'Yeah, my wife's pretty high up there and she got a free car.' And [he offered] incentives for me to join with them. That's the only time he really talked to me."

As a result of being friends with Chris on Facebook, Brown saw all Shanann's voluminous postings. Finally he blocked her.

"It would be updates of her trying to [promote] Thrive," he said. "And 'I did the laundry today. Got the kids packed for school. Lunch made. Cleaned house.' And I'd get five or six [posts] a day through his Facebook."

David Colon also defriended her on Facebook.

"She posted every three minutes," he said. "It was just kind of crazy."

Even Cindy Watts tuned out her daughter-in-law's Facebook videos, knowing her son was faking it.

"There were so many videos out there," she said. "I

couldn't watch poor Christopher going through the motions and looking so uncomfortable."

Ever since she was a little girl, Shanann had suffered from crippling migraines. They had now become so bad that she decided to have arthroplasty neck surgery to fix a degenerative disc. In mid-August, her friend Cristina Meacham flew in from Hawaii to help her through the surgery and take care of the girls. Cristina brought along her daughter, Koral, who was the same age as Bella.

"She's like my sister," said Cristina. "I [would be] her right-hand person until she was healthy enough."

Although Cristina had met Chris casually at several lifestyle getaways, it was the first time she'd spent a prolonged period with him and Shanann. She thought they were perfect together.

"They had a great marriage," said Cristina. "It was amazing to see how they were as parents and as a couple."

Over the two months she lived with them, Cristina was impressed by Chris's devotion to his two small daughters.

"He [would] come home from work and help get them showered and ready for bed," she said. "A very active father. Very caring. Very loving and very attentive to them."

She also observed how he always deferred to Shanann, whom Cristina thought somewhat OCD in the strict, regimented way she organized the household.

"She was the person in charge and he followed through," said Cristina. "He did what she wanted, but they seemed to be . . . very lovey-dovey."

On Sunday, August 20, Shanann cooked a meal for just her and Cristina. It was one week before the surgery and Shanann had been told by her doctors to stop taking Thrive.

During the meal, the two talked about their goals over a bottle of white wine.

Shanann confided that she and Chris were struggling

financially, especially since her complicated spinal surgery would cost them $25,000 and put them into debt.

"I know that they struggled," said Cristina, "but I don't know to what point."

Chris drove Shanann to the Littleton Adventist Hospital in Littleton, Colorado, where she underwent anterior cervical discectomy and fusion surgery (ACDF) to remove a degenerative disc in the neck. Doctors made a one-inch incision in her throat area and removed the disc, which was pressing on her spinal cord. A graft was then inserted to fuse together the bones over and under the disc. A plate was screwed into the front of her spine until it healed.

A day later, Chris announced the surgery had been a success.

"This is Chris," he posted on Shanann's Facebook page. "I wanted to let everyone know Shanann's neck surgery yesterday went well. She is going to be staying another night. She's in a lot of pain, but she's doing good. She's strong and still trying to help others. Thank you everyone for prayers and checking up on her!"

While she healed, Shanann had to wear a neck brace, which she hated, as it made her self-conscious. The surgery had also left a visible scar on her neck. But during her recovery she never slowed down with her Thrive business; from her hospital bed within hours of the surgery, she had earned her airfare for an upcoming getaway to Mexico. Although she was busy putting together trial packs for prospective new customers, she was unable to take any Thrive on doctor's orders.

The third week of September, Shanann and Cristina Meacham took a road trip to Las Vegas for the Team Relentless Training Party. They left at three o'clock in the morning, tiptoeing out of the house so as not to awake Bella and Celeste.

Cristina drove Shanann's white Lexus for the eight-hundred-mile journey through Utah and Arizona.

"I have the BEST hubby ever," wrote Shanann. "This weekend Cristina and I drove down to Vegas for our team's yearly Celebration/training and Chris is taking care of the 3 munchkins."

"Great job Chris," commented his father-in-law.

At the training party at Stoney's Rockin' Country, on Las Vegas Boulevard, someone told her to pretend she was wearing the brace because she'd been bitten by a shark in Australia.

"So I did that for the rest of the day," she said, "and the looks I got from everyone was Priceless!"

In early October, Cristina and Koral flew back to Hawaii and Shanann took off the neck brace. She was preparing for the next trip, to Puerto Vallarta, with her mother flying in to look after the girls.

"In less than 48 hours," she posted, "Chris and I will be on the beach sipping on margaritas! [This is] our 4th trip . . . in the last 12 months. Seriously, pinch me!"

Since he'd started wearing the DUO Burn, Chris had lost even more weight. Shanann was delighted, posting a video of him stripped to the waist mowing their yard.

"My yard guy is sexier than yours," she quipped.

The climax of the trip was to be an eighties-themed party, and Shanann bought her husband a Bon Jovi–style glam-rock wig to wear.

On October 12, they flew to Mexico, and after checking into their hotel room overlooking the ocean, Shanann and Chris went live on Facebook.

"So Chris has already cracked open a beer," she said. "He's excited."

"Yeah!" squealed Chris in a high voice, waving his beer can at the camera. "What's up?"

During the four-day getaway Shanann posted dozens of romantic photographs in an album titled "Love traveling the world with Chris." Usually shy and reserved, he stuck out his tongue for one photo at the eighties party, wearing his glam-rock wig.

"Chris and I are having an incredible time," she wrote, accompanying a Facebook Live video of them French-kissing in the pool. "Life is so short not to be this happy and feel this blessed."

16

"I'LL SEE YOU NEXT YEAR"

On Christmas Eve 2017, Chris Watts once again put on his Santa Claus outfit with a huge white beard and a large red sack of presents. The beard completely obscured his face. Shanann was going live for Santa's annual visit, but things weren't going according to plan. For a brief moment a glimpse of what was really going on in the Watts household leaked out to the world.

Celeste was crying hysterically, and Bella, wearing her green elf outfit, looked distracted as Shanann turned on the Christmas tree lights and went live. That was Chris's cue to enter through the front door.

"Santa's here," announced Shanann, "but the kids are freaking out. Hey, Santa, where's your phone?"

"On top of your car in the garage," replied Chris unenthusiastically, as Shanann flashed him a disapproving look.

"I needed it for the pictures," she said as she went into the garage to retrieve it. Then with her iPhone camera still running, she reversed the lens onto herself.

"My husband's a genius," she snapped. "Doesn't listen!"

After retrieving his phone she returned to the front room and placed her iPhone on the floor, so Santa and the tree were in focus. Then she went off to find Bella, who did not want to meet Santa.

"Come on, Bella," coaxed her mother. "Santa has presents."

When Bella came into the living room, Shanann tried to coax her into going over to Santa for her presents. But the little girl just stared at him in bewilderment.

"Merry Christmas, Bella," said Santa. "Have you been expecting me tonight?"

Then Shanann's parents came online from North Carolina and tried to get Bella to at least acknowledge Santa. Celeste could be heard crying off camera.

As Bella started opening her presents, Shanann left to find Celeste for family photos. A few moments later, Shanann returned and placed her on Santa's lap next to Bella.

"Hello, Miss Celeste, how are you?" asked Santa, waving his arms.

Finally, after taking half a dozen photographs of Santa and the girls, Shanann had had enough.

"All right, let's say goodbye to Santa," she said, gathering Celeste into her arms.

"Goodbye, girls," said Santa. "Ho, ho, ho. Enjoy your gifts."

As Santa walked toward the front door, he turned back to address his daughters. "I'll see you next year. I'll make sure I wave goodbye on the reindeer."

17

"SUCH A BEAUTIFUL COUPLE"

On New Year's Day, Shanann Watts vowed to double her team's 2017 sales. She had sold $720,699 of Thrive in 2017, more than twice as much as the year before.

"I am focused on doubling with my team in 2018," she announced in a Live, "because I want to . . . show my two little girls how to achieve their dreams and inspire them."

On January 6, she held her annual vision-board party at the house. She posted a photo of Bella holding up her 2018 vision board complete with pictures. The four-year-old wanted a Pony watch, gymnastic lessons, and trips to Disney and North Carolina, to see her two sets of grandparents.

Four days later Shanann celebrated her thirty-fourth birthday on Facebook Live with Chris and the girls. As they all sang "Happy Birthday," Frank and Sandi Rzucek joined in from Aberdeen.

A couple of days later Shanann posted a photograph of her and Chris sharing her birthday dinner.

"Such a beautiful couple!" commented Amanda Thayer. "Inside and out!"

* * *

Three weeks later, Shanann and Chris flew to Las Vegas for their fifth lifestyle getaway. They met Sandi Rzucek at Denver Airport, who had flown in to babysit.

"Nonna came to take care of the girls," Shanann posted, "while PopPop holds down the house in NC! We are blessed."

After landing in Vegas and checking in to the Wynn Hotel, Shanann and Chris were reunited with Cristina Meacham. They were also joined by their Thrive friends Samantha Pasley, Addy Molony, and Cassie Rosenberg and her husband, Josh.

The following morning Chris and Shanann test-drove a Tesla Model S, as part of a Le-Vel event. Shanann went first, with Chris streaming it live on Facebook. Then Chris got behind the wheel for his test-drive.

"Ever driven a Tesla?" asked the salesman.

"Never driven one," replied Chris. "I've worked on cars for a long time but never any of these."

As the representative described how the all-electric car went from zero to sixty miles per hour in just three seconds, Chris steered it out of the Las Vegas Convention Center and into traffic.

Then the salesman asked if he wanted some music.

"He likes Britney Spears," joked Shanann.

"No," said Chris, "we'll get a little Metallica, if you have anything on there."

"Anything specific?" the salesman asked.

"Can we do 'Justice for All'?" asked Chris.

As the heavy-metal beats of Metallica pounded through the speakers, Chris revved up the car onto the freeway.

"That felt pretty good," he said. "That felt pretty smooth. It'll sneak up on you . . . rolling down the Strip."

Metallica's "The Unforgiven" came on next, and

Chris started tapping the steering wheel in time with the music.

After test-driving the Tesla Model S, which starts at $78,000, Chris and Shanann agreed they'd prefer the top-of-the-line Model X, almost $10,000 more.

A few days later, back in Colorado, Chris good-naturedly subjected himself to the Pie Face Sky High! game. He went down on his knees and put his head through a hole at the top of the three-foot-high machine. Directly below was a container of whipped cream, which Bella would launch by hitting the baseplate with a plastic hammer.

As Bella prepared to cover her father's face in whipped cream, Shanann went live on Facebook as her mother cheered her on.

"Hit it down there," shouted Sandi.

"Hit it hard, Bella," said Shanann.

Then she hit the baseplate with all her strength, sending the whipped cream straight into her father's face, to Bella's delight.

"Nice, nice, nice," said a smiling Chris. "Do it again."

She did, scoring another direct hit.

"Nice," said her father, as he proudly high-fived her.

In the wake of Las Vegas, Shanann decided to trade in the Lexus for something better, out of her and Chris's combined $1,600 car allowance from Le-Vel. Shanann said she loved driving a Tesla, but what she really wanted was an Audi.

"I think I'm an Audi girl," she told her Facebook followers, "because they're awesome."

On social media Shanann and Chris appeared to be living the good life, but in truth they were drowning in debt. Although Shanann was now earning around $60,000 a year and Chris $62,000, they were still living well beyond their means.

They paid around $25,000 a year for the Primrose School, as well as mounting medical bills from Shanann's neck surgery and the girls' overnight hospital stays. They now lived paycheck to paycheck, owing thousands in credit card debt.

In March, they received a warning letter from Chase Bank for being three months behind with mortgage payments. In desperation Shanann took out a $10,000 loan against Chris's 401(k) to try to catch up. They also owed the Wyndham Hill Master Association a year of monthly dues and faced a civil court action.

"She was stressed-out about it," Chris would later explain. "That's why we took the 401(k) loan out. That was the max we could do and just put it all towards the house and get[ting] caught up."

But there was no hint of any problem in Shanann's aspirational social media postings.

"Turning in Explorer tomorrow," she wrote at the end of February, "and deciding on Audi Q7 or Tesla X."

A week later she posted photographs of Audis at a dealership in Broomfield.

"Coming back tomorrow," she wrote, "to test drive some of these beauties! Then maybe hit up Tesla dealership."

On February 23, Shanann became an 80K VIP Brand Promoter, just one rung below the highest ranking, the 200K VIP level. She would now earn a 4 percent commission on the eight levels of customers and promoters below her.

She had around two hundred customers beneath her, including fifty promoters. Under the Le-Vel hierarchy,

Addy Molony was her team leader, who in turn reported to Sam Pasley. Dubbed the Rockstar team, it did almost a million dollars in annual sales.

On March 12, Bella was back at the Children's Hospital ENT with breathing problems. Two days later she and Celeste both underwent surgery to remove their adenoids. The night before the operations their mother posted photographs of Chris cuddling the girls.

"Celeste and Bella are ready for their bilateral ear tubes and adenoidectomy," she wrote. "These girls share everything."

While they were in surgery, Shanann updated her Facebook followers.

"Had about 2 hours of sleep last night," she wrote. "I had a lot on my mind with girls surgery today."

Later that day she posted photographs of Bella and Celeste on their way home.

"Girls' surgeries went well," wrote Shanann. "Thanks everyone for prayers."

That spring of 2018, Shanann told friends she was trying to get pregnant again and that Chris wanted a boy.

"They were planning on having a third kid," said Jennifer Lindstrom. "She [told me] she knows the great dad that he is and that he'd always be there to help."

Shanann was also planning to take Bella and Celeste to North Carolina for an extended trip. It would be the first time she'd been back since their marriage.

"She wanted to come and visit everyone," said Frank Rzucek. "It went from a week . . . to two. And then she says, 'No, let me do six weeks [and] just spend the summer.'"

* * *

On April 26, Shanann flew to New Orleans for Le-Vel's annual Thrivepalooza, leaving Chris behind with the kids. It was a big weekend for Shanann, who had been profiled in the first edition of *Strive,* Le-Vel's new glossy magazine. The feature, titled "Time for a Reset," carried a full-page color photograph of her, Chris, and their daughters.

"After being a caretaker for everyone else," it began, "Shanann Watts started taking care of herself. And she's never been happier."

During the five-day trip, Shanann shared a hotel room with half a dozen Thrive friends, including Kellie Ann Burke, Cassie Rosenberg, and Nickole Atkinson.

"It was six of us in a room having fun," said Shanann, "chitchatting, girl talk."

Every morning Shanann started the day by dancing on everybody's bed to Justin Timberlake's "Can't Stop the Feeling."

"I got up super-early and woke everybody up," she said. "They loved me."

It was a busy five days with training during the day and social events at night. On the last night, Shanann donned a sexy leopard-print dress with a slit up the side.

During the evening, Shanann was called up onstage to receive a blown-up framed copy of her *Strive* magazine profile from Le-Vel joint CEOs, Paul Gravette and Jason Camper. She was terrified.

"It was the scariest thing ever," she said. "Like walking onstage in front of twenty-five thousand people I'm like, 'Holy crap, am I going to trip in these heels? Am I going to bust my face?'"

But it all went perfectly as Shanann took the stage to thunderous applause.

"Good to see you," Gravette told her as he handed her

a bouquet of white roses and she posed for pictures with the two Le-Vel founders.

"Dreams do come true!" she wrote on Facebook next to a photograph of her holding her *Strive* profile. "I'm beyond BLESSED!"

PART TWO

18

"OOPS . . . WE DID IT *AGAIN*"

On Mother's Day, Chris Watts presented Shanann with a plaque he'd had specially made, listing all the important dates of their lives in embossed gold lettering. It read:

> Shanann Cathryn—01.10.84;
> Christopher Lee—05.16.85;
> Our Wedding—11.03.12;
> Bella Marie—12.17.13;
> Celeste Cathryn—07.17.15.

"Chris did great!" a delighted Shanann posted on Facebook. "I love my Mother's Day gift! Thank you Chris."

That same week they started trying to have a baby, posting photos of Bella and Celeste with the caption, "I wonder what 3 would be like!"

Chris had now lost so much weight that his wedding ring no longer fit, so he stopped wearing it. He did not get it resized. Although he told Shanann he wanted another child, he had fallen out of love with her and felt trapped in the marriage.

He hated the way she criticized him in front of Bella and CeCe, who had now started parroting her angry words back to him. Passive-aggressive by nature, Chris was now bottling up his anger and wanted to start a new life without Shanann.

Early one morning their neighbor Melinda Phillips was leaving for work when she saw Chris and Shanann having a raging argument in their driveway across the street.

"But they caught my eye and suddenly everything changed," Phillips later told *People* magazine. "They started talking a lot more calmly. He even gave her a hug."

This astonishing transformation happened in just the few seconds it took Phillips to load up her car.

"From a full-blown fight to hugs in less than a minute," she said. "It was incredible. They were putting on a show."

At 3:40 P.M. on Tuesday, May 29, Shanann Watts set up her iPhone and began filming in her kitchen. Chris was on his way home from work and she had a special surprise for him.

First she stepped in front of the camera to show off her new T-shirt with the words OOPS . . . WE DID IT *AGAIN.*

Then Dieter padded toward the front door to welcome his master with a loud bark. Chris walked in wearing sunglasses, stopping midstride as he looked in his wife's direction. He seemed confused but started grinning when he saw her T-shirt.

"We did it again?" he asked, walking toward her and giving her a hug out of camera shot. "I like that shirt. Really?"

"Really."

When he came back into the frame, Chris was holding a pregnancy test and staring at it. "So pink means . . . ?"

"That's just the test."

"I know it," said Chris. "Is pink going to be girls?"

"I don't know, it's just a test."

"That's awesome." Chris leaned in and kissed her. "I guess when you want to, it happens. Wow!"

Shanann was delighted to be pregnant and called her friends and parents with the good news. But some of them, who knew how much she struggled with Bella's and Celeste's health issues, were secretly concerned.

"She told us she was pregnant again," said her father. "She had problems with Bella [and] Celeste and we were worried about her health."

Although it was Chris's idea to have another baby, he would later admit to being "scared."

"We had talked about it," he said. "It happened fast. It was like once or twice and she was pregnant. [I was] surprised."

The next morning he told his boss, Luke Epple, that Shanann was pregnant, swearing him to secrecy.

"He hadn't told hardly anyone," said Epple. "He was pretty excited."

Soon afterward, Chris told his parents.

"We were shocked," recalled Cindy Watts. "I thought, 'Well, they must really be doing good to have a third child.'"

Word soon got out at Anadarko, and a few mornings later Chris walked into the office and was congratulated by Troy McCoy.

"No one knew what he was talking about," said Anthony Brown. "And then Chris was waving his hand with three [fingers]. And he's like, 'We're having another baby.' And everyone in the room congratulated him."

Later that day while they were working in an oil field, Brown asked Chris how he felt becoming a father again. Chris seemed totally unemotional and asked Brown, whose wife had recently had several miscarriages, if he wanted another child.

"I was honest," said Brown. "I told him I don't think it's in our cards."

Then Chris looked at him and said, "Well, *do* you want one?"

"[He was] implying that I can have one of his," Brown later told detectives. "I thought he was joking [but] that was kind of a weird comment."

19

"MY DADDY IS A HERO"

On June 1, Chris Watts had problems with a computer app controlling the gas-monitor sensors out in the field. He went to health-and-safety representative Nikki Kessinger's office for help. It was the first time they had ever spoken.

"I had seen him before in the lunchroom but I didn't talk to him. So that day we just started talking," said Kessinger. "It was pretty casual [and] he didn't have a wedding ring on his finger."

Five days later, Kessinger emailed Luke Epple, Chris Watts, and several other Anadarko team members on her progress with the sensor problem.

Watts replied on his Anadarko email: "Thanks Nikki. Have a great rest of your day!!"

After that, they started running into each other in the office hallway.

"It was always hit-or-miss," she recalled. "It wasn't an everyday thing."

On June 8, Shanann put her husband on the newly released Thrive BURN patch, with dramatic results. Early the next morning, she reposted a text message from Chris, wearing a SUPER DAD T-shirt.

"I cannot stay still," it said. "I vacuumed kitchen, entry

ways and mopped them. Vacuumed downstairs and now moving upstairs."

Shanann listed her husband's accomplishments since he'd started infusing from the new patch.

"Chris, just said he's been more talkative since he started #Burn! Talking to random strangers. #Hesaintrovert."

She also posted more photographs of Chris stripped to the waist and mowing the lawn.

"I love my sexy man," she wrote.

On Monday, June 11, Shanann posted the "Oops . . . We Did It *Again*" video on Facebook with the caption, "How Chris found out. Hot Off The Press."

Then she went Live with Bella and Celeste, who were sitting together on the couch. Chris was shooting the video.

"Guess what, girls," she began. "Mommy has a baby in her belly. Are you guys excited?"

Both girls jumped up and started dancing with joy.

"Oh my goodness," said Shanann. "I love you girls."

"I want to give the baby a hug," squealed Bella, as she put her tiny head on her mother's stomach, as her father could be heard laughing off camera.

"So sweet," said Shanann. "Give me a kiss."

Shanann also staged an Instagram photograph of "teacher" Bella pointing a ruler at a blackboard on which she'd written, "Big Sister 101," for her "pupil" Celeste.

"Ready or not, Celeste" was the caption. "Here comes Baby Watts #3."

The next morning, Chris and Nikki Kessinger had their first real conversation. He explained how he had moved here from North Carolina and had two daughters. Then he took out his cell phone, showing her a photograph of Shanann and the girls on its lock screen.

"He started talking about his kids," remembered Nikki, "and then mentioned, 'Yes, I have a wife, but we're getting separated.'"

Nikki was impressed as Chris proudly showed her photographs of his daughters on his phone.

"I thought it was kind of cute," she said. "It was right around Father's Day, too."

A few hours later, Kessinger sent him an email: "Chris, Thank you for being honest with me this morning. Truthfulness is so underrated in our culture. Saludos Cordiales, Nikki."

An hour later, Chris replied, "Nikki, I'm a straightforward guy. Lying just complicates things. I think you're absolutely stunning and from what I've learned about you so far you seem like an amazing person. I hope to continue to get to know you better since we have a lot in common."

"It is always nice to find people you can relate to," Kessinger replied. "I enjoy talking to you as well. I feel understood. I'm looking for someone to build a beautiful life with (seems so simple but it is unrealistic sometimes). Build something similar to what you have done with your wife and those cute little girls. I do believe in karma so out of respect for myself, you and your family I think it is best if we keep that friendship at work."

Less than two hours later, Watts replied, "Yes, a beautiful life is something that is hard to find in this world since people always seem to have an agenda for everything. I do believe in karma so I agree with that as well. Any conversations we have will stay between us, no need to worry there."

He then gave her his work number in case she needed to get ahold of him in the field, saying the email service could be "spotty" out there.

"I have an early morning meeting," he told her, "and

then I'm [working] for a construction crew on various sites all day so if I don't see you tomorrow, I hope you have an amazing day!!!'"

That was the last message they would exchange using the Anadarko email.

On Father's Day, June 17, Shanann and the girls gave Chris a T-shirt they'd had especially made for him, with the words I'M A PROUD DAD OF TWO AWESOME DAUGHTERS WHO LOVE THE STEELERS.

Shanann also posted another montage of family photographs on Facebook, with a touching Father's Day message:

"Chris, we are so incredibly blessed to have you! You do so much everyday for us and take such great care of us. You are the reason I was brave enough to agree to number 3! You are incredible and we are so lucky to have you in our life! Happy Father's Day!"

She also filmed Bella, strapped in the back of the Lexus, singing a special song for her dad, which she had memorized as her present to him:

> *My daddy is a hero,*
> *He helps me grow up strong,*
> *He helps me snuggle,*
> *He reads me book,*
> *He ties my shoes,*
> *You're a hero through and through,*
> *Daddy, Daddy, I love you.*

Shortly afterward, Watts added Nikki Kessinger's mobile number to his work-phone contacts, knowing Shanann constantly checked his iPhone. He was smitten with Kessinger, but he was waiting for Shanann and the girls to go to North Carolina for the summer before he made his move.

"I thought it was just flirting," Chris later said. "I didn't think that something would actually happen. I've never been pursued by anybody before."

The week before he and Shanann went to San Diego for another Thrive getaway, Chris had several flirtatious conversations with Kessinger on his work phone. Then she told him only to use his personal phone, so no one at Anadarko would know they were talking.

As they got to know each other better, Chris started coming out of his shell. He felt comfortable with Nikki, and unlike his wife, she seemed really interested in what he had to say.

"It was just kind of feeling each other out," he said. "[Then] it just went to a different level and she was talking about meeting up after I got back from San Diego."

One morning, Lauren Arnold arrived at Shanann and Chris's house with her kids for a playdate. She walked in to find Shanann busy preparing for her six-week trip to North Carolina.

Shanann, saying she would be finding out her baby's gender while she was away, asked Lauren how her pregnancy was going.

"And I said, 'Well, I'm having a boy,'" said Lauren. "'So you have to have a boy.' She was excited and very happy."

On June 19, Shanann had a doctor's appointment and posted a sonogram of her new baby.

The baby's due date was January 31, 2019, and Shanann changed her iPhone password to 013119.

"Little Peanut," she wrote on Facebook. "I love Chris. He's the best dad us girls could ask for."

On June 21, Frank Rzucek flew in to take care of his granddaughters while Shanann and Chris were in San Diego. It was the first time Rzucek had visited for some time, and he immediately noticed a difference in Chris.

"They were going through this new Thrive stuff she was selling," he later told detectives. "And he started getting himself all built up and lost a lot of weight."

The usually passive Chris also seemed "sterner" with Bella and Celeste and was now "yelling" at them.

"What was he getting mad at the kids for?" asked Rzucek. "I looked at him like, 'Is that you yelling at the girls? I've never heard you do that.' It just caught me off guard because he never did it."

On Friday, June 22, Chris and Shanann flew to San Diego for their sixth lifestyle getaway. During the flight, Chris secretly added Nikki Kessinger's cell phone number into his iPhone contacts, under the listing "APC Health Safety Environmental."

They checked in to the Manchester Grand Hyatt and had dinner with Cristina Meacham, Nickole Atkinson, Addy Molony, and the Rosenbergs.

It was the first time Molony had seen Chris in six months, and she couldn't believe his dramatic physical transformation from "dad bod to buff."

While in San Diego, Chris visited an old friend, Mark Jamieson, who was stationed at the naval base nearby. The two had grown up together and Chris considered him his best friend.

"I told him about Nikki," Watts would later tell detectives. "I just came out with the whole story . . . that there was this girl at work I've been talking to. But I didn't tell him that I was going to meet up with her."

During the four-day trip, Chris and Shanann seemed as devoted as ever.

"[They were] lovey-dovey," said Nickole Atkinson. "I have tons of pictures of them on my phone."

Shanann posted many romantic pictures of her and Chris, including one of him tenderly massaging her shoulders in the swimming pool.

On Tuesday, June 26, they flew back to Denver. They arrived home to find a letter from the Wyndham Hill Master Association, ordering them to appear in Weld County Court on August 24 for failing to pay $683.80 in homeowner's dues. The association was now suing them for a total of $1,533.80, including attorney fees and court costs.

That afternoon Chris drove Shanann, her father, and the girls back to Denver Airport for the flight to Charlotte, North Carolina. Then he returned home and immediately called Nikki Kessinger, arranging to meet her the following afternoon after work.

20

"ELECTRIC WOMAN THAT TAKES MY BREATH AWAY"

Less than twenty-four hours after dropping off Shanann and the girls, Chris Watts met Nikki Kessinger at a nature preserve near her house in Northglenn, Colorado. Earlier, they had exchanged texts setting out some ground rules.

"Promise!" said Nikki. "I'm about loyalty, truthfulness and being dedicated. I don't like playing games . . . unless it's role playing. 😉"

"If you want me there I will be there," replied Chris.

In late afternoon they sat down on a bench by a lake. It was the first time they had been alone outside of the Anadarko office.

Nikki asked when he had decided to separate from his wife. Chris said it had been in late March, and since then they no longer slept together. He said they were putting their house up for sale and sorting out their finances.

"I asked why he had decided to separate from [Shanann]," recalled Nikki. "He told me she was bossy."

When Nikki asked what he meant by "bossy," Chris replied that she was controlling and belittled him in front of their children. He said the final straw had come when Bella and Celeste started to repeat Shanann's words back to him.

"[Chris] said that she was all about appearances in all

aspects of her life," said Nikki, "and that in front of her friends she was occasionally bossy, but she would turn it into a kind of a joke."

They hardly ever argued, he told her. The only time he tried to stand up for himself, she had thrown him out of the house for the night, so he had avoided any further confrontations. Nikki asked him when things had started going bad in his marriage.

"[Chris] said six years," she recalled, "and the last year or two were the worst. He said he tried to talk to her many times but it 'fell on deaf ears.'"

He complained that Shanann often ignored him, preferring to talk on the phone or go on Facebook. When Nikki asked if they had tried counseling to mend the marriage, Chris said they had not.

After several hours, they went back to Kessinger's house. Chris had brought two packets of condoms, one unopened and the other partially used. When she questioned why one of the packets was open, he said he got them when he and Shanann were still having sex, and they had been gathering dust in a closet.

When Nikki questioned why he used condoms with the mother of his children, Watts replied that Shanann did not like to "get messy."

The next day after work, Watts drove back to Kessinger's house and they went to bed again. Later, she informed him that she was leaving town for a few days and would be back for her birthday on July 3.

"I'm still going to see you!" she later texted him. "It won't be as often as we like but I will make it happen. You think you're the only one addicted right now? I'm so hooked on you."

Watts texted back, "Sleeping without your warm body next to me isn't going to be fun tonight."

On June 30, Watts went online and googled the Bandi-mere Speedway. Previously they had discussed their love of cars and drag racing and going to see a race together. Shanann had never showed any interest, and he was delighted to find someone who did.

"I have an idea btw," he texted her. "I have a free hotel stay at the holiday inn . . . not sure if you can swing it this month but we can road trip to the mountains or southern Colorado for a day or two if you want."

"Won't cost a dime lol," replied Nikki. She asked what his wife would think.

"She supports me," he replied. "It won't bother me. I'm not going to stop seeing you."

"I made up my mind," Kessinger texted back. "Are we bad people?"

Chris was infatuated with his new girlfriend. Shanann, Bella, and Celeste were fast receding from his mind. He was ready to move on.

"Being in your life is something that I crave," he texted Nikki on Sunday afternoon, July 1.

"I enjoyed our conversation tonight," she replied a few hours later. "I hope you have a great night. Sweet Dreams!"

Tuesday, July 3, was Nikki Kessinger's thirtieth birthday, and Chris arrived at her house bearing flowers and a birthday card with a poem he'd composed:

> *Your Energy is so insane,*
> *You heat me up, you make me melt, and*
> *Then you cool me down like rain.*

He also wrote her a love letter on pink paper, looking forward to their future together.

"Big things will happen this year," it read. "Dreams

will come true. That smile (that stare), that laugh (that giggle) gets me every time!! You are truly an amazing, inspirational and electric woman that takes my breath away every time I see you!"

Nikki Kessinger would later say she told Chris she wanted to take things slowly until his divorce came through.

"He was like in fifth gear the entire time," she said. "Maybe it was up to me to hit the brakes . . . but he was so kind to me . . . why was I going to push him away?"

She also laid down some parameters for their relationship: that he would always come to her house, where she lived alone with her dog.

"So I used to tell him," she said, "'This is our space.' I felt it was better to be in my place."

Chris finally felt as if he could be himself with Nikki, for the first time in his life.

"I was just always so nervous [with Shanann]," he said. "With Nikki it was just different. I was more in control."

The next morning, July 4, Chris woke up in Kessinger's bed to find Shanann had called a dozen times. He went outside to call her back, and Shanann said the girls wanted to talk to him. When he told her he was asleep, she angrily replied, "Screw you!" and slammed down the phone.

He told Nikki he had to go home. She was taking a shower and told him she was disappointed, as they had planned to spend the day together.

"I had to calm her down," he recalled. "It made her take a step back and wonder what she was doing. And I just told her, 'Just because I had to leave doesn't mean [anything].'"

Back at home, Chris called Shanann and the girls. He then called Kessinger and invited her over to help him set up a new fitness app she had told him about. She arrived to find him busy doing the housework.

"He had just cleaned his carpets, and the furniture was in the way of the door," she recalled.

When he took her into the living room, she saw a framed picture of Shanann holding Bella and Celeste.

"I said, 'My God, she's so beautiful and your little girls are beautiful, too,'" recalled Kessinger. "And we laughed."

She asked why he wouldn't want to fix his marriage, as he seemed to have the perfect life.

"And he's like, 'I don't really want to,'" said Kessinger. "'It's just not working out.'"

Chris took her on a tour of the house, and she wondered how the family could possibly afford such luxury.

"Everything in there [was] very nice," she said. "Like it all came with a very expensive price tag."

When they went upstairs past the master bedroom, Kessinger couldn't resist a peek inside at their ornate wooden four-poster bed.

Chris took her down in the basement, where there was exercise equipment and a bed, which he said he had been sleeping in since their separation. Nikki weighed him for the fitness app and he said Thrive was responsible for his drastic weight loss and suggested she try some.

"I never wanted to," she said. "I was uncomfortable with it . . . and I even looked on their website and still didn't completely understand it."

During their time together, she never saw Chris without at least two Thrive patches on his biceps, triceps, or lower back. Although she never questioned it, she remembered him saying that one was enough.

"He always wore two," she said. "Always. I remember thinking, 'I thought you only needed one of these. Why are you using two?'"

Then she fine-tuned his MyFitnessPal app and helped him set up a fitness regime.

After lunch, Kessinger left to go to a baseball game, and later that night Watts met Nick and Amanda Thayer to see the July 4 fireworks in nearby Thornton. Nick asked how Watts was coping with the bachelor life. He replied that it was "weird" being in an empty home, but he was working out all the time to take his mind off Shanann and the girls.

Nikki Kessinger had set up two dates on the eHarmony app for that night, but when neither turned up, she invited Chris over to her house. He came straightaway, apparently unconcerned that she was still dating.

Over the next five weeks, Chris Watts spent every night at Kessinger's house, having sex and watching movies with her. He only went home after work to change his clothes and eat dinner.

Shanann's calls now mostly went unanswered, and Chris seemed distracted during their nightly FaceTime sessions. Shanann intuitively knew that something had changed in their relationship, although she couldn't pin it down.

"She would FaceTime every night because of the children," said Frank Rzucek. "A few times she did catch Chris off guard, because she was like, 'What's going on? Are you going to pay attention to the children?' [It was] like he was in another world."

On Friday morning, July 6, Cindy Watts picked up Shanann and the girls to stay with the Wattses for a weekend. Before arriving in North Carolina, Shanann had given both sets of grandparents a list of preapproved foods for Celeste that wouldn't set off her allergies, stipulating that no nuts could be anywhere in the house.

"She had two EpiPens that she had to carry with her," said Frank Rzucek. "Little Celeste has severe allergies to tree nuts . . . so she told us all, 'Get rid of anything that's got nuts.' No problem. My wife cleaned the whole house out."

But when they arrived at her in-laws', Shanann didn't approve of the food there and went to the grocery store, spending $375 on food her daughter could eat.

That same night, Chris Watts took Nikki Kessinger out to see the new *Jurassic Park* movie in Westminster, Colorado. The 7:00 P.M. show was sold-out, so they bought tickets for the next one and walked around the Orchard Town Center outdoor mall.

"That was our first date," remembered Kessinger.

The night marked a new stage in their relationship, as Chris declared he was in love with her. He said that she made him feel comfortable for the first time in his life, and he wanted a loving relationship.

"He really enjoyed talking to me," said Nikki, "[because] he felt he could get out of his shell. And it wasn't just in his home life but in general. He said with me it made him feel like he could really just start talking about things that excited him."

But Kessinger was still hesitant about their future.

"I told him, 'If we're going to build a relationship . . . you are getting a divorce. I'm not ready to meet your children.'"

The next night they had a dinner date at the Rusty Bucket restaurant. Shanann called Chris all night and left several messages. He hardly noticed, as he was so entranced with his new girlfriend.

Finally at 5:15 A.M. on Sunday, he texted Shanann from Kessinger's house: "I'm sorry Boo. I fell asleep as soon as I got home. That heat killed me yesterday. I love you so much!!!"

21

NUTGATE

On Monday, Chris's sister, Jamie Lynn Williams, brought her two children, Dalton, ten, and Dylan, seven, over to her parents' house for the afternoon. Bella and CeCe played with their two older cousins and everything seemed fine until Dylan went to the fridge for some ice cream.

Shanann walked into the kitchen and was horrified to find Celeste about to eat the ice cream, which Shanann later claimed contained extracts of tree nuts.

"You're trying to kill my child," she screamed at her mother-in-law, who insisted it was just plain vanilla.

But Shanann rounded up her daughters and called her father to come and get them immediately.

"She . . . said, 'I've got to go,'" recalled Frank Rzucek. "'We had a blowout because she's got nuts on the table.'"

As Shanann was waiting for him to arrive, she furiously vented on Facebook about her in-laws: "Oh I'm not coming back. I don't have a car since I flew here so I'm waiting for my dad to get here to pick us up. This is the last time my kids step foot in her house. My heart is still racing 30 minutes later."

As soon as she got to her parents' home, she called Chris to tell him what had happened. He told her to calm down and that he would take care of it.

That night Shanann was back on Facebook: "My 2.5 is severely anaphylactic to almost all tree nuts, and we are visiting in laws. I specifically said we can't have them in the house when we stay. My mil stated we don't buy them. I arrived and on the floor shelf of her center island was a bag of pistachios (big bad one). I removed immediately.

"Today she lets her other grand daughter eat an ice cream that has all tree nuts in front of . . . my 2.5 year old child that can't have them. I said I don't appreciate it and removed my daughter. I'm beyond furious and she's telling me I'm overreacting when my child's life is at risk."

A few hours later, Shanann updated her post, saying that Chris had now confronted his mother about putting their daughter at risk.

"Her response to my husband was, this is a learning experience to my 2 year old to realize she can't always get what she wants! FU."

Shanann texted Chris strict instructions on how to handle his parents: "You should call your dad and tell him you did not appreciate your mom putting your daughter at risk today, nor do you like that she teased our girls. You should also say you don't appreciate her saying they have to learn they can't always get what they want!"

A few minutes later, Chris texted Shanann, "I will call him and tell him what I think about this. It's not fucking cool at all because it is the kids. I will set this right."

When Ronnie and Cindy Watts saw Shanann's angry posts, they blocked her on Facebook.

The next day, Shanann called Chris after work. She again told him to confront his parents about "Nutgate," as it was now being called. But he was evasive. Always non-confrontational, Chris hated challenging his parents, and it only put more distance between him and Shanann. He was now avoiding her calls and they communicated mainly by text.

"You ok?" Shanann texted him later that night. "It's like you don't want to talk. I kept trying to talk and I had to dig it out of you."

"I'm fine baby," he texted back. "The last few days at work have put a lot of responsibility on me with new people. I didn't mean to seem short Boo. I love you to the moon and back."

Meanwhile, Nikki and Chris were exchanging nude selfies of each other. To make sure Shanann never found them, Chris had downloaded a secret calculator app onto his iPhone, with a password required to reveal his hidden photographs and videos.

On Saturday, July 14, Watts and Kessinger went on a date to the Shelby American Collection museum in Boulder. It celebrated the legendary race-car driver and entrepreneur Carroll Shelby, who had designed Chris's beloved Shelby Ford Mustang.

He gave her a tour of the exhibits and photographed the classic Mustangs on display.

During the two hours they were there, Shanann called four times, all of which went unanswered. A few minutes after they left the museum she called again, and Chris had a brief conversation with her. Then Kessinger drove him back to his house and went inside with him as Shanann repeatedly called.

"I felt uncomfortable," Kessinger later told detectives, "as if I didn't belong there."

She saw all the beautifully posed family photographs in the front room and once again wondered why Chris wanted to trash it all. It just didn't make sense that he would walk out of such an apparently perfect life.

"I took a step back," she recalled. "This man has a gorgeous house, he has beautiful babies, he has an awesome job—why would he want to leave this?"

That night, Chris Watts spent almost two hours looking online for a special present for his new girlfriend. He searched the high-end Denver dealer Dave Bunk Minerals and was particularly interested in dioptase, also known as the gem of the Congo. A healing crystal, dioptase helps build confidence, further spiritual attunement, and stimulate memories of past lives.

On Sunday, July 15, Shanann threw a birthday party for Celeste, inviting all Shanann's old friends from North Carolina. Notably absent was Chris's family, who were upset by Shanann's continuing attacks on Facebook.

"She just pounded and pounded every day about the allergy thing," said Cindy Watts. "I told Ronnie, 'You go if you want to. I just can't be around her family. I don't want something to be started on CeCe's birthday.'"

Ronnie was planning to go with a load of birthday presents, but the morning of the party Shanann posted yet another attack on Facebook.

"There's no way in hell we'll show up there," said Ronnie, "and everybody [would be] looking at us like we were trying to kill CeCe. I ended up sending the birthday presents to Colorado by UPS."

During the party Shanann FaceTimed Chris so he could wish CeCe a happy birthday. He did his best to put on a good show, but his heart wasn't in it.

After the party, Cassie Rosenberg texted Shanann to see how it had gone.

"Great," replied Shanann. "In laws no show."

"I'm sorry they no showed."

"Their loss not mine. They are out of my kids' life now. I don't ever want to see them again."

One night, Shanann visited with her old friend Sandra Gironda, whose parents owned the pizzeria where Shanann used to work in high school.

"She appeared to be very happy," recalled Gironda, "absolutely glowing with pregnancy."

Over dinner, Shanann complained that her in-laws had never accepted her. She accused Cindy Watts of trying to undermine her as a wife and mother.

"I asked her how Chris handled the situation," said Gironda. "She said that Chris was her rock, always supportive, always put her and the girls first. That was a real point of contention between her and her mother-in-law."

Shanann claimed her in-laws had told her she would never be good enough for Chris and still blamed her for taking him away to Colorado.

"I suggested that she let Chris lead the way in dealing with his family," said Gironda. "She said her heart [broke] for Chris . . . because she [saw] firsthand how it hurts him and affects their marriage."

The following Saturday, July 21, Chris Watts took his girlfriend to watch drag racing at the Bandimere Speedway. Before leaving for the track, he transferred his latest batch of nude images of Kessinger into his secret app. Then he texted Shanann, "Headed out to the track Boo. I will text you when I get there."

On the way to the racetrack, the lovers had a romantic lunch at the Roof Top Tavern in Morrison. As usual, Chris paid for the meal with a gray Anadarko reward card, so there would be no record for Shanann, who still handled all their finances, to find.

At the Bandimere Speedway, they watched the Mile-High Nationals and stayed until the very end. Chris was in heaven, as it was the first time he had been to a drag race since he'd gone as a young boy with his father.

22

THE BACHELOR LIFE

At 1:17 P.M. on Tuesday, July 24, Nikki Kessinger googled *Man I'm having affair with says he will leave his wife*. She apparently now had hopes that the relationship could lead to marriage, as she spent the next several days online searching for wedding dresses.

Shanann was becoming increasingly suspicious because Chris rarely answered his phone. She even had her mother call him a dozen times, and when he still didn't reply, Shanann texted him to see if he was all right.

"Tire light came on when I was leaving King Soopers last night," he replied. "Got the tires aired back up."

"You could have answered or texted back," wrote Shanann. "Thought something happened. But you don't care about others feelings. . . . Or think you're with another girl, or worse. No consideration of others."

Chris did not reply, as he was busy googling the Victoria's Secret website.

Not getting a response, Shanann fired off another text: "I realized [during] this trip what's been missing in our relationship! It's only one way emotions and feelings. You don't consider others at all, nor think about others feelings."

Chris then apologized and said he loved her.

"I try to give you space," Shanann replied, "but while

you are working and living the bachelor life I'm carrying our 3rd and fighting with our two kids daily and trying to work and make money."

She said it was easy for him to text that he loved her and missed her, but if it was a lie, they needed to talk.

"I kept looking at my phone all night and no response from you," she said. "Like seriously! We didn't just start dating yesterday! We've been together 8 years and have 2.5 kids together."

A few hours later she met Sandra Gironda again for dinner at Vito's Pizzeria. They spoke about CeCe's birthday party and how Shanann's in-laws were no-shows.

Gironda told her to stay positive and not let them ruin her trip.

"She said she just wished her mother-in-law . . . would just get over it already," said Gironda. "That they would accept that they have a great marriage, beautiful little happy girls, and a new baby on the way to look forward to."

When Nikki suggested a camping trip to the Great Sand Dunes National Park, Chris was delighted. He had never been camping before and had always wanted to. It was also their last weekend together, before he left for North Carolina for a week with Shanann and the girls.

Kessinger would pay for gas and snacks, while Watts took care of the campsite, meals, and firewood with his Anadarko gift card.

On Saturday morning, they set off early in Kessinger's Toyota 4Runner for the four-and-a-half-hour drive south to Alamosa, Colorado. To cover his tracks, Chris told Shanann that he was going on a weekend hike with a co-worker and would be out of cell phone contact.

"We set up camp," said Kessinger, "and then we went to the national park. It was superwindy [and] the sand hurt so bad."

It started raining but they toughed it out, taking selfies of themselves kissing with the sand dunes in the background. In the photos, Chris looks as if he were in heaven.

Watts took a short video of their yellow tent with the Jon Langston song "Forever Girl" playing in the background. They sheltered in the tent for the rest of the night, proclaiming their love for each other.

"He told me he loved me," she later recalled. "I said [I loved him] and I meant it. It was just all very new to me."

On Sunday morning, they went sandboarding. On the way there Chris replaced his iPhone home screen of Shanann and the girls with a photo of the sand dunes.

Over the next couple of hours, he took more photographs and videos of his lover sandboarding in the dunes.

"So damn sexy," he can be heard saying.

Then he video-recorded Nikki telling him what a great weekend she'd had: "Thank you so much for coming out here with me, Christopher. I'm having a wonderful time. You mean a lot to me and I'm glad that you're having a blast."

Then she blew a kiss at the camera.

They began the long drive back in late morning, stopping off at BJ's Brewhouse in Colorado Springs for lunch. Watts left his wife a voice mail: "Finished the hike. Packing up and heading home."

Then he ignored a string of calls from Shanann, who finally texted him that afternoon: "I'm assuming you're safe, considering it's been 3.5 hours."

"There was a car fire," he replied, "and the Renaissance Festival traffic in Colorado Springs. Just got our car. Headed home."

It was another two hours before he finally answered her calls.

After hanging up, Shanann sent him a sarcastic text:

"Sorry you're so tired, but I haven't talked to you in 48 hours and I had a hard weekend . . . if you care."

Ten minutes later, he responded, "I'm sorry you had a hard weekend Boo. I will make it up to you I promise. I'm sorry I'm out of it tonight."

"It would have been nice for my husband to show interest in how the girls and I are, and the baby," she told him. "I'm done with begging for you to talk. See you Tuesday."

Monday was Chris Watts's last day at work before going to North Carolina.

Before leaving to spend one last night at his girlfriend's house, he texted his wife: "Letting Dieter out and going to bed Boo. I love you."

He arrived at Kessinger's bearing flowers, a card, and a love letter.

7.30.18

Nikki,
Wow, where do I even start? The first day I saw
you, you took my breath away. The first day I
had the guts to talk to you, I got lost in those
stunning green eyes. The first day we went out
in the park together, I knew I was addicted. The
first time we kissed, I knew I had met the most
amazing, unique and electric woman EVER!!
    We have had a lot of FIRSTS together Nikki.
And I want to keep having them with you!!
Love, Chris

23

"WORST SUMMER EVER"

Early the next morning, Chris Watts arrived at Denver International Airport, dropping off the Lexus at the long-term parking lot. Then he took a photo of the car-park sign and texted it to Shanann with the words "At the Airport."

While waiting at the gate, he transferred dozens of photos and videos of Nikki Kessinger at the Great Sand Dunes into his secret app. He also deleted his "APC Health Safety Environmental" iPhone contact for her.

At 4:46 A.M. he texted Shanann, "On the plane. Love you Boo." She immediately texted him back, complaining that the long-term car park would cost $16 a day.

"You never ever listen to me," she told him angrily. "$130 we can't spend at the beach."

Five hours later, Watts landed at Raleigh-Durham Airport and texted Shanann, who was there waiting with the girls.

"[Let me know] when you are coming down escalator so I can record girls," she texted him.

Although it was the first time Chris had seen his family for five weeks, he seemed cold and distant when they reunited.

"He was acting really standoffish," said Frankie Rzucek. "I'm like, 'I bet you guys missed each other.' And they were like, 'Yeah.'"

That night, they all went out to dinner at Vito's Pizzeria. It was the first time that Sandra Gironda had ever met Chris.

Over a long Italian dinner, he hardly spoke and appeared distracted.

"The girls were clearly happy to see their daddy," Gironda recalled. "Chris was quiet [and] did not say much. When we spoke of the possibility of a baby boy on the way, he lit up with a smile."

Back at the Rzuceks' house, Chris and Shanann went outside to talk on the porch. She had immediately noticed that he had replaced the photo of her and the girls on his iPhone lock screen with one of sand dunes. When she asked why, he was evasive.

Later, he refused to have sex with her, saying he didn't feel like it. Then he left her in the bedroom, going back outside to call Nikki Kessinger.

At around 2:00 A.M. Frankie heard strange noises coming from Shanann's bedroom and went to investigate.

The light was on and he peeked in to find his sister vomiting and asked if she was all right.

"And I was like, 'Is that pregnancy stuff?' And she [said], 'Yeah, probably.'"

Sandi came in to try to help.

"Shanann was vomiting all night," Sandi said, "and Chris didn't get up to see how [she] was. This was his wife."

Early the next morning, Shanann posted on Facebook for the first time in several weeks. Since arriving in North Carolina, she had drastically scaled down her output on social media.

"I'm so excited about August!" she wrote. "Girls and I Fly home August 7th! I fly to Scottsdale Aug 10-12 for an amazing weekend with my Le-Vel family! Gender Reveal for Baby Watts #3! Lots of excitement, Lots to be thankful for."

After breakfast, Shanann took Chris and the girls to downtown Aberdeen, where they visited the Hair Jazz salon, where Sandi worked.

"She was glowing," said Stacey Fowler, who worked at the salon and had gone to high school with Shanann. "She was very excited. She told me she was pregnant and they were having a gender-reveal party."

Another stylist, Darnell Search, said Chris said nothing during the visit and did not seem to want to be there. "Chris was very standoffish. I said hi to him and he kept his head down."

Later that morning, Frank Rzucek drove Shanann, Chris, and his granddaughters to Myrtle Beach in South Carolina, where they had rented two condos for a five-day vacation. The plan was for Frank to stay a couple days and go back to Aberdeen, then Sandi would join for the rest of the time.

Ronnie Watts had taken a week off work so he and Cindy could join them, but Shanann refused to allow it. Chris had been looking forward to spending time with his parents and felt Shanann was punishing them for Nutgate. It was Bella's and Celeste's first time at the beach and they were excited. But their father simmered throughout the trip, furious that Shanann had put a wall between him and his parents.

Back at the condo that night, Chris went out for a walk and spent more than an hour on the phone with Nikki Kessinger. Meanwhile, Shanann called Cristina Meacham in Hawaii to complain that she no longer recognized her husband, who refused to touch her and was pushing her away all the time.

The next morning Shanann texted Meacham that she thought Chris might be angry.

"He's been so closed off and only focus[ed] on his food," Shanann wrote. "Kissed me once since he's been here. No grabbing my ass, hug or anything. I want [to] cry."

Cristina wondered if it had something to do with the new BURN patch he was using and advised Shanann to tell him how she felt.

"He said nothings [*sic*] wrong," she replied. "5 weeks away from me and not touching me doesn't make me feel good. He got me pregnant. I just want to cry."

Shanann said she and Chris were now sleeping apart, questioning if he was turned off sexually because of the weight she had gained during pregnancy.

"He wanted this baby," she said. "That means I gain weight. I'm not feeling wanted."

Later, Chris went off by himself to look for presents for his girlfriend. He snapped a photograph of a necklace, which he immediately transferred into his secret app. He and Nikki were continually communicating through the app, sending nude selfies to each other.

That night, while Shanann stewed in their bedroom, the lovers spent almost an hour and a half talking on the phone. Again, he refused to have sex with Shanann, preferring to do push-ups in the bedroom.

"Kids in bed," a frustrated Shanann texted Cristina. "I took a night shower (means I want sex and he knows it) he's over here doing [a] push up challenge instead of discussing anything or fucking me. I'm over here crying in silence."

"Gurl stop him," replied Cristina, "and tell him. Don't cry in silence that's not good for you baby."

"I can't do this," Shanann texted back. "Not 3 alone.

He's never been like this. 5.5 ducking weeks no sex. Unless he is getting it somewhere else."

On Friday, August 3, Frank Rzucek went back to Aberdeen and Sandi arrived for the rest of the vacation. Shanann had now confronted Chris about what was wrong, and "begged" him to talk to her. He told her that he was upset that his parents had been banned from coming to Myrtle Beach.

"He looks up to his dad," she told Cristina. "His dad is his hero and he doesn't understand why his dad deleted the whole family [from Facebook]."

Shanann was also texting Nickole Atkinson in Colorado for feedback and advice.

"She didn't know what was going on," Nickole later recalled. "She hadn't seen him in five weeks . . . and he wasn't even sleeping in the same bed as her, which I [found] really odd."

Nickole asked if he had been affectionate before she left for North Carolina, and Shanann said everything had been fine.

"She said they were screwing like rabbits," said Nickole, "and he couldn't get enough of her. And they were doing it in the pantry while the girls were in the other room. So to go from that extreme to 'I don't want to touch you' is odd."

Later that day, Chris got up the nerve to assert himself and invited his parents to Myrtle Beach to see the kids. When Shanann found out, she was livid and he backed down immediately, but he was becoming even angrier with his wife.

"I told him over my dead body," Shanann later told Cristina. "They [don't] get to disrespect me and him and his kids and get rewarded."

She also complained that Chris had been too weak with his parents about Nutgate.

"Chris is so submissive," she told Cristina, "and gives in so easy. It's like he brushed this off. What if Celeste died?"

That night, Chris defiantly called his parents, saying he wanted a separation.

"He said, 'She will not let me see you guys,'" said Cindy. "'She won't allow it and she doesn't want you to have anything to do with [Bella and Celeste].'"

Then he called Nikki Kessinger. Although it is unclear what they discussed, she spent two hours after the call googling wedding dresses again.

Late that night, Chris finally told Shanann that he had had enough of her alienating him from his parents. A bitter argument ensued and they retired to different bedrooms.

"It got ugly," Shanann texted Cristina Meacham. "Truth [came] out."

Getting no reply from Cristina, who was six hours behind in Hawaii, Shanann wrote a long text to Chris, expressing exactly what she thought.

"Truth came out last night," it began. "I didn't create [a] dagger between you and your dad. That was done by your mom and your dad. And I won't change a thing. My daughter's life is way more important."

She told him that his parents' home was no longer a "safe zone" for Bella and Celeste.

"You can let them tell you what you want," she wrote. "You can believe I created this dagger but I didn't do that. These kids are my world and I have to protect them from the evil of the world. I shouldn't have to protect them from evil family."

Then she confronted Chris about his recent behavior toward her and the children: "Something changed when

I left. You may be happier alone and that's fine. You can be alone!"

She chastised him for failing to acknowledge her pregnancy or her feelings.

"The first trimester is the scariest and most dangerous," she told him. "We can lose this baby at any point till delivery. I'm not going to be treated this way for having the balls to protect our family and kids. I should get a gold ducking medal for handling it the [way] I did."

Several hours later Shanann added, "If you want to go hang out with your parents today, by all means do so, but without us. Don't put it on me why you can't go. You are your own person."

Although staying in the same condo, Shanann and Chris were now solely communicating via text so they didn't argue in front of their daughters and Sandi.

"These kids mean the world to me and always will," Chris replied early Saturday morning. "I'm sorry for the way I've been acting, it's just been in my head and I haven't been right at all."

Before replying, Shanann forwarded his message to Cristina, commenting, "He's feeling like shit."

"I do not deserve to be treated the way you have," Shanann texted him back. "I have defended our daughter."

Chris then thanked Shanann "a million times a million" for protecting CeCe, adding that his parents still wanted to be in their granddaughters' lives.

"I'm not used to [not] having a relationship with my dad," he wrote. "I should have called him before it got to this point. I didn't and that's my fault."

Shanann demanded that his parents apologize for not attending Celeste's birthday party. She told him that they did not appreciate him the way she did, and maybe he should move back and live with them.

"No one ever protected you from your mom," she texted, "and someone should have before me. I'm done with being the bad guy in all this. Especially when I had more balls to stand up for you a long time ago with them."

When there was no reply by lunchtime, Shanann sent another text: "While it's on my mind . . . you not standing up for us and the girls is not cool. You just make it so they feel they did no wrong and brush it under the rug."

Three minutes later she followed up again: "I'm not asking you to choose who to be with. I shouldn't have to ask you to choose right from wrong. [If] You are not happy, then you know where to go. . . . Worst summer ever."

Shanann continued to text Cristina, providing regular updates on her escalating battle with Chris. Shanann lambasted Chris for being weak and not challenging his parents enough about Nutgate.

"I'm tired of him not having balls to stand up to his family," she wrote. "He's so worried of what his dad thinks."

Cristina agreed, saying Chris needed to "protect his family no matter what."

Shanann then accused her in-laws of ruining everything, starting with Chris's proposal, the engagement party, and their wedding. She said she was "sick" of it and Chris needed to toughen up and stand up for her and the girls.

"This is the worst it's gotten and I can't do this," she texted Cristina. "I can't fight my own husband. I'm 14 weeks pregnant and he hasn't once touched my belly or asked me how my pregnancy is going. He wanted this pregnancy."

Chris Watts would later admit that he had become so desperate to leave Shanann and start a new life with Nikki

Kessinger that he ground oxycodone tablets into her Thrive protein shakes in an attempt to make her miscarry. He rationalized that it would be easier to be with Nikki Kessinger if Shanann lost the baby.

Several times that week, Shanann texted Cristina Meacham that she felt physically ill and didn't know why. Several times she complained of chronic constipation, which is caused by opioids.

On the last day of the disastrous Myrtle Beach trip, Chris and Shanann took Bella and Celeste back to Pavilion Park, putting on a cheerful face as if nothing were wrong. They shot videos and photographs of the girls playing on trampolines, and Shanann posted a photograph of a smiling CeCe playing on the beach in a bikini.

"The older she gets the more scared I am," she wrote next to it, "to let her out in the real world. The world of evil, the world of hate. The world is a very scary place."

24

"YOU FELL OUT OF LOVE WITH ME"

That night the couple drove back to Aberdeen in silence, the girls asleep in the back of the car. After arriving back at Frank and Sandi's house, Chris went outside to call his girlfriend while Shanann updated Cristina on the deteriorating situation.

"Drove 3 hours in silence," she wrote. "I told him to find a place when we get back and I'm putting house on market. He said nothing."

Shanann was now preparing for a future without her husband.

"I need to move out of Colorado," she said. "Too expensive to live alone with 3 kids. I'm not moving to NC."

"Omg and he says nothing!!" replied Cristina. "Wtf is wrong with him . . . he needs to wake up!"

"He just said, 'I love the kids.' This is not the man I married."

On Sunday afternoon, Shanann texted Chris to see if, before going to visit his parents, he still planned to see Maw Maw, his ninety-four-year-old grandmother, Margaret Watts, who was in a nursing home with dementia. Shanann said that she and the girls would accompany him to see Maw Maw, but would not go to his parents' afterward.

"I'm standing strong with your family," she told him.

"You can use the truck and see both. But I just need to know. I'm not going to be the reason you don't see them."

Chris texted back that Bella and Celeste would love to see their great-grandmother one last time, asking if he should have someone pick him up at the nursing home and take him to his parents, as they only had one car.

Shanann replied that he should have his parents drive him there as she was not taking any chances of running into them.

"I'm not kidding Christopher," she told him. "I'm having a bad experience these last few days with my pregnancy and I'm spotting. I'm not dealing with it. Have your parents pick you up . . . then do what you need to do."

That night, Shanann sent Chris a screenshot of a quote by Seventh Day Adventist church elder Isaac Kubvoruno.

"Husbands," it read, "stand up for your wife and protect her from the attacks that come from people close to you. From the day you said 'I do' your wife displaces your parents, friends and siblings. Apart from God, your wife now occupies and assumes the privileged first place of honor in your life."

Two hours later, Shanann followed it up with a wrenching text: "I don't know how you fell out of love with me in 5.5 weeks, or if this has been going on for a long time, but you don't plan another baby if you're not in love. Kids don't deserve a broken family. . . . [When] I left you, you [couldn't] take your hands off me. You show up and I have to practically ask for a kiss in airport."

The text arrived when Chris was in the middle of a ninety-minute call to his girlfriend. Getting no response, Shanann desperately sent another:

"Being away from you, I missed the smell of you, you touching me when I'm cooking, you touching me in bed, you touching me period! I missed holding you and

snuggling with you. I missed eating with you. Watching
TV with you. I missed staring at you. I missed making
love with you. I missed everything about you."

She said she had been so looking forward to his coming to North Carolina, to celebrate the eight-year anniversary of their first date.

"If you are done," she told him, "don't love me, don't
want to work this out, not happy anymore and only staying because of the kids, I NEED you to tell me."

Around midnight, when there was still no response,
Shanann sent one final message: "I just don't get it. You
don't fall out of love in 5 weeks. How can you sleep? Our
marriage is crumbling in front of us and you can sleep."

A few hours later, Chris drove Shanann, Bella, and Celeste
to visit Maw Maw in the nursing home. She was having a
good day, and they all spent time together walking up and
down the hall. She recognized Chris and lit up when she
saw her great-granddaughters.

Then Shanann drove the girls back to Aberdeen, and
Ronnie Watts collected Chris and took him home for the
family reunion. Chris arrived to find his sister, Jamie, there
with her husband and children. It was the first time Chris
had seen his whole family together for many years, but
they were upset that Bella and Celeste had not come.

"We finally saw the Christopher that we loved," said his
mother. "The old Chris. He was so happy. He talked about
the girls [but] he didn't really mention the baby that much."

He told his family that he wanted a separation from
Shanann and would soon file for joint custody of Bella and
Celeste. He seemed optimistic for the future, as if a huge
weight had been lifted from his shoulders.

"He was ready to move on," recalled Ronnie. "He said,
'Dad, she already knows I want a divorce [and] the house
is up for sale.'"

He spoke enthusiastically about getting a small two-bedroom apartment with bunk beds for Bella and Celeste.

"He had his game plan," said his father. "He looked at me and said, 'Dad, I don't need that big ass house [and] make payments all the time.'"

His sister said it was the first time she had seen her brother that happy in years.

"He just seemed strong and for once normal," she recalled. "He wanted to take Bella to the races and do things that he hadn't been able to do with them."

Throughout the visit, Chris would go off on his own to text Nikki Kessinger and transfer some new erotic selfies she was sending. His sister intuitively knew something was going on, but kept quiet.

"It made my radar go off," said Jamie. "'I know you're not texting Shanann, so who are you texting this much?' But I didn't ask him because I didn't want to rock the boat."

A heavy storm that night caused power outages all over North Carolina. At 6:45 P.M. Chris texted Shanann that his father didn't want to drive the sixty-six-mile round trip to Aberdeen in such bad weather. Shanann offered to come and collect him.

"It's up to you," Chris replied. "He's cool bringing me back first thing in the morning early."

Shanann was furious.

"We fucking leave tomorrow," she fired back. "I need help. I will be there in an hour."

Chris told her not to bother as he had persuaded his father to drive him back.

Back at the Rzuceks', Shanann took Chris outside on the porch to find out what his family had said about her. The conversation was strained, and when she tried to hug him, he walked away. Then he coldly told her he did not want their new baby. Shanann burst into tears.

A few minutes later, she texted her husband: "I was trying to get you to fucking hug me. Make me feel safe. This is much deeper than 'lack of conversation!' Make me feel like everything is going to be ok."

"It will be ok," Chris calmly texted back. "This will all get fixed."

"No. I don't need words damnit. You just told me you don't want this baby. Something changed in the last 5 weeks . . . something you won't say."

"I am scared ok. You wanted the truth and I told you how I felt."

At 5:17 A.M. the next morning, Shanann desperately texted Addy Molony that Chris no longer wanted their baby. Addy tried to reassure her that he was probably just scared.

"He has changed," Shanann said. "I don't know who he is. He hasn't touched me all week, kissed me. . . . What if he doesn't love me anymore?!"

Addy asked if he might be resentful that she had spent so much time in North Carolina with the kids.

"He was totally on board," Shanann answered. "We decided it together. Quality time with everyone."

She told Addy, "I just want to cry. We've never had a problem in our relationship like this. No Joke. NEVER. THIS IS TOTAL LEFT FIELD."

Shanann also told Cristina Meacham that Chris had now changed his mind about their new baby.

"Chris doesn't want this baby?" Shanann texted. "Said he's scared to death. I said, 'Do you want me to abort?'"

Before leaving for the airport that afternoon, Shanann had second thoughts about going back to Colorado. She was still trying to find out what was really going on.

"Something else is wrong that you're not saying," she texted Chris, "because lack of communication doesn't cause you not to be present, or touch me or love me. This fucking sucks. I really don't want to leave here."

While his wife was floundering, Watts told Nikki Kessinger that his divorce would soon be finalized. He said Shanann had spoken to a Realtor about selling their home and was already looking for a new place to live. Kessinger offered to help him find an apartment in Brighton, which was near his work. They even discussed nearby gyms. She later told detectives he was "gung ho" about moving on.

A few hours later, Kessinger finally went public with their relationship, sending a photograph of Chris to her best friend, Charlotte Nelson.

Before going through security at Raleigh-Durham Airport, Shanann filmed her brother, Frankie, saying goodbye to his nieces.

"I gave [Bella] one last hug and kiss as they were leaving," he recalled. "I said, 'Make sure you slow down on getting so big.' She said, 'I love you, Uncle Frankie, why are you crying?'

"I said, 'Because I love you and I'm going to miss you guys,' as tears streamed down my face. She didn't want to let me go . . . neither did I."

At 11:00 P.M. that night, Chris and Shanann arrived back home. After they had put the girls to bed, Shanann texted Cristina that she wanted sex but was feeling insecure and scared of being rejected.

"He's in the shower," she wrote. "I just got out. I'm so horney [sic]. I'm sure even if he hates me. Sex is sex."

Cristina told her, "Stay naked and go for it."

"How do I approach him?"

"You should jump in shower with him. Go wash his back."

"Ok, he's getting out. Pray I get sex tonight."

A couple of hours later, Shanann texted that Chris had spurned her advances, and she'd been bawling her eyes out for an hour and was still trembling.

"Just went . . . and woke his sorry ass up," she wrote, "and asked him who he was sleeping with. He denied anyone."

25

NICO LEE WATTS

On Wednesday morning, Chris Watts went back to work, and Shanann posted on Facebook for the first time in more than a week. There was no sign that anything was amiss, and she appeared her usual positive self as she raved about the effects of her Thrive patch.

But hours later she poured out her true feelings to Sara Nudd, who used to work with her at Children's Hospital.

"[Chris] told me he doesn't want this baby," she texted. "I'm so sick to my stomach. Tried to have sex with him last night . . . and he rejected me."

She said she was having an ultrasound that night to find out the baby's gender, and that Chris wanted her to abort.

Sara asked if she thought Chris was having an affair.

"Honestly no," replied Shanann, "but what else would make him do a complete 360. . . . We couldn't get enough of each other before I left."

When he arrived at the Anadarko headquarters that morning, Chris went straight into Luke Epple's office and closed the door. He told his boss that he and Shanann were having issues.

"[He said] that if I saw anything goofy on his [Anadarko

truck] GPS," said Epple, "that it may be because he was going to be staying with a friend."

Watts also asked for Friday off to take Shanann to the airport, as she was going to Arizona for a Le-Vel training weekend.

After getting off work, Chris drove to Nikki's house. It was the first time they had seen each other in more than a week, and they made love. After he left to take Shanann for her ultrasound, Kessinger googled *Marrying Your Mistress*.

Shanann's appointment was at 6:45 P.M., and Nickole Atkinson arrived early to look after the girls. When Chris came home, he was remote and uncommunicative.

"He did not acknowledge me at all," recalled Nickole, "which is not normal for him. [Usually] he'll like give me a hug . . . or say, 'Hey, how are you doin'?' And then go on his merry way. He did not talk to me at all that night."

During the ultrasound session, Shanann grabbed Chris's hand for reassurance. He did not respond. As they left, they were given a sealed envelope with the baby's gender inside.

Back at 2825 Saratoga Trail, Shanann gave the sealed envelope to Nickole to bring to the upcoming gender-reveal party.

Later that night, Shanann had a big argument with Chris, and she called Nickole saying she had canceled the party.

"She said, 'Can you tell me what I'm having?'" remembered Nickole. "'I need some happy news.' And I said, 'Yes, I can. Are you sure?'"

Nickole offered to drive over and tell her in person, but Shanann said it could wait until the next morning.

While Chris was in the basement speaking to his girlfriend, Shanann created a group text with Cassie and Josh

Rosenberg and Nickole to plan for Shanann's future. They discussed the possibility of the Rosenbergs and their two daughters moving into 2825 Saratoga Trail, as Shanann would no longer be able to afford to support three kids alone in Colorado.

"We got this, girl," Cassie assured her.

"And believe me you will come out stronger and better," Nickole told Shanann. "Your [sic] not alone."

"Love you ladies," Shanann replied.

Then she pointed out that the mortgage was in Chris's name.

"Fuck him," replied Cassie. "You get the kids and can't go without a home. Everything will work out right."

Just after 6:00 A.M. on Thursday morning, Shanann sent Chris a text. She said she still wanted to repair their marriage, trying to get him to open up and tell her what had caused his sudden change.

"Do you want to find out together with me tonight the baby's gender?" she texted.

"Yes," he replied.

"Please take 5 mins today to write me," replied Shanann, "and tell me how you are feeling! I love you Chris more than you know."

That morning, Chris Watts deleted his Facebook account, as he had decided what he must do to start a new life with Nikki Kessinger. When his father asked if he had really done so, a jubilant Chris replied, "Yes Sir! Liberated."

At 11:44 A.M. he sent Shanann a bizarre photograph of one of the girls' dolls lying on their sofa, with a sheet covering it like a burial shroud. Puzzled, she immediately posted it on Facebook, saying, "I don't know what to think about this. . . ."

After receiving the eerie photograph, Shanann messaged

an ultrasound image of her unborn baby to Sara Nudd. She also sent a photograph of a letter she had just written to Chris, saying she hoped he would reply.

My Dearest Chris,
I don't know where to begin. I am so lost for words. I can't even explain how hard this pain is. The last 5 weeks have been the hardest. I missed everything about you. I missed your morning breath, your touch, your lips/kisses. I missed holding you! I missed smelling you in the sheets. I missed talking to you in person. I missed watching you laugh and play with the kids that I love so much about you. I missed seeing you naked and on top of me making love to me. OMG. I missed having you around when I felt alone and upset. I just flat out missed the hell out of you. We haven't been away from each other that long since 2012.

I really don't know how we fell out of compatibility or if that is someone else's words. The only thing that changed this was everything going down with you[r] family. I can't change what happened, but can try to work things out with you with them. But there has to be a mutual respect for everyone. I definitely deserve an apology because of Celeste. I can suck up her going against everything I said to our kids but our daughter's life . . .

Then Shanann went on Amazon and ordered Dr. Sue Johnson's bestselling self-help book *Hold Me Tight: Seven Conversations for a Lifetime of Love,* to be delivered to Chris on Saturday, while Shanann was in Scottsdale. She also bought an ebook of it for her phone, so they would be on the same page.

On Thursday afternoon, Shanann arranged for Bella to go back to school the following Monday. She had missed much of the summer semester and was looking forward to seeing her friends again. Although Chris usually left early for work on Monday mornings, Shanann asked if he could come, too, for Bella's first day of kindergarten.

"I can make that happen," he texted back.

That night, Shanann and Chris had their own gender-reveal party, which she recorded and later posted on Facebook. She seemed upbeat and positive for the first time in weeks.

"Nico Lee Watts," Shanann texted Cassie Rosenberg. "We are not telling the world [until] Monday. Tonight has been the best talk yet."

At around 10:30 P.M., Sara Nudd asked how Chris had reacted to the letter, and Shanann replied that Chris had now agreed to try to work things out.

"We talked," wrote Shanann. "He told me he loved me back. Still cold, but not as cold. He even kissed me before going to sleep in the basement."

Down in the basement, Chris called Nikki Kessinger, and they talked for more than an hour. Then he googled prices for an Audi Q7 car, before transferring his latest batch of nude selfies from Kessinger into his secret app.

26

"SWEET DREAMS MY SEXY EMPANADA"

At 4:30 A.M. Friday, Nickole Atkinson collected Shanann to take her to Denver Airport for the promoter-training weekend in Scottsdale. After going into the basement for a farewell hug, Shanann left her handwritten letter for Chris on the kitchen counter. Then she wheeled her suitcase outside, where Nickole was waiting in her car.

Shanann texted Chris while she was waiting to board: "Thank you for everything last night. I miss and love you so much! I am still in shock we are having a little boy! I'm so excited and happy! I really thought it was another girl. Thank you for letting me hold you this morning. It felt good! Your letter is on the counter."

Instead of reading Shanann's letter, Chris called Nikki Kessinger to set up a Saturday-night date. He explained Shanann was out of town on a business trip, and he was getting someone to look after his daughters. Then he called Jeremy Lindstrom to see if his seventeen-year-old daughter, McKenna, would be available to babysit, saying that he had won a work raffle to go to a Rockies game.

During the two-hour flight to Phoenix, Shanann read the *Hold Me Tight* ebook, telling Nickole Atkinson that Chris would be getting his copy tomorrow. After landing, they got a taxi to the Embassy Suites Hotel in Scottsdale, where the training sessions would be held.

When all her Thrive friends saw Shanann, they were shocked by the state of her. She looked "a wreck" instead of the usual "ray of sunshine" they were used to. She was not eating or drinking properly, and they spent the weekend coaxing her to do so.

Once in her room, which she was sharing with Cassie Rosenberg, Shanann took a selfie of her growing stomach, sending it to friends with the caption "15 Weeks Baby Is The Size of an Orange."

Then from the hotel, she messaged her Realtor, Ann Meadows, saying she and Chris were thinking about moving to nearby Brighton or Fort Lupton.

"Hey Love," Shanann texted, copying Chris, "Chris and I would like to talk to you about possibly selling the house. Before I paint baby's room and more, I think it's better to see where we are at and options."

She asked if they could all meet early next week, but Meadows texted back advising that they first get preapproval for a loan.

Around lunchtime, Shanann received confirmation from Amazon that the *Hold Me Tight* book had been delivered. She then texted Chris to check his mail—which he did, throwing the unopened package straight into the garage dumpster.

Soon afterward, Ronnie Watts texted his son to see if he and Cindy could FaceTime Bella and Celeste that night, since Shanann wouldn't be around.

"Do you think that's a good idea?" asked Ronnie. "Don't want to get anything started."

Chris replied that he did not think so, as Bella would likely tell her mother.

"That's what I'm afraid of," Ronnie replied. "If she

finds out she would probably have a fit. Don't want to make things worse."

Just after 3:00 P.M., Chris Watts pulled into the Safeway parking lot in Fort Lupton to meet Troy McCoy, who had agreed to show Chris how to work his new Amazon Fire TV Stick.

"Bella and CeCe were in the backseat," recalled McCoy, "happy and laughing."

As they were talking, McCoy received a call from Kodi Roberts, an operator in their Anadarko team. Roberts said there was a leak on the bypass line on the Cervi 319 oil well, but it could wait until Monday to be fixed.

Overhearing the conversation, Watts immediately volunteered to go out to the oil well first thing Monday morning to repair it, although he had promised to take Bella to the Primrose School for her first day of kindergarten.

That night, Shanann had dinner with her promoter friends at the Yard House in Scottsdale. Cindy Derossett, who was running the training weekend, could not believe the change in Shanann, who told them about the problems she was having in her marriage.

"She was just so distraught . . . and about to break down," said Derossett. "She [didn't] want to lose her marriage."

Back in Frederick, Chris fed the girls before he put them to sleep. Then he went online to plan his date with Kessinger. While he was googling upcoming shows at the Comedy Works in Denver, Shanann was searching Groupon for hotel deals in Aspen, hoping she and Chris could use the vacation to work on their marriage. She booked a room for two the following weekend at the Westin Snowmass Resort.

Chris Watts loved playing sports as a young boy and his father, Ronnie, always cheered him on from the sidelines. *(Courtesy of Cindy Watts)*

Shanann Rzucek's 2003 senior photo and yearbook page. *(Courtesy of Pine Crest High School)*

Shan'ann Rzucek

FCA; Key Club; Teacher Asst.; Powderpuff; Softball; Spectrum Staff; Superfans; Relay for Life; Young Life; Campaigners; ITS

"FRIENDSHIP, is the hardest thing in the world to explain. It's not something you learn in school. But if you haven't learned the meaning of friendship, you really haven't learned anything."

Muhammad Ali

Shanann worked so hard that she was able to buy the luxurious 1000 Peninsula Drive in Belmont at the age of twenty-five. *(Courtesy of John Glatt)*

Shanann and Chris's engagement party, where a heated argument broke out between their parents. (*Courtesy of Cindy Watts*)

Shanann and her brother, Frankie, at her wedding in November 2012. The only member of Chris's family to attend was his grandmother. (*Courtesy of the Weld County District Attorney's Office*)

Shanann and her mother-in-law, Cindy Watts, made an effort to get along, but their relationship was often strained. (*Courtesy of Cindy Watts*)

After moving to Frederick, Colorado, Chris and Shanann bought this beautiful house at 2825 Saratoga Trail. (*Courtesy of John Glatt*)

Shanann's lifelong dream of being a mother came true when Bella Marie was born in December 2013. *(Courtesy of Cindy Watts)*

In July 2015, Shanann gave birth to another daughter, Celeste Cathryn. *(Courtesy of Cindy Watts)*

After the girls were born, Shanann made peace with her in-laws. Ronnie and Cindy Watts visited Colorado several times a year to see their granddaughters. *(Courtesy of Cindy Watts)*

Sandi Rzucek was a devoted grandmother to Bella and Celeste. She and her husband, Frank, moved into Shanann's house after Celeste was born. *(Courtesy of the Weld County District Attorney's Office)*

The Wattses were passionate Pittsburgh Steelers fans and never missed watching a game on television. *(Courtesy of the Weld County District Attorney's Office)*

Shanann loved posing with her beautiful daughters for photographs, which she would post online for her legion of Facebook followers. *(Courtesy of the Weld County District Attorney's Office)*

Shanann radiated beauty and self-confidence to everyone, although she was naturally shy. *(Courtesy of the Weld County District Attorney's Office)*

Bella and Celeste happily playing at Ronnie and Cindy's house in July 2018, a few days before "Nutgate." *(Courtesy of Cindy Watts)*

While Shanann was away in North Carolina, Chris started a passionate affair with his coworker, Nikki Kessinger. *(Courtesy of the Weld County District Attorney's Office)*

Chris wrote many love letters to Kessinger, swearing his undying love. *(Courtesy of the Weld County District Attorney's Office)*

Kessinger would constantly send Chris sexy photos that he would save in a hidden app on his iPhone. *(Courtesy of the Weld County District Attorney's Office)*

The last photo ever taken of Shanann, at dinner during a business trip, a few hours before her murder. *(Courtesy of the Weld County District Attorney's Office)*

A nervous Chris Watts and his neighbor Nathaniel Trinastich look at surveillance video after Shanann went missing. "He's not acting right at all," Trinastich told Officer Scott Coonrod. *(Courtesy of the Weld County District Attorney's Office)*

The Missing poster for Shanann, Bella, and Celeste Watts. *(Courtesy of the Frederick Police Department)*

MISSING MOM & DAUGHTERS

CASE WARRIORS

Last Seen: Aug 13, 2018
FREDERICK, COLORADO

SHANANN WATTS
34-years-old
15-weeks pregnant

DAUGHTERS
Bella & Celeste
3 & 4-years-old

- Shanann just returned from a trip to Scottsdale, AZ at 2am, Aug 13
- Husband left for work at 5am
- Girls not dropped off for school on Aug 13
- Phone, purse & children's medications at home
- No vehicle associated at this time

CBI Agent Tammy Lee gave Chris Watts a polygraph test that would break the case and lead to his confession. *(Courtesy of the Weld County District Attorney's Office)*

The drone photograph of Cervi 319 with Watts's markings of where he left the bodies of Shanann and his daughters. *(Courtesy of the Weld County District Attorney's Office)*

The oil tanks that Watts dumped his daughters in. *(Courtesy of the Weld County District Attorney's Office)*

Chris Watts's mug shot after he was arrested for the murders of Shanann, Bella, and Celeste. *(Courtesy of the Weld County District Attorney's Office)*

The gravesite of Shanann, Bella, Celeste, and Nico, in Bethesda Cemetery in Aberdeen. *(Courtesy of John Glatt)*

At around 9:00 P.M. Watts called Kessinger, announcing that his divorce was proceeding well, and he and Shanann had now agreed to split everything fifty-fifty. He told Kessinger that his and Shanann's "transition" would begin on Monday, when she returned from her business trip.

"It was like a sealed deal," Kessinger recalled, "getting everything finalized."

At 12:40 A.M. Saturday morning, Watts texted his girlfriend: "Hope you had a great night beautiful. Miss you! Get home safe! Sweet Dreams my sexy empanada."

Early Saturday morning, Shanann messaged her husband: "Good morning baby! Are the girls up?"

Watts replied that they were in bed watching cartoons, then texted Shanann his plans for Saturday night: "McKenna . . . is coming to watch the girls for a few hours while I go to that Rockies game."

At 9:30 A.M., Nikki Kessinger started preparing for her upcoming date. She spent forty-five minutes googling anal sex and how to prepare for it. Then she went on Pornhub looking for *threesomes with double penetration* and *interracial porn*.

In Scottsdale, Cassie Rosenberg and Nickole Atkinson looked after Shanann the entire weekend. Now fifteen weeks pregnant, she was complaining of severe migraines, dehydration, and constipation, all possible side effects of the oxycodone Chris claimed to have given her.

Nickole carried a water bottle for Shanann's headaches, for which she was taking Imitrex. Cassie was a trained nurse and feared Shanann's blood sugar was dropping as she wasn't eating properly.

"She would take a couple of bites and say she was full

up," said Nickole. "Normally we'd go out and do something [but] we stayed in the hotel the entire weekend."

Although Shanann gamely attended training sessions, she spent most of her time alone in her hotel room, reading *Hold Me Tight* and writing another letter to Chris about how to mend their marriage.

At 4:25 P.M. Jennifer Lindstrom dropped her daughter McKenna off to babysit Bella and Celeste. Chris gave her a tour of the house, before giving Bella and Celeste, already in their pajamas, their medicine.

He instructed McKenna to put them to bed at 7:00 P.M., showing her the baby monitor hooked up to cameras in their rooms so she could keep an eye on them. Then he ordered a pizza from Papa John's.

"He told me to distract the kids while he left," recalled McKenna, "so they didn't get upset."

All through the evening Shanann texted McKenna, checking in on the girls. Shanann even had her take a photo of Celeste, which Shanann later posted on Facebook. She also asked McKenna to babysit the following Friday, as she and Chris were going to Aspen for the weekend.

Chris Watts drove straight to Nikki Kessinger's house, dressed casually in a white T-shirt and jeans. He apologized that he could not stay over that night, explaining that the babysitter didn't do overnights.

After they had sex, Kessinger weighed him to update his fitness app that she'd helped him set up. He had lost thirteen pounds since the beginning of July and was now down to 180 pounds.

"I was concerned that he was losing so much weight," she said. "It was kind of fast. And I'm like, 'Oh, my God. It's because he's doubling up on all the Thrive stuff.'"

Over a salmon dinner that night, they discussed Chris's

plan to rent a two-bedroom apartment when he moved out. Kessinger had already found a couple of nice ones in his price range, but he now said he could not afford the deposit.

"[I was] trying to make sure that he got a place that was close to where his ex-wife would be staying," Kessinger explained, "so he could have a good working relationship with her and the kids."

Chris got the check and paid for it with a light blue credit card, one linked to his joint account with Shanann. It was the first time that he hadn't used his Anadarko rewards card for a date, and he must have known she would see the charge.

Then he went back to Kessinger's house, where they had sex again before he left, explaining he had to relieve the babysitter at 10:00 P.M.

Back in her Scottsdale hotel room, Shanann received an alert from her bank that their credit card had been used. She immediately checked her bank statement, seeing that Chris had spent $68 on his dinner. She thought it seemed unusually high for just one person.

Just after 10:00 P.M., she texted McKenna and discovered that Chris was not home yet, noting that the Lazy Dog restaurant, where the card had been used, was only fifteen minutes away from their house.

Shanann called Chris, who by then was on his way home, asking what he had eaten for dinner. He said salmon and a beer. Then she went on the Lazy Dog website, finding the meal would cost less than $30. She was immediately suspicious.

Later, Shanann sent him a text asking him to keep the Lazy Dog receipt, so they could write it off in taxes.

27

"FELT THE BABY MOVE TWICE THIS WEEKEND!"

On Sunday morning Shanann pretended everything was normal, so as not to tip Chris off that she was suspicious about his dinner the previous night.

"Can you do me a favor today if you have time?" she asked. "Can you get the girls backpacks ready for tomorrow with blankies and spare clothes, please? If not I can do it in the a.m."

Chris replied that he would be happy to.

She sent her husband a text saying she loved him, with a smiling emoji. An hour later she asked how Bella and Celeste were, and he replied that they were drinking shakes.

"Miss you guys!" she replied. "Give them kisses for me."

Chris promised to do so and then called his girlfriend for a thirty-minute conversation.

Shanann did seem to be in better spirits. She texted Addy Molony that it would be a busy week and she was looking forward to going away with Chris to Aspen.

She had now almost finished the *Hold Me Tight* ebook and had given much thought on how she could improve the marriage. She decided that she didn't give Chris and the girls enough "family time," and that she should be nicer to him.

"I sometimes can be bitchy," Shanann texted Addy. "I have control issues. He said the other night he wishes I'd just let him hang up a picture."

Shanann was also attempting to see things from Chris's perspective, observing that he never complained about the way she treated him.

"He never calls me out," she told Molony. "He never fights me, just goes with the flow. [We] know I like things done in a certain way, but I never thought about how that may make him feel as a man. I don't even know if this is what's bothering him. He still hasn't said."

She said she prayed he had written her a letter describing his feelings, as he expressed himself best in writing.

"I'm the pusher and he's the withdrawer," she explained. "He has strengths that are my weaknesses and vice versa."

Shanann also told Addy of her deep frustration by Chris's total lack of communication: "He doesn't communicate! But I say things just to get him to react in any way since he doesn't react and that's not good. He was NEVER close to anyone but his dad!"

Shanann and Nickole Atkinson had stayed in Scottsdale an extra day to go sightseeing. But Shanann felt so sick that, after checking out at 11:00 A.M., they spent the rest of the day in the hotel lobby.

"Ready to get home to Chris and the girls," Shanann posted on Facebook.

A few hours later she posted again. "Felt the baby move twice this weekend!"

After having such a good time with Chris on Saturday night, Nikki Kessinger told her friend Charlotte Nelson more about her new boyfriend.

"Keeping it a secret," she texted. "Dude loves to eat pussy. Never met a man who does til now. I just let it happen lol."

"Where did you meet this man?" asked Nelson.

"I think he really likes me. It's the best sex I've ever had. I'm hooked." Kessinger sent a photograph of her and Chris Watts together. "Like he seems too good to be true. He's very handsome. And he works out so he's super sexy."

"And u look really happy!"

Kessinger said her only concern was that he was coming out of a marriage with two young daughters, and she didn't want to always be "second place" in his life.

"Like he's been there done that," she texted. "It's early though, we will see. He is very kind to me though."

"Second is not bad. It's after the first fuck up a person learns what they rly want in a human being."

"Don't tell nobody. I haven't made up my mind on him yet."

"How old is he?"

"33 I think. He's all about his kids. The fact that he takes care of his kids is a good thing I think."

At midday, Chris got Bella and Celeste ready for Jeremy Lindstrom's son's fourth birthday party. Chris did their hair in little ponytails and helped them dress.

At the party, he took photos of Bella and Celeste playing with water balloons and sent them off to Shanann, saying they were having fun.

During the party, Jennifer Lindstrom asked Chris if he needed a crib for the new baby. Chris said no, as he already had that taken care of.

Chris also texted Kessinger from the party to arrange their next date at an IMAX cinema, saying his kids were soaked from water balloons.

At 4:00 P.M., Chris drove Bella and Celeste home, feeding them cold pizza from the night before. While they were eating dinner, Shanann's parents FaceTimed them from North Carolina.

The girls told their grandparents how excited they were that their mom was coming home and would be there the next morning when they woke up.

Just after five o'clock, Chris Watts texted Kodi Roberts about his plans to check out the oil leak the next morning. Investigators now believe that he was putting into action his plan to get rid of Shanann and his daughters.

"I'm gonna go straight out there from my house," he told Roberts. "No sense in both of us going out there Lol."

Nine hundred miles away, Shanann Watts was having an early dinner with her friends before boarding the plane home. As soon as they sat down, she showed them her bank statement with Chris's $68 charge for dinner.

"She thought that was a little suspicious," said Addy Molony, "so she asked us what we thought [and] if he was with somebody."

Shanann ordered a chicken Caesar salad and some water with lemon. Her flight back to Denver had been delayed because of a bad storm, and all the restaurant lights went out for a few minutes.

"She was really anxious to get back," said Molony. "She was supernervous she wasn't going to get back and be able to talk to him and work things out."

At the end of the meal Shanann and the others posed for a photograph, giving the Le-Vel sign. Shanann posted it on Facebook, commenting, "Best way to leave Arizona . . . with loss of power while eating dinner."

* * *

Two hours later Shanann was at the gate at Phoenix Airport, still waiting to find out when her flight would be leaving. She texted Chris and asked him to send pictures of the girls from the party.

He replied with a picture of Bella.

"Great job on Bella's hair," she told him. "Really bad dust storm, rain, thunder and lightning. Praying it doesn't cancel the flight."

She then called him, but Watts was angry that she had interrupted his workout and said he had to go.

"Sorry I bothered you," she texted back. "I just wanted to talk to you."

While she was waiting at the gate, Shanann composed a rough draft of what she planned on telling Chris when she got home. She sent it to Addy Molony for feedback.

"Can you please tell me something," it read. "This is making me crazy. I know you need time. I want to give you what you're asking for and respect your space."

She said her being in a bad place was unhealthy for her and their new baby.

"I need you to give just a little bit of what I did, or didn't do, so I'm not going crazy in my head to figure it out. I know I can't fix this by myself; that, we are going to have to work together."

At 9:28 P.M. Shanann called Chris, but he didn't answer as he was in the midst of a two-hour call to his girlfriend.

Almost two hours later, she finally boarded the flight back to Denver.

"Ready to be home with Chris and the girls," she posted on Facebook. Then she texted Chris: "Finally on plane and about to take off. Thank God! Prayers for safe flight! Love you."

After finishing his call to Nikki Kessinger, Watts finally

replied, "Holy crap. Sorry, I passed out on the couch. That's gonna be late."

Shanann and Nickole finally arrived at the Denver Airport at 12:45 A.M. on Monday. At 1:25 A.M. Shanann texted Cassie Rosenberg, "Landed."

On the drive back to Frederick, Shanann told Nickole that she would not wake Chris up when she got home. She would just put her arms around him and feel close.

PART THREE

Exactly what happened that morning, only Shanann and Chris Watts will ever know—and only one of them survived. Investigators believe that Watts began carefully planning out what he was going to do the previous Friday, after learning about the leak at Cervi 319. It provided the perfect opportunity. His decision to use one of their joint credit cards to buy dinner for Nikki Kessinger on Saturday night, according to police, showed he had moved past his marriage for a new start with her.

Chris Watts claims it was entirely spontaneous. He says it was as if a bomb suddenly went off in his head and he was powerless to stop it.

At 1:48 A.M. Shanann Watts entered 2825 Saratoga Trail through the front door. She kicked off her flip-flops and left her suitcase at the entrance. Then she went into her office to buy some hair-care products, but her credit card was denied. She tiptoed upstairs, careful not to wake Bella and Celeste, who were both light sleepers.

Chris Watts was lying in bed in the master bedroom when he heard Shanann come up the stairs. He looked at his iPhone to check the time.

"I felt her get into bed," he later told detectives. "I could feel her stirring around a little bit."

By now he was certain Shanann knew about his affair, after she'd questioned Saturday night's Lazy Dog charge on their credit card.

"She started rubbing her hand on me," he said, "and we ended up having sex."

Watts thought Shanann was testing him to see if he had been faithful, as it was the first time they had made love since she'd left for North Carolina.

"I felt totally strange," he remembered. "I didn't know who I was. I didn't know who I'd become. [It] didn't feel right with me."

After they finished, they went to sleep.

A couple of hours later, Chris woke up and put on a blue fire-resistant shirt, pants, and a pair of old boots. He went downstairs into the kitchen to prepare his lunch.

Then he came back to the bedroom and woke Shanann up, saying they had to talk.

"I told her," he recalled, "'I don't feel like this is going to work. Can we cancel the trip to Aspen?'"

Shanann told him that she knew there was someone else and started crying. She said she was leaving with Bella and Celeste and he would never see them again.

Then, according to Watts, he told her that he didn't love her anymore as he put his hands around her neck and began to strangle her. Using all his strength, he stared deep into her eyes and watched them turn bloodshot as tears of mascara ran down her face.

Shanann never struggled during the two to four minutes it took her to die. The sheer horror she must have felt, staring helplessly at the man she loved and the father of her children as he choked the life out of her, is unimaginable.

Bella, who had been woken up by all the commotion, walked into the bedroom and saw her mother lying dead on the bed.

"What's wrong with Mommy?" she asked.

"Mommy don't feel good," replied her father.

Then he took the top sheet off the bed and wrapped Shanann's body in it, leaving the pillows and comforter on the floor. He attempted to pick her up and carry her downstairs, but she was too heavy. He dragged Shanann's lifeless body down the stairs and into the garage as his four-year-old daughter trailed behind.

"She was crying a little bit," Watts recalled. "She's like, 'What's wrong with Mommy?' I said she doesn't feel good, but she's a smart girl and she knew what was going on."

At 5:17 A.M., Watts opened the garage door with his remote. He backed his Anadarko truck into the driveway in front of Shanann's white Lexus, where it remained for the next twenty-eight minutes.

He put his wife's body in two black garbage bags, one over her head and the other over her feet. He lifted her into the back of the truck, dropping her on the floor behind the driver's seat.

Then he went back inside the house and grabbed his lunch box and water jugs and put them in the truck, along with a gas can. He could hear Celeste and Bella walking around upstairs, so he went back up to collect his daughters, bringing along CeCe's pink blanket and her favorite barking-dog toy. Then he turned out all the lights and went into the garage.

"I grabbed the kids," he said, "and put them on the bench seat in the back. [Shanann] was on the floor."

The girls kept asking if Mommy was okay, and Watts reassured them that she would be fine. At 5:45 A.M., Watts reversed out of the driveway and onto Saratoga Trail, closing the garage door behind him.

It was still dark when Chris Watts turned right onto Wyndham Hill Parkway. He took another right on County Road

7 and then a left to County Road 52 out of Frederick, for the forty-mile journey to the Cervi 319 oil well.

As he drove the deserted roads, the girls were in the back, whimpering and falling asleep in each other's lap, their feet resting on their mother's dead body.

"They were pretty quiet," Watts remembered. "They just laid next to each other. When we were driving . . . Bella said, 'Daddy it smells.'"

As Watts drove through Hudson and turned north onto I-76, it began to get light. Dry, flat scrubland was on both sides of the road.

At 6:29 A.M., he turned off onto the rural Route 386 to Roggen and began reaching out to his coworkers to ensure that no one would disturb him for the next couple of hours at Cervi 319. He made the first of three unanswered calls to Kodi Roberts, before texting him, "Where you at?"

"Just got fuel in Kersey," Roberts immediately replied.

"Ok. I'm in Cervi," tapped Watts. "Where you going first?"

"DPC state."

Watts responded with a thumbs-up emoji.

Roberts said he was calling Chad McNeil to see if he was still planning to go to the Cervi oil wells to pump one out. At 6:39 A.M., afraid that McNeil might disturb him at Cervi 319, Watts called his cell phone, but there was no answer.

"You headed out to Cervi?" Watts texted McNeil. "I'm out here. . . . Kodi said something about pumping out the 10-29."

"Well since you're out there," McNeil texted back, "you want to fire it up?"

"Ok I will."

At 6:53 A.M. Chris Watts drove through the front gates of the Cervi Ranch and out to the 319 oil well. He unlocked the gate and proceeded through the barbed-wire surround into the three-quarter-acre well site. He parked by the well heads of the twin tanks.

Telling Bella and Celeste he would be back soon, he got out, opened the back of the truck, and lifted out Shanann's body.

"What are you doing to Mommy?" asked Bella.

There was no reply.

He dragged his wife's body, shrouded in the garbage bags, across the parking lot and out into some scrubland a few yards away and dumped it there. He walked back to the truck and got in the back.

Then, as Bella watched in horror, he smothered Celeste, his hand wrapped inside her favorite blanket. Using all his strength to push her against the back seat of the truck, he forced the life out of her.

After he had finished, he pulled his youngest daughter's body out of the truck, leaving Bella behind. He calmly carried Celeste across the parking lot to the towering twenty-foot-high oil tank on the right and walked up the stairs. At the top he opened the thief hatch and slowly lowered Celeste feetfirst through the eight-inch opening. He dropped her inside, hearing her tiny body make a splashing sound as it hit the crude oil below.

After closing the hatch he walked back to the truck where Bella was waiting.

"What happened to CeCe?" she asked softly. "Will the same thing happen to me?"

"Yes," her father coldly replied, as he grabbed the blanket and came toward her.

"Daddy, no! Daddy, no!" screamed Bella, as his hand went over her mouth. Unlike her mother and sister, Bella fought desperately for her life, biting her tongue multiple times before taking her last breath.

"I felt her head moving back and forth," Watts would

later remember. "There was a grunt here and there [as she was] trying to breathe."

He then picked up his daughter's dead body and carried her up the stairs of the right tank and across the catwalk to the one on the left. He put Bella's body down as he opened the hatch.

Bella was too big to fit, so he had to force her body through the eight-inch opening, scraping the skin off her shoulders and buttocks. He remembered her making a slightly different-sounding splash, as there was less oil in that tank.

Then he turned his attention to Shanann's body. He walked over to it and started raking away some weeds. He picked up his shovel and dug a hole twenty-seven inches deep. When he had finished, he pushed her body into the shallow grave. He glanced down and saw that she had miscarried their son, Nico. He covered them both in earth, smoothing over the ground to make it blend in with the rest of the scrubland.

After he finished burying her at 7:40 A.M. he sent a text to Shanann's iPhone: "If you take the kids somewhere, please let me know where they are at!"

Then, coldly, methodically, Chris Watts began contacting his Anadarko team to cover his tracks. Despite the absolute horror of what he had just done, Watts had already detached himself from his family and compartmentalized the act, carrying on as if it were just another morning at work.

He first made a two-minute call to Troy McCoy, to see how far away he and the other members of his crew were. McCoy replied that he was about forty minutes away and would see Watts soon.

Then Kodi Roberts texted Watts to see if he would come over and join him at the nearby Cervi 10-29.

"Yea, I'm at 319," Watts texted back. "One sec."

Then he took a photograph of the leaking pipes by the wellhead and sent it to Roberts.

"10-4," replied Roberts. "How's it look?"

"Fresh—lol."

Over the next few minutes, Watts calmly chatted to his boss Luke Epple and to Chad McNeil, updating them on his progress at Cervi 319 and making small talk, without a hint of anything being wrong.

At 8:25 A.M. Watts called Shanann's phone again, leaving a twenty-three-second voice mail.

Then he googled the Primrose School and called the main number. The owner, Shannan Meyer, answered, and Watts announced that Bella and Celeste would not be returning to school, as he and Shanann were moving out of the area. He asked if his daughters had come to the school that morning. Meyer checked and said that they weren't clocked in.

She told him they would be missed by their teachers, asking if he wanted to put them on the waiting list in case anything changed. Watts replied that she might as well and hung up.

Five minutes later, Chad McNeil and Melissa Parrish arrived at Cervi 319 to find Watts digging a small hole with his shovel where the bypass line was leaking. He seemed to be in good humor, chatting about his weekend and describing the Rockies game—which he had not gone to—as "epic."

A few minutes later, Troy McCoy pulled into Cervi 319, immediately noticing Chris Watts's truck was parked far away from the bypass line he was working on. He also saw Watts was dressed far worse than usual, wearing an old pair of lace-up boots instead of the smart new pair of Red Wings he was so proud of.

"I was like, 'What, are you slumming it today, Bud?'" recalled McCoy. "And he laughed."

McCoy was also surprised that Watts kept complaining he was hot, as it was a cool, fresh Colorado morning in the fifties.

At 8:28 A.M., Watts strolled over to his truck and called Realtor Ann Meadows, asking if Shanann had been in touch yet. Meadows replied that Shanann had texted her a couple of days earlier from Arizona, and she'd advised that the Wattses get the loan preapproval before proceeding.

Watts then informed the Realtor that he and Shanann were getting a divorce.

At 9:30 A.M. Chris Watts and his team left Cervi 319 and moved on to another well, UPRC 10-29, which was just ten minutes away. Troy McCoy would later recall Watts walking past his truck and stopping for a last look at the two oil tanks, now containing his daughters. Then he turned around, got into his truck, and drove off.

They arrived at UPRC 10-29 in separate trucks and started working at that oil well. For the next couple of hours, Watts periodically went back to his truck to make calls or to get on the internet.

At 10:10 A.M. he made half a dozen Google searches for the lyrics of the Metallica song "Battery," about killing a family.

> *Lunacy has found me . . .*
> *Cannot kill the family.*

While he was reading the lyrics, Sandi Rzucek texted him, "Is Shanann ok?"

Watts then called his mother-in-law, explaining that they'd argued that morning and Shanann had taken the kids to a friend's house, but he didn't know who.

Then he googled hotels in Aspen and called the Westin

Snowmass Resort to cancel Shanann's booking for the following weekend.

Over the next several hours, Chris Watts started fielding calls and texts from Shanann's friends, who were concerned they couldn't contact her. Nickole Atkinson was particularly alarmed that Shanann had missed her doctor's appointment, and that the girls had not turned up at school. Nickole was now on her way to 2825 Saratoga Trail to make sure she was all right.

Just after midday she arrived at the Wattses' house with her teenage son, Nicholas, and two-year-old daughter, Madison. She was on a conference call with Shanann's mother, Cassie Rosenberg, and Cristina Meacham.

At 12:10 P.M. Nickole rang the doorbell, but there was no answer. She entered the code to open the front door, but it only opened an inch because of a safety latch that had been installed to stop Celeste from getting out.

Nickole then peered inside and saw Shanann's favorite black flip-flops and luggage in the hallway. She and Nicholas shouted Shanann's name a few times through the crack in the door, but there was no reply.

Then Nickole pulled her car up to the garage. Nicholas climbed on top and could see Shanann's white Lexus in the garage with the girls' car seats still inside. He tried to open the garage door and set off the alarm.

29

"HE'S NOT ACTING RIGHT"

Forty miles away, Chris Watts received an alert on his cell phone that somebody was at his front door. He opened his Ring app to see Nickole Atkinson. A few minutes later she called him three times before he finally picked up.

"He said they were going on a playdate," said Nickole. "But if they're on a playdate, how did she get them there?"

Watts told her that one of Shanann's friends must have picked them up, but he did not know which one.

"I'm busy and I'm at work," he told Nickole sharply. "Are you messing with the door?"

She apologized for setting off the alarm, saying she was worried about Shanann.

"She's on a playdate, Nicki," he snapped. "I don't know what to tell you. I'm at work. I'll try and contact her. Would you please leave and stop messing with my doors."

Then he hung up.

Cassie Rosenberg, who was in Arizona, had her husband, Josh, text Watts to see if he would be more forthcoming with him.

"Hey bro," Josh texted. "Cassie asked me if I've heard from Shanann today. I guess her and Nicki can't get hold of her. Have you heard from her today?"

"I just talked to Nicki," Watts texted back a few minutes later. "Shanann went to a friend's house with the kids today. I haven't heard from her since. I will keep you updated though."

All through the morning, Watts had been in contact with Nikki Kessinger. He assured her everything was moving forward for his divorce.

At 12:43 P.M., Cassie texted Watts again, determined to get a straight answer. She had now spoken to Cristina, Sandi, and Nickole, discovering Chris had given them each different versions of where Shanann and the girls were.

"This is Cassie," she texted him. "Shanann is in a very bad way emotionally and I'm worried about her. . . . I know you are having issues, but I don't know [to] what extent, but I do know I've never seen her so broken to an extent I am worried."

"She went to a friend's house with the kids," Watts texted back. "She won't tell me where though. When I get home I will update you."

A few minutes later, Cassie sent him another text: "Sweetie, her car and shoes and everything is at the house. What the heck is going on with you guys that she would totally shut out everything? It's not like her."

Watts then told her that he and Shanann had agreed to split up last night, sell the house, and downsize.

"Separation would be best right now," he explained, "if we can work thru the issues. I really don't want you to think I'm a bad person Cassie."

"Right now I don't care about you, or your relationship," she replied, "or what type of person you are or not, or what I think of you, and I'm not trying to be rude when I say that."

In between texts to Cassie, Chris was also messaging

his Realtor, providing updates to help put the house on the market.

Finally at 1:03 P.M. Cassie told Watts that Nickole was calling 911.

"Right now I'm worried about [your] damn wife and her well being," she told him. "Nicki is calling the police. Period. [Shanann] is broken emotionally. Her blood sugar dropped due to not eating and it could cause her to pass out. So unless you want the police to bust your damn door down you get home and check on your family."

"I'm going home Cassie. On my way. Don't call the police. I will be there in 45 minutes."

Just after one o'clock, Watts told Troy McCoy he was going home. For the last several hours Watts had sat in his truck fielding calls about Shanann, telling McCoy that nobody could get ahold of her. But he didn't seem too concerned or in any rush to leave.

"He's like, 'Hey, guys, I've got to go,'" recalled McCoy. "'Something's not right at home.' It wasn't like he was in a panic."

But first he said he needed to defecate, pulling his truck over to the holding tanks for some privacy. Later investigators would question if he was trying to get rid of evidence.

At 1:36 P.M. Nickole Atkinson called the nonemergency line of the Frederick Police Department, who transferred her to the Weld County Dispatch Center.

"My name is Nickole," she told the dispatcher, "and I'm calling because I'm concerned about a friend of mine. She's not answering the door, she's not responding to text messages, phone calls. And there's no movement in the house whatsoever."

Four minutes later, Officer Scott Coonrod of the Frederick Police Department was dispatched to 2825 Saratoga Trail to carry out a welfare check. He pulled up at 1:50 P.M. and turned on his body cam. Nickole and Nicholas Atkinson greeted him.

Visibly worried, Nickole told him that she and her friend Shanann had been out of town for the weekend on a business trip, and Nickole had dropped her off at about two o'clock that morning.

"She's fifteen weeks pregnant," said Nickole. "She wasn't feeling well and she had a doctor's appointment this morning at nine and she didn't go. She's got two little girls and she was very distraught over the weekend."

She then told Coonrod how Shanann's husband, Chris, was now telling everyone that they were separating.

"But she didn't know this," said Nickole. "She thought they were just having issues."

When she'd called Chris to ask him if he'd heard from Shanann, he said she'd taken the girls on a playdate. But Nickole pointed to the garage, asking why Shanann's car was still inside with the girls' seats in the back.

"I've called. I've texted," she told the officer, as they walked over to the front door, which was open a crack. "Her shoes she wears every single day are right [here]."

"Okay," replied Officer Coonrod. "No answer on the phone? Her husband's on his way?"

"Supposedly," said Nickole, adding that he kept changing his arrival times.

Then the officer asked Nickole to call Chris for the garage pass code and permission to enter. She did, telling Chris that the police were at the house and couldn't get in.

Watts said he was only five minutes away and didn't

want them to break down the door. Then he hung up and sent another message to Shanann's iPhone: "Where are you?"

While they were waiting for Chris Watts, Officer Coonrod walked around the house with Nicholas, checking the windows and knocking on the side of the house. Nicholas asked why he couldn't just break in.

"I've got to have more unless I get consent from him to go in," said Coonrod. "You've got your Fourth Amendment rights to the house. I can't violate that."

When Coonrod came back to the front of the house, Nickole had on her speakerphone Sandi Rzucek, who provided the key code to open the garage.

"He told me Shanann was at her girlfriend's house," Sandi told the officer.

"Do we know who that is?" asked Coonrod.

"He didn't say," replied Sandi. "He seemed to be acting funny."

Officer Coonrod walked back to the front door and started to knock loudly. Then he asked for Chris's phone number and called him.

"Hey, Chris, Officer Coonrod from the police department."

"How's it going?" Watts replied casually.

"Pretty good. So do you have any idea where your wife is?"

Watts said he didn't and would be there in ten minutes.

Although he was only forty-five minutes away, it took Watts almost twice as long to get home. On the way he stopped off near a construction site and changed into clean clothes, throwing his dirty ones into a dumpster. Then he went to a gas station to buy some snacks, where a CCTV camera caught him flirting with the attractive cashier.

As they waited for him, Nicholas told Officer Coonrod that he was suspicious of Chris Watts.

"We know he's been lying," said the teenager, "because his story's not adding up. He's been telling us a lot of different stories."

"I mean I don't see anything out of place," said Coonrod. "I'm not hearing kids. I'm not hearing anything."

Then Officer Coonrod knocked on the front door again, shouting, "Shanann. Are you home? Police department! If anyone's inside, make yourself known!"

The only sound from inside was Dieter barking.

At 2:07 P.M., Chris Watts pulled up outside in his Anadarko truck. He calmly strolled over to Officer Coonrod, introduced himself, and shook hands. Wearing shades and a baggy gray Ariat sweatshirt, he opened the garage with his remote and went inside, where Shanann's white Lexus was parked.

He then entered the house alone through the garage, leaving everyone outside. A couple of minutes later, he opened the front door from the inside.

"Mind if I come in, Chris?" asked Officer Coonrod.

"No objection at all."

"Do you mind if I look around?"

"No." Dieter started barking. "Go ahead. I'm going to get the dog."

Officer Coonrod first took a cursory look around, going into the pantry and the living room. Then he went down into the basement with his flashlight, before coming back upstairs and going up to the top floor, where Watts was waiting.

"All the girls' blankies are gone," Watts observed with an air of concern. "They don't leave anywhere without them."

"Nothing else seems to be missing though?" asked Coonrod.

"No."

Watts led Officer Coonrod through Bella's bedroom and then into Celeste's. Downstairs in the living room, Nicholas found Shanann's iPhone, with its distinctive green case, under a pillow on the couch.

"She works from home," said Watts, rushing over to turn it on, "and this is her lifeline."

"It was shut down?" asked Coonrod.

"Yeah." Watts nodded as he paced around nervously.

Coonrod asked for Shanann's pass code.

"It's the baby's due date," answered Nickole.

"That's one, thirty-one, twenty-nineteen," said Watts, punching in the digits.

"What does she do for work?" asked Coonrod.

"She works for a direct-sales company called Thrive," replied Watts.

Then Nickole told him to check his security camera and see what time Shanann had left, noting he'd told her Shanann had gone on a playdate with the kids, but had said to Addy Molony that she'd left in the middle of the night.

"Oh, no," said Watts dismissively. "She didn't leave in the middle of the night."

"Yeah," replied Nickole, unconvinced.

Then Officer Coonrod asked when he had left for work.

"I usually leave between five thirty and six," answered Watts.

"And was Shanann here then?" Coonrod asked.

"Yes." Watts paced back and forth as he checked Shanann's iPhone for messages.

"You guys have any kind of marital issues?" asked Coonrod.

"We're going through a separation."

"You are," said Coonrod. "You guys filed yet or just talking?"

"No. We're going to have to sell the house and have a separation."

"How's that going? Civil for most part?"

"Civil," Watts mumbled, as he checked Shanann's phone.

Then he went into the master bedroom for a few seconds, suddenly reappearing with Shanann's wedding ring on his finger. "I found it on the nightstand. That's weird."

They all walked into the master bedroom, where the curtains were drawn and all the bedding was piled up in the corner.

Nickole immediately heard warning bells.

"Bad thoughts were going through my head," she later explained. "[Chris] does all the laundry, so if he left for work, why was the bed stripped . . . if Shanann was still there sleeping in it?"

"Is there any of her clothes missing?" asked Coonrod, as they walked into her huge closet, resembling a clothing store with its racks of dresses neatly hung up—the word GORGEOUS painted on the purple wall.

"No," said Watts, "it would be hard to tell if she took a little bit."

"Okay," said Officer Coonrod. "Did she say anything about leaving? Moving out?"

"Not moving out. The last time I talked to her was this morning. She said she was going to take the kids to a friend's house . . . but the car's still here. Unless someone came and picked her up."

"Any kind of behavioral changes?" asked Coonrod.

"We're going through a separation. That's been the only change."

A few minutes later, Officer Coonrod and the others went next door to neighbor Nathaniel Trinastich's house, to watch his CCTV camera video of the driveway outside the Watts's garage. They all gathered around his television in his living room as Trinastich played his surveillance video.

The video started at 5:17 A.M. that morning, when the camera's motion detector began recording the Anadarko truck backing into the driveway.

"This is him at five seventeen," said Trinastich, as Watts's truck came on-screen.

"I loaded my stuff up with my coolers, my water jugs," explained Watts, as he nervously played with his iPhone. "My bug bag. Some of the tools I had from the toolbox. I knew I was going to have to do some pumping in the rubbers today, because I was out so far.

"I usually park out there on the side," said Watts, his hands on the back of his head and not looking at the screen. "I just went to get . . . all the tools I had to bring in."

After several minutes he asked what was going to happen now.

"My detective just showed up," said Coonrod, who had summoned backup. "So he'll probably want to talk to you."

As Trinastich flipped through his remote, he stopped at the 1:48 A.M. mark, when the camera was activated by Shanann's walking into the house. He said those were the only two times anyone had accessed the house that day.

"But if any action would have happened," said Trinastich, "any cars or [anyone] left your house, it would have picked it up."

"Nothing for the rest of the day?" asked the officer.

"No, that's it."

"She's pregnant as well," observed Watts, as he toyed with his phone.

"How far along?" asked Coonrod.

"Fourteen, fifteen weeks," Watts replied with his arms folded. "That's why her friend said it was low blood sugar."

"Did you go and check whether anything was missing around your house?" asked Trinastich.

"There was nothing," Watts replied. "Her wedding ring was on the nightstand. Her phone was still there."

After several more minutes of nervously fidgeting, Watts shook his neighbor's hand and thanked him before walking out.

"He's not acting right at all," said Trinastich, shaking his head. "He's rocking back and forth, and he never moves his stuff in and out of the garage ever."

"Right," replied Officer Coonrod.

"To be completely honest with you," whispered Trinastich conspiratorially, "my wife and I were kind of wondering when she was on vacation if something happened. Because I've heard them full out screaming at each other at the top of their lungs . . . and he gets crazy."

"Does he? And that's pretty recently?"

"Yeah. Well, that's why we thought she went and visited people, because she wanted to get away from the situation."

Then Nickole Atkinson came in saying Shanann's mom wanted them to check the GPS on her son-in-law's truck, as she thought he had done something.

"He's acting so suspicious," said Trinastich. "He's nor-mally quiet and well subdued and never talks. So the fact that he's over here blabbing his mouth makes me kind of suspicious."

At 2:35 P.M. Detective Dave Baumhover from the Fred-erick Police Department arrived at 2825 Saratoga Trail. He was briefed by Officer Coonrod, who told him that Shanann's cell phone, purse, wallet, and wedding ring were still in the house. Then they went upstairs and into the master bedroom, where the bedding lay on the floor.

"Officer Coonrod and I both checked the bedding for signs of foul play," Baumhover later wrote in his report, "but found nothing."

The detective asked Chris Watts when he had last seen his wife and daughters. Watts said she had arrived home from the airport at 1:48 A.M., when he'd received a door-bell camera alert to his iPhone.

"At approximately 0400 hours," wrote Baumhover, "he informed Shanann he wanted to initiate a marital separa-tion and they were both upset and crying."

Watts said that Shanann had then informed him she was taking the girls to a friend's house that day and did not say who.

"It should be noted when I asked Watts a second time to recall his day," reported the detective, "he told me he worked out in his basement for fifteen minutes that morning before returning to the bedroom to speak with Shanann about the marital separation."

Watts then said that they were having financial diffi-culties and planned to downsize and sell their house.

"I asked if they were planning on living together during the separation," wrote Baumhover. "Watts said he would get an apartment somewhere and Shanann and the girls could move into a smaller house and they would share custody of their kids."

Watts showed the detective an email from Realtor Ann Meadows on his cell phone, to prove they wanted to sell the house. He also pointed out an alert that his garage door was left open at 5:27 A.M., as well as another for the basement door earlier.

"He appeared to be puzzled by both alerts," noted Baumhover.

Asked where he had gone that morning, Watts said he had driven to an oil well site near Hudson, but could not remember the name of it.

"I asked Watts if anyone could vouch his arrival," wrote the detective. "He said no one else was at the site until later, and he had gone early to check on a repair before starting his normal duties."

Detective Baumhover then interviewed Nickole Atkinson, who said Shanann could only have left the house through the garage because the front-door safety latch was still on. She also told him that Watts never backed his truck up to the garage, as the noise woke up the girls.

"Nickole was adamant Shanann would not leave the house without her phone or medications," noted the detective, "or take the girls anywhere without their car seats."

Officer Coonrod requested Weld County Dispatch to issue a BOLO (be on the lookout) for Shanann, Bella, and Celeste Watts. For the next several hours Coonrod canvassed the neighborhood, knocking on doors and looking for any leads. He also left business cards at any nearby houses with video surveillance.

Soon afterward, Cristina Meacham texted Chris Watts for any news about Shanann: "What's going on??? We are so worried."

"Cops are here," he replied. "Call you when I know."

At 2:55 P.M., when she hadn't heard anything further, Cristina sent him another text: "Anything?"

"Police searched the house up and down. Missing persons report filed in the morning more likely."

"This is so unlike her. I'm extremely worried. We are praying for all of you!"

"Thank you, Cristina. I'm praying so hard right now."

30

"PLEASE PRAY!!"

At 3:45 P.M. Chris Watts asked Nikki Kessinger to call him. She had just gotten home from work and had a friend over.

"He told me [Shanann] was gone and he didn't know where she was," Kessinger recalled. "'My wife and my kids aren't home.' And I was just like, 'Okay.'"

As Watts seemed unconcerned, she didn't take it too seriously, thinking Shanann had probably taken the girls out shopping.

Twenty minutes later, Nick Thayer texted Watts to see if he wanted to go running.

"Not sure man," Watts texted back. "I can't find Shanann or the kids. Haven't heard from them all day. Cops are here. I will keep you posted."

"Whoa. That is crazy man," replied Thayer.

"I don't know. It's very odd right now."

That afternoon, Frankie Rzucek made an emotional appeal on Facebook: "Please say a prayer for my sister and nieces. They're missing, no one knows where she is. Her phone and car are home. We don't know what to think at this moment. I pray it's nothing. Shanann Watts please be ok."

Sandi Rzucek also went online with an appeal to her daughter: "Where are u my baby."

Shanann's Thrive team leader Sam Pasley posted, "Please pray!! Please share and please help us find our dear friend and her sweet girls. Shanann Watts we love you so much and are praying [for] you and the girls."

When Jeanna Dietz saw all the Facebook appeals, she texted Watts.

"He was vague," she remembered, "and saying, 'Pray for my family,' or sending me emojis of praying hands."

She then offered to come over and organize a search for Shanann and the girls, but Watts said that was not a good idea.

"Everybody wanted to do something," said Jeanna, "so a lot of people [were] saying, 'Well, can we start a search?' He said the police told him that he was not allowed to do that."

All of Shanann's friends who had seen how upset she was in Arizona about her marriage were now in constant contact. They all suspected that her husband had something to do with his family's disappearance.

When Addy Molony asked if there was any news of Shanann, Watts replied, "I'm so worried."

She then sent out a group text: "The police need to look at Chris' cell!!!! And computer."

Josh Rosenberg also confronted Watts about everyone's suspicions: "You know how this looks."

Watts said he was aware that everyone was "mad" at him, but did not know how they could think he would do something to harm Shanann and his daughters.

At 4:20 P.M. Officer Matthew James arrived at 2825 Saratoga Trail to search the house with Officers Coonrod and Jared Brakes. Chris Watts signed a consent form, waiving his right to a search warrant, saying they had "free rein to do whatever you've gotta do." Then he left, saying he was going out for a walk to clear his head.

A few minutes later, he came back and waited outside on the porch with Dieter as his house was searched.

"The house was very well kept and organized," wrote Officer James in his report. "I did not observe anything obviously damaged or anything that would indicate a struggle in the bedroom."

Watts was then asked to check their bank accounts for any recent activity by Shanann. He said he didn't know how to log in, as Shanann handled all the finances, but would call their banks.

Questioned about all the bedding lying on the floor of the master bedroom, Watts explained that Shanann "usually jumps into bed" after returning from a trip and washes the sheets the next morning. He said although he had been sleeping in the basement during the separation, he had slept with Shanann last night. In the morning, he said, they had discussed separating and selling the house.

After the search, Officer James gave Watts his business card, telling him to have Shanann call him immediately if she turned up.

"Chris was very cooperative," wrote James, "and answered questions appropriately. Nothing was readily observed inside the residence that would indicate a struggle."

All afternoon, Sam Pasley had been texting Watts for any updates.

"I'm praying so hard," he told her. "I'm sick to my stomach. Cops searched the house up and down and drilled me pretty hard. I have no idea where they can be."

When Pasley asked why they were drilling him, Watts

replied, "They are just being thorough. They gotta do all the digging they can."

Soon after the officers left, Nick and Amanda Thayer arrived to offer support. Chris brought them into the kitchen, nervously pacing back and forth as he answered their questions. He said that he had just finished calling hospital emergency rooms to try to locate Shanann and the girls. But he seemed more concerned with himself than what had happened to them, saying it was "bizarre" that Shanann had not taken her cell phone.

"It's empty here," he told the Thayers. "I need my family back."

While they sat at the kitchen table brainstorming what to do, Watts suddenly asked, "Do I walk out into the field to look for someone?" Someone suggested he contact the media to run a story about Shanann going missing, but Watts was against it. He said they might pry and make him "public enemy number one."

Then Lauren Arnold arrived after seeing all the Facebook posts that Shanann and the girls were missing.

"[Chris] answered the door and gave me a hug," she recalled. "I asked the logical 'Are you okay?' questions. He said, 'No.'"

Then Lauren saw Shanann's flip-flops and suitcase by the stairs, and a toy under a chair in the living room.

"And then I just glanced upstairs," she said. "And he said, 'I had to close all the doors [upstairs] as I can't handle going up there and seeing all the toys and stuff.'"

She asked if he had gone out to search for them, but Nick Thayer replied that the police had told them not to. Amazed, Lauren asked Watts why he was not out searching for them.

"And he said, 'No, they told me not to,'" she said. "That [didn't] really seem logical to me, but okay."

Lauren was also struck by his lack of concern and that he was planning to go back to work tomorrow.

"He wouldn't make eye contact with me while we were talking," she later told detectives. "He looked at the floor the whole time. His behavior was very suspicious."

Nick and Amanda Thayer finally left at around 8:00 P.M. They immediately called the Frederick Police Department and left a message. During their three hours with Chris, something seemed wrong and they felt it was their duty to report it.

After they left, Watts called Nikki Kessinger.

"He was calm," she later told police, "but you could just hear it in his voice that he was concerned for his kids."

The lovers talked on and off for the rest of the night, spending several hours on the phone together.

At 9:00 P.M. Luke Epple texted for any updates.

"He called me back immediately," said Epple, "and said, 'They're still gone. The police came and searched my house. They had a warrant. They searched the vehicles.'"

Watts said he planned to work tomorrow morning, so he wouldn't have to stay at home.

"It's like something out of a movie," he told his boss. "She's just gone. And her purse is here. Her ID is here. Her car is here. The kids' medicine is still here. She just disappeared."

Late Monday night, Jeremy Lindstrom saw Sandi Rzucek's Facebook post asking for prayers for Shanann and the girls. He then called Dave Colon, who also hadn't heard about Shanann's disappearance. Both men decided to go to Chris Watts's house and offer support.

At around 9:30 P.M. Colon arrived to find Watts vacuuming the carpet.

"He was keeping himself busy," said Colon. "I totally

understood that. And then about thirty minutes later Jeremy showed up."

As Watts made a protein shake in the kitchen, he matter-of-factly described how Shanann and the kids had been there when he left for work, but were gone when he got back.

"He was pretty blank," recalled Colon. "He was not like, 'Oh, I knew this was coming. I don't know why she did this.'"

Then Lindstrom asked if the girls' medicine had been left behind, as he knew about Celeste's allergies. Watts said it was all still there.

"I didn't want to grill him with questions," said Lindstrom, "because obviously he's going through something."

Then Watts said he just wanted to finish cleaning the house and go to bed.

"I'm like, 'Okay, I guess some people get nervous. Get weird. Start cleaning,'" said Lindstrom. "I don't know."

After they left, Chris Watts FaceTimed his girlfriend. He was lying on a bare mattress in his master bedroom, wearing a black-and-white wifebeater shirt. He explained he was cleaning the house to keep his mind occupied.

"He wanted me to talk to him," she remembered, "He's like, 'I just wanted to see your face.'"

Then Kessinger asked why there were no sheets on the bed.

"He said, 'I had to wash the kids' sheets,'" said Kessinger. "'They smelled.' I'm like, 'This man keeps that house so clean . . . why would his kids' sheets smell so bad?'"

Then Kessinger said she would call back, as he was making her feel uncomfortable.

"It was kind of weird," she recalled. "I [didn't] really

know where this [was] going. He was just, like, really fix-
ated on me."

Kessinger called him back at 11:09 P.M. and they spoke
for almost an hour. It was past midnight when she got off
the phone and immediately googled *Shanann Watts*.

Back at the Frederick police station, Officer Matthew
James was calling Shanann's friends for more information.
They all told him how worried she was about her marriage
and that Chris was having an affair.

Cindy Derossett described how upset Shanann had
been during their training trip to Arizona: "She was
about to break down. He's been saying things, that
they're not compatible anymore. That she was blindsided
by him."

Derossett said that Shanann would never have left
without the girls' medicine, her purse, or her cell phone.
"She's the most OCD-like, really routine person that I've
ever met. She's like a helicopter mom [and] would never
have left the house without the girls having everything they
needed. We're trying to be reasonable and not hysterical,
but none of this makes any sense at all."

Derossett also told the officer about the bank alert
Shanann had received, after Chris had supposedly eaten
dinner alone after the Rockies game. "He spent more
money than he should have for his own meal. That was just
curious to her . . . her suspicions are everywhere."

Addy Molony told Officer James that if Shanann
had gone on a playdate, she would definitely have taken
Bella's and Celeste's car seats and medicine.

"She's the best mom that I know," Molony said, "and
he's always been a great dad. This is why this is so alarm-
ing. I don't even know what to say. I just hope that we find
her."

Cristina Meacham said when she had stayed in the Wattses' house, Shanann never varied her routine. "Nothing adds up. That the latch was on doesn't make any sense to me, because she comes in and out of that door every day. The routine was completely off. And that's not normal."

The officer then asked if Shanann planned to leave Chris or try to mend the marriage.

"She wanted their marriage to work. And I just told her, 'You just need to talk to him, give him space, and work things out.' Because Chris is very, very quiet. You don't see many emotions from Chris."

Like the rest of Shanann's friends, Cristina had wondered if Chris might be responsible. "I don't think Chris has it in him. I think Chris is a good guy, so it's kind of hard for me to even imagine that he would hurt his family . . . especially those girls."

That night, Frederick PD patrol officers continued canvassing the neighborhood, without any results. Several officers were also discreetly watching 2825 Saratoga Trail in shifts, from a vantage point one hundred yards north on Steeple Rock Drive. Their brief was to log and document any unusual activity. Watts was seen packing up blankets and a cooler inside the white Lexus before closing the garage door.

Before going off duty, Detective Dave Baumhover decided to call in the Colorado Bureau of Investigation (CBI) and the FBI if Shanann and the girls had not turned up by morning. The detective now had Chris Watts firmly in his sights and was certain that he knew more than he was saying.

"I knew something was really wrong when I went out there," he later explained, "and so did Officer Coonrod, which is why he called me. And it's just a matter that you have to check off certain things."

Detective Baumhover said he had to consider whether Shanann had taken the kids just to "mess with his head" after Watts asked for a separation, or if it was murder.

"I had already made the decision that if she had not returned by the morning," said Baumhover, "we were going to initiate a full-blown investigation."

Frederick police officer Ed Goodman had already started preparing a missing persons report for Shanann and the girls. At 2:00 A.M. he called Chris Watts's cell phone several times for their physical details. The line was busy, as Watts was talking to his girlfriend.

A few minutes later, Watts called him back on his work phone, explaining something was wrong with his iPhone.

"Has anything else come to mind," asked Officer Goodman, "to help us try to figure out what's going on? Where she is?"

"Nothing's come across," Watts coolly replied. "Just a bunch of text messages from friends reaching out to me and just seeing if they could help. But nothing new."

"It should be mentioned," wrote Officer Goodman in his subsequent report, "that he did not ask me if I had been calling because I had any information concerning his missing wife and daughters. Or if I was calling because they had been found."

After the call, Goodman sent the information to the Weld County Dispatch Records Office, who officially listed Shanann, Bella, and Celeste Watts as missing persons.

At 4:38 A.M., after a sleepless night, Sandi Rzucek anxiously called Officer Goodman, saying she was convinced it was "foul play."

"She honestly believes," wrote Goodman in his report, "that her son-in-law [is] involved in the disappearance of her daughter and granddaughters."

Shanann's mom said her son-in-law was acting "weird," planning to go to work tomorrow, even though his family was still missing. She told the officer that he might have poured oil on their bodies to dispose of them, and that Shanann would not have been able to put up a fight because of her lupus.

31

"WE HAD AN EMOTIONAL
CONVERSATION"

At seven the next morning, Detective Dave Baumhover issued a press release, appealing for any information about
Shanann, Bella, and Celeste Watts. It was emailed to all
local newspapers and television stations, along with a photograph of Shanann, Bella, and Celeste.

MISSING PERSONS—Be on the Lookout (B.O.L.O.)

> On August 13, 2018 the Frederick Police De-
> partment was notified of 3 missing persons.
> Shanann Watts 34 years old, and her two
> daughters that are 3 and 4 years old, are miss-
> ing as well. Shanann is also 15 weeks pregnant.
> There is no vehicle associated at this time.
> If you have any information regarding this
> case, please contact Det Dave Baumhover or
> the Frederick Police Department with any in-
> formation regarding this BOLO.

Within minutes, reporters started calling Shanann's family and friends for any further information.

"I started getting all the phone calls . . . from reporters," said Lauren Arnold, who had posted on Facebook

about Shanann's disappearance. "So a lot of Tuesday was spent . . . being driven crazy."

When Nick and Amanda Thayer received calls from the media, they drove to 2825 Saratoga Trail to see how Chris Watts wanted to handle it. They arrived just after 9:00 A.M. to find him "tired, not himself, and over-whelmed." He was frustrated that Anadarko had ordered him to stay home until his family was found.

Then the three of them sat around the kitchen table, discussing if and when Chris should do media interviews.

Soon afterward, a reporter from Denver's Fox 31 TV station called, and Watts gave a brief phone interview.

"My heart is racing a mile a minute," he told the reporter. "It's not something I could ever, ever fathom would happen in my lifetime."

Back in Aberdeen, Shanann's parents and brother were being bombarded with media requests and appointed a cousin, Lu Valentino, as family spokesperson.

She posted a press release online: "PLEASE HELP MY FAMILY BRING HOME OUR MISSING PREGNANT COUSIN SHANANN WATTS & HER 2 DAUGHTERS BELLA & CELESTE—They've disappeared from Frederick, Co on Monday. We just want them all home safe."

At around 9:00 A.M., Officer Dave Egan set up an incident command room at the Frederick Police Department, to gather information and coordinate the search. Detective Dave Baumhover, who had now been appointed lead detective, then called in the CBI and the FBI for assistance.

As the hunt for Shanann and the girls intensified, Chris Watts was busy transferring a new batch of seminude selfies Nikki Kessinger had just sent onto his secret app.

By 11:00 A.M., more than twenty local and national media outlets had contacted the Frederick PD for more information. A fifteen-weeks-pregnant mother and her two little daughters going missing had all the makings of a major national story. Sergeant Robert Bedsaul sent out the release again, writing:

"This is the press release for the Shanann Watts case that is being inquired about. You can contact me with questions. We don't have any additional information we can release at this time.

"A majority of our department is working on the case. I will send out any updates . . . today at about 3pm."

Twenty-three minutes later, Fox 31 broke the story online with interviews from Chris Watts and Nickole Atkinson, who was not named.

The story said that police were releasing little information and refusing to say if foul play was suspected. It quoted "a close friend" as saying she had dropped off Shanann at home at about 2:00 A.M. Monday after returning home from a work trip and seen her go inside. They were supposed to have met later, but Shanann stopped answering her phone.

The story quoted Chris Watts, saying he hoped his wife and daughters were okay.

"She said she was going to a friend's house with the kids," he said, "and that's the last thing I heard, and that was it. It was very vague."

During her lunch break, Nikki Kessinger went online and read the fast-breaking news stories. She was shocked to learn that Shanann was fifteen weeks pregnant.

"When I read the news," she later told detectives, "I thought, 'If he was able to lie to me and hide something that big, what else was he lying about?'"

She immediately confronted him, and he denied that the baby was his, asking if this would "ruin" their relationship.

"And I was like, 'You need to focus on finding all three of your kids,'" she said. "I kept emphasizing he had three kids."

Finally Watts admitted the baby was his and he had known about it the whole time. Once again he anxiously asked if this would "ruin" their relationship. Kessinger said no.

"And in the back of my head, it's like, 'Yeah, I'm done,'" she later said. "But his situation is so critical right now . . . I'm not going to ruffle his mental feathers."

For the next four hours, Kessinger closely monitored online news coverage, realizing that everything Watts had ever told her was a lie.

"I got so sick," she said. "I packed my stuff and left work and went home. I just needed some time to process what was going on."

Over numerous texts and calls to his girlfriend that afternoon, Watts showed zero emotion about his missing family. He swore that he would never hurt them.

"It seemed off," said Kessinger. "He was telling me so many lies that I eventually told him that I did not want to speak to him again until his family was found. I told him, 'I'm scared because I feel like I don't know who you are anymore.'"

Then she deleted all his texts, photos, and videos from her cell phone, as well as anything she had ever sent him.

At around midday, Officer Katherine Lines of the Frederick PD and three search-and-rescue dogs arrived at 2825 Saratoga Trail. Watts had obviously been cleaning up, and the television was tuned to a sports channel. Watts gave permission for the K9s to search his home.

"I immediately noticed a strong odor of cleaning chemicals," Officer Lines later reported. "The home appeared spotless and the carpet had noticeable vacuum lines."

Told that the specially trained dogs would need scent samples from Shanann's and the girls' untouched dirty clothing and shoes, Watts apologized, saying that he had touched everything.

"Chris mentioned that he had made the girls' beds that morning," wrote Officer Lines, "and done the laundry."

When the officers tried to empathize, saying that they couldn't imagine what he was going through, Watts seemed flat and emotionless. He never once asked a question or offered help.

"Chris's facial expressions rarely changed," observed Officer Lines. "However, when they did, he seemed to smile/smirk inappropriately."

After escorting the officers around his house, Watts remained outside while a cadaver dog went inside to search. Several times the dog picked up scents where there might have been "trauma or struggle," but nothing definitive.

One of the cadaver dogs was taken to Watts's work truck, parked outside. The dog detected something, but did not enter the vehicle, as it was locked.

While the cadaver dogs were inside his house, Chris Watts was on the porch outside giving media interviews. He appeared to relish all the attention.

"Doing interviews with the news," he texted Cristina Meacham. "Dogs swept the house for a scent and they are on a patrol. My heart is racing honestly, so much activity here."

When KMGH-TV reporter Tomas Hoppough arrived with a cameraman, Watts seemed calmly detached from the whole situation. He explained the North Carolina Tar Heels football T-shirt he was wearing was a gift from Shanann.

"We go into the interview," recalled Hoppough. "We were just going to ask the husband, 'Do you know where

she could have went? Are you afraid for their safety?' It's
one of those type of stories."

Usually reticent and monosyllabic, Watts was surprisingly verbose.

"What's going on right now at your house?" Hoppough
asked.

"Well, right now it's K9 units [and] the sheriff's department. Everybody's doing their best right now to figure
out . . . where they went. They're going through the house
trying to get a scent, and hopefully they can pick something up."

Then the reporter asked what had happened when
Shanann came home early Monday morning.

"She came home from the airport [at] two A.M. And
[when] I left around five fifteen, she was still here.
And about twelve ten that afternoon her friend Nickole
showed up at the door."

Watts said he had texted his wife several times and
gotten no reply, but wasn't concerned. However, that she
wasn't returning calls from the people she worked with
had worried him. He said he had come straight home
after getting the call from Nickole.

"And then I walked in the door and nothing. Just vanished. Nothing was here."

As several neighbors gathered outside to see what was
going on, Hoppough asked if Watts thought Shanann had
just taken off with the kids.

"I just don't want to throw anything out there. I hope
she's somewhere safe now with the kids. But, I mean,
could she have vanished? Could she have just taken off?
I don't know."

He told the reporter that he wanted them back immediately.

"That's the not-knowing part," he said. "If they're not
safe."

Watts described last night as "traumatic," saying he had left every light on in the house. "I was hoping that I would just get run over by the kids, running in the door and barrel-rushing me. But it didn't happen."

"This might be a tough question," said Hoppough, "but did you guys get into an argument before she left?"

"It wasn't like an argument," replied Watts nervously, as he rocked back and forth with his arms folded. "We had an emotional conversation, but I'll leave it at that."

Finally, Hoppough asked what Watts would say to Shanann and the kids if they were watching.

"Shanann, Bella, Celeste"—Watts stared into the camera—"if you're out there, just come back. If somebody has her, just bring her back. I need to see everybody again. This house is not complete without anybody here. Please bring her back."

Over the next hour, Watts did more interviews, with KUSA-TV and KDVR-TV.

"When I got home yesterday, it was like a ghost town," he told the KUSA reporter. "She wasn't here. The kids weren't here. It's like a nightmare I can't wake up from."

The reporter then asked if he was worried people might think he had done something.

"I mean, everyone's going to have their own opinion," he answered. "I just want people to know I want my family back."

Watts was then asked about his two missing daughters.

"Celeste"—he smiled wistfully—"she's just a bundle of energy. I call her rampage because she's got two speeds—go or she's sleeping. And Bella . . . she's the more calm, cautious, mothering type. She's more like me. But Celeste has definitely got her mom's personality to where she's always just gung ho and ready to go."

Asked by a KDVR-TV reporter how the police had responded so far, Watts was highly appreciative:

"They've been amazing. They've been on top of everything."

In the early afternoon, half a dozen special agents from the Colorado Bureau of Investigation and the FBI arrived at the Frederick Police Department to be briefed by Detective Dave Baumhover. They set up a command center in the tiny Fifth Street police headquarters and began working the case.

CBI agent Tammy Lee immediately upgraded to a Missing/Endangered Alert for Shanann, Bella, and Celeste. She called Anadarko and arranged to get Watts's work cell phone information and truck GPS information as soon as possible.

She also requested that AT&T, Verizon, and Facebook preserve all of Shanann's and Chris's records. For the next several days, agents would interview all of Shanann and Chris Watts's family and friends searching for any leads.

Frederick PD officers fanned out over Wyndham Hill, setting up checkpoints and handing out missing persons flyers to motorists. TV news crews set up camp outside 2825 Saratoga Trail, talking to anyone who knew the Watts family. Nick and Amanda Thayer and Nickole Atkinson all did interviews.

Close friends and family were also fielding calls from the *Today* show and *Good Morning America,* with both planning segments now that the case had been upgraded to an Missing/Endangered Alert.

"*Good Morning America* has contacted my sister," an excited Chris Watts texted Addy Molony. "News crews are doing live updates on the corner of the street."

"I can't imagine what you're going through," Molony replied. "Stay strong. You will get through this!!"

"I will stay as strong as I can."

"Are you a believer in prayer?"
"Always."

Just before 4:00 P.M., Nick and Amanda Thayer left to collect their daughter from school. They had invited Watts to spend the night at their house, so he wouldn't have to be alone. He agreed and said he would soon be over.

When he failed to arrive, Nick Thayer called him. Watts explained that Fox News reporters were in his front yard, and he didn't want to be seen leaving with a bag of clothes, as it would look suspicious.

32

"THE TALE OF TWO CHRISES"

All four local networks led off the six-o'clock news with dramatic Chris Watts interviews.

"We begin tonight with breaking news," intoned KMGH-TV, Denver 7, anchor Tom Mustin. "The disappearance of a pregnant Frederick woman and her two children has captured the nation's attention."

Then several segments of Watts's interview were played, including his admission of "an emotional conversation" with Shanann right before she went missing.

Fox 31 also carried a tearful interview with Nickole Atkinson about her friend's disappearance.

"Shanann, if you're hearing this or you're out there," sobbed Nickole, holding her daughter, Madison, "please let somebody know you're okay."

Then Chris Watts came on the screen, nervously rocking back and forth on his porch.

"I have no inclination of where she is," he said listlessly, without a hint of emotion. "She said she was going to a friend's house with the kids, and that's the last thing I heard."

Special Agents Tammy Lee and Grahm Coder watched the Chris Watts interviews with Detective Dave Baumhover at Frederick Police Station. If they had been suspicious before, they were now certain he was lying.

"It didn't look good," recalled CBI agent Lee. "We all watched it together and went, 'This might be bad.'"

Detective Baumhover asked FBI special agent Coder to conduct a formal interview with Watts. Agent Lee would also offer Watts a polygraph test.

At 6:46 P.M., Baumhover called Watts and asked him to come to police headquarters as soon as possible. Watts agreed to do so. Immediately after putting down the phone, he called his father, asking him to fly out to Denver.

"Christopher called us," said Cindy Watts. "He said, 'Tell Dad I need him to come down.' I said, 'What about me?' He said, 'No, Mom, just send Dad.'"

Nikki Kessinger, who had diligently deleted anything on her cell phone or computers that could link her to Chris Watts, now asked him to do the same. Late Tuesday afternoon, she began researching how long phone companies keep text messages and if the police could trace them.

Shortly before 7:00 P.M., Chris Watts walked into the police headquarters on Fifth Street in downtown Frederick. He had been tailed by police officers from his house.

Detective Baumhover greeted him and introduced him to Agent Coder.

"Hey, good to meet you," said Coder casually. "Thanks for coming in. Grahm Coder. I'm from the FBI."

"Okay," Watts replied.

"Really appreciate it," said Coder, "I think you're gonna . . . be able to help us."

Coder brought him into Squad Interview Room 2 and told him their interview would be recorded. CBI special agent Tammy Lee sat at the nearby command post, watching on a live video feed.

"So I work missing-children cases," began Coder, "and I'm very sorry for what you're going through. Right? I'm a father, too."

He handed Watts a written statement sheet, asking him to write down all the events leading to Shanann and the girls' disappearance.

"Okay," Coder told him. "Thank you for your willingness to help. Start from the beginning, please include everything you can remember and tell us what happened."

"Feel like I'm in high school again," said Watts, smirking.

Coder then left Watts alone to write out the statement, telling him to call Detective Baumhover's cell phone when he had finished.

Chris Watts's handwritten statement read as follows:

1:48 AM	Door Bell detected visitor, neighbor's camera that faces driveway didn't pick up anyone walking up to the house
2:00 AM	Shanann gets into bed with me
4:00 AM	My alarm goes off for work and I proceed to get ready for work
4:15 AM	I slide into bed and begin having a conversation with Shanann. The conversation involves putting the house up for sale. Shanann had contacted our realtor a week prior via email about this as well. The conversation also involved moving along with the separation. This was an emotional topic due to the fact that we have 2 beautiful daughters and another baby on the way. We spoke about the fact that we didn't feel that connection that we used to. We spoke about the notion that

the love that we had at the beginning was no longer there. We spoke about just staying together for the kids, but realizing that normally doesn't work. It was a very emotional conversation with crying on both parts. When I got off the bed to go downstairs she told me she was going to a friends [sic] house and taking the kids there, but also that she would be back.

5:00 AM	Downstairs and I made a protein shake, packed my lunch box, filled my water jug.
5:15 AM	Backed my truck in to load up my book bag, lunch box, water jug, container with O-ring kit and loaded up various open ended wrenches from my personal toolbox.
5:30 AM	Departed for work
7:40 AM	Texted Shanann and asked if she could tell me where she was taking the kids
12:00 PM	Texted Shanann to call me
12:10 PM	Doorbell visitor [Nickole Atkinson] was at my door
12:20 PM	Called Nicole [sic] to see what was going on and she told me she couldn't get ahold of Shanann either and that her shoes were next to the door and her car was in the garage.
12:40 PM	A few more efforts by Nicole [sic] to reach her
1:00 PM	I'm on my way home to check on my family
2:00 PM	I arrive home, open the garage door and get inside the house. Shanann, Bella and Celeste are not in the house. Shanann's wedding ring is on her nightstand, her phone is on the couch, her purse is still here, the medicine for the kids is still here, the car with the car seats are still here. There is no sign of them anywhere.

3:00 PM	Frederick Police Officer and Detectives are asking Nicole [*sic*] and I questions about where she could've gone or who she could be with.
4:00 PM	Police check neighbors security footage and question them as well.
5:00 PM	Officer, Detective and Sergeant come by to search the house and ask some more questions.
6:00 PM	Begin calling around to anyone that I know that could know something or maybe seen Shanann. Calling local hospitals and hotels as well.
7:30 PM	Friends Nick and Amanda come by to show support.
8:00 PM	Lauren Arnold comes by to show support.
9:00 PM	Friends Dave Colon and Jeremy Lindstrom come by to show support.
10:00 PM	I lay in bed and proceed to take calls from Friends and Family for the rest of the night.

After Watts had finished, Agent Coder came back and started talking him through each part of his statement in detail.

"I'm going to sit next to you," said Coder genially. "So we can look at it together."

For the next three hours, the trained FBI interrogator methodically sifted through Watts's account, questioning Watts on everything. Although he was a suspect, Watts seemed nonchalant, acting as if he were under no pressure whatsoever. He never once asked how the investigation was progressing.

About an hour into the interview, Agent Coder remarked that Nickole Atkinson seemed far more worried about his missing family than he did.

"So when I work investigations like this," Coder told Watts, "I have to keep an open mind on everything."

"Okay," said Watts.

"And part of keeping an open mind is listening to you talk about your wife and your marriage. And the day she goes missing is the day that you guys have marital discord. So you can understand what I'm thinking about you."

"Yeah."

"What do you think about that?" Coder looked him straight in the eye.

"It makes me sick to my stomach, honestly. I've talked to a few of my friends [who are] like, 'You know this stuff's not going to look good on you.' I know you have to look at every, every vantage point. This is something I would never do to my kids or my wife."

Agent Coder just sat there without saying a word, as the clock above ticked away.

Watts finally broke the silence. "I'm not sure what I could do to make people believe that. Just because they knew we were having marital discord, they would automatically look at me. But there's no way I would harm anybody in my family. . . . I promise you I had nothing to do with any of this."

"Are you telling me the truth?"

"Absolutely. The absolute truth."

"Why should I believe you?"

"Because I'm a very trustworthy person." Watts nervously gesticulated with his hands. "I'm a person who's never going to be abusive or physical in any kind of relationship. I would never harm my kids. I would never harm my wife."

"We're talking about things that might offend you. You know that we have to get to the bottom of this. You know that?"

"Yeah."

"Would you take a polygraph?"

"Sure."

"Okay, would you take it tonight?"

"If that's what you want me to do. I've never done one."

"Do you know what the purpose of one is?"

"It's for a lie detector test."

Agent Coder suggested they take a break, as he had a lot more questions for Chris. Coder assured him that he was not being arrested and was free to walk out of the interview at any time.

"Having said that," said Coder, "if you want to talk, I have a lot more questions for you."

"Okay," said a visibly nervous Watts.

"Do you know where your wife is?"

"I do not know where my wife is," Watts replied emphatically.

"Are you telling me the truth?"

"I am telling you the absolute truth."

Then at 9:17 P.M., two hours into the interview, Special Agent Coder left Chris Watts alone to stew, saying he wanted to look over his notes. The video feed remained on and captured Watts staring blankly at the wall.

Twenty minutes later, the seasoned FBI agent returned to the interview room, placing a photograph of Shanann, Bella, and Celeste on the table in front of Watts.

"How are you feeling?"

"Looking at that picture," answered Watts wistfully, as he picked it up, "Celeste wore those shoes even though they were winter shoes."

He said Shanann had wanted to sell them on Facebook when they returned from North Carolina, but Celeste wouldn't let her.

"And Bella," he continued, "always wore some flip-flops, she always will. She loves that dress."

Coder asked him about his daughters. Watts spoke without emotion as the FBI agent watched him intensely.

"Celeste, she's rampage," replied Watts in a flat voice. "She's either go or asleep. She's a tiger. And Bella . . . she's just the sweetest little girl, she's the one that favors me more than Celeste, who's the one that favors Shanann more."

"When you say 'favored' you, you mean look like?"

"Yes."

"Oh, okay. Are they little daddy's girls?"

"That one is." Watts pointed to Celeste in the photograph. "Because the first one I wasn't really good at it yet. Second one I knew what I was doing and she bonded with me. Right from the start.

"I remember [Celeste] just wore that dress not too long ago, and I unbuttoned the back of it so I could get her pajamas on. And Bella loved those spaghetti-strap dresses. She is a girlie girl. Always."

Coder asked what Watts was thinking about while he was left alone in the interview room.

"How much I want to see these two girls and my wife again. I just want them to come home."

Agent Coder then informed him that he had some uncomfortable questions to ask about Chris's marriage and infidelity.

"Okay."

"Tell me about it?"

"I have never cheated on my wife," replied Watts resolutely.

"Yeah."

"I've always been a trustworthy person. I fully expect if we ever thought about straying another way, that we would tell each other before it happened."

"I think that sounds ridiculous, because in the history of the earth, nobody ever does that."

"Okay, I . . . I . . . ," stammered Watts, "that's what I would like to think. . . ."

"Okay."

"I mean . . . I'ma—I-I know mistakes happen . . . but that's what I would think in my head . . . I would hope would happen."

Agent Coder again told him that sounded "ridiculous," but if Coder were in Watts's shoes, he'd probably say the exact same thing.

"You can imagine in my job I meet all kinds of people," Coder said. "There are people who have Saturdays with their girlfriends and Sundays with their wives."

Coder said that he didn't care if anyone else was in the relationship, and that, if there was, it would stay between them. He then asked if Shanann could be having an affair, and Watts said that he didn't think so.

"Okay," said Coder. "Now let's talk about you. On your end. I gotta ask . . . what's her name?"

"I—I don't have another one," Watts replied nervously.

"You sure?"

"I'm sure."

"Okay. Would you tell me if you did?"

"Yes." Watts fidgeted with his hands.

Agent Coder then observed what good physical shape Watts was in, saying that often happened when people start cheating. "So tell me about it."

"Uuuuh . . . I did not cheat on my wife."

"Okay."

"Thrive helped me. I went from two hundred forty-five pounds to about—"

"You were two forty-five?" asked Coder incredulously.

"I was two hundred and forty-five pounds."

"Jesus . . . [good] for you, man."

"Thank you. And I'm one eighty-five . . . one eighty

now. And I've been eating cleaner. Thrive has helped me a lot."

"Okay, and I've got to imagine that maybe there was a girl [that] inspired that?"

"No."

Coder then asked why Watts had fallen out of love with Shanann.

"I was like walking on eggshells. You feel you're always doing something that's wrong."

"The timing doesn't make sense to me."

"Okay, but you can't be yourself around your wife, who can you be yourself around?"

"I've got to tell you, that sounds like a load of horseshit. What about the girls?"

"Bella and Celeste are the light of my life. I'd do anything for those girls. I'd step in front of a bullet for those girls."

As they entered the third hour of the interview, Agent Coder asked how he could help Chris walk out of the interview room without looking guilty.

"You have to trust me," Watts replied. "Just seeing these pictures . . . I need them . . . I want them to just run through that front door and just . . . knock me to the floor. Bust my head open . . . I don't care. The amount of love I have for my family is exponential, and it's never going to die . . . and I need . . . I want them back."

Special Agent Coder looked unimpressed.

"So let's have that hard conversation again," he said, pushing the photo of Shanann and the girls back in front of Watts. "So can we talk about two Chrises?"

"Two Chrises?" Watts looked increasingly uncomfortable.

"The tale of two Chrises, okay. And you need to help me know which Chris I am looking at today, and which

Chris you really are. So Chris number one is right here. Right? And fell out of love with his wife. So he started wondering what it might be if he didn't have a wife . . . and the girls to take care of."

Coder hypothesized that one Chris enjoyed being alone when his family was in North Carolina and wanted out of the marriage.

"He's looking at a bachelor pad," said Coder, "and did something terrible to his wife and kids."

"That's not the Chris you're looking at right now," answered Watts defensively. "No. The Chris you're looking at is the man who loves these kids and loves his wife and would never, ever do anything to harm them."

Coder then asked why someone else had to call 911 instead of him, and why he had called the Primrose School to say Bella and Celeste were not coming back. "We're back to this tale of two Chrises, Chris."

"I care . . . I promise."

"Nothing you've told me tonight makes sense. Nothing you've told me tonight feels like the truth. I think that there's something that happened that got maybe a little bit out of control."

Coder then asked what should happen when who was responsible for his pregnant wife's and daughters' disappearance was found.

"Life in prison would be the best," said Watts. "That's what I think. There are two kids involved."

"What if he hurt them?"

"The death penalty."

At 10:30 P.M. Agent Coder suggested they break for the night, telling Watts not to go home, as it was being searched again.

"I want to talk to you again tomorrow," said Coder. "I

want you to get a good night's sleep and a good breakfast and a good workout . . . whatever your morning routine is."

"My dad flies in at about eight or nine . . . from North Carolina."

Coder told him to pick up his father at the airport and then come back to the Frederick Police Station at around 11:00 A.M.

"I would love you and me as a team to talk tomorrow," Coder told him. "To do a polygraph and move past me wondering which Chris I'm talking to. I just want to get it behind us, and our talks are going to be a lot more comfortable than they were tonight."

Then Coder took Watts's cell phone away to extract its data, telling him that he had done "a really good job tonight."

Agent Coder said, "Let's get everything out of the way, and then we're going to send you on your way and we're back to the old Chris. The good Chris."

Just after 11:00 P.M., Chris Watts walked out of the Frederick Police Station, adding Grahm Coder to his list of contacts. Nick and Amanda Thayer, who had arrived four hours earlier, were still waiting outside, and he followed them back to their house to spend the night.

33

THE POLYGRAPH

At 6:00 A.M. Wednesday, Lead Detective Dave Baumhover and Officer Steve Walje met CBI special agent Matthew Sailor and Crime Scene Analyst Dave Yocum outside 2825 Saratoga Trail for a forensic search of the house. A Frederick police officer had spent the night outside on guard.

After calling Chris Watts for the security code for the front door, they all went inside. Officer Yocum first photographed every room in the house. Then a Bluestar luminol was sprayed in the bedrooms, bathrooms, stairs, and entryway into the garage to test for blood. None was found. In his report Agent Sailor would observe how "neat and orderly" the house was, to the point of obsessiveness.

"The items in the kitchen cupboard were organized and labelled," he wrote. "I noted that the clothing in the closets [was] arranged by clothing type and color."

He also noted how both girls' beds were now made, although they had not been during previous searches. The master bedroom's pillowcases and the top sheet were in a trash can in the kitchen, but the matching fitted sheet was missing.

"The bedsheet and one pillowcase had an unknown dark substance that appeared to be smeared on them," reported Agent Sailor.

The officers also seized computers, iPads, Apple

watches, and an Amazon Echo, logging them into evidence. The *Hold Me Tight* book Shanann had sent her husband, to try to help repair their marriage, was found dumped in the recycle bin, still in its unopened Amazon packaging.

That morning, Shanann and the girls' mysterious disappearance made front-page news all over the country, with millions seeing Chris Watts's interview on NBC's *Today* show.

Denver's ABC-11 featured an exclusive interview with Shanann's old high school friend Lauren Arnold.

"Shanann has a schedule . . . and she does not deviate," said Arnold. "A dead cell phone is not an option for her. She always has her communication with her."

At 8:00 A.M. CBI agent Tammy Lee received a phone call from Anadarko security, saying Chris Watts's work emails showed he was having a romantic relationship with another employee, identified as thirty-year-old Nichol "Nikki" Kessinger. They worked out of the same Anadarko office in Platteville, and the relationship had started in June 2018.

Later that morning the security department forwarded the emails to Agent Lee, who ordered a full workup on Kessinger.

At around the same time, Nikki Kessinger called the Weld County Sheriff's Office, saying that she had important information on the Shanann Watts case. When Detective Dave Baumhover called back a few minutes later, she admitted to being in a relationship with Chris Watts and offered her full cooperation.

Just after nine o'clock, Special Agent Coder texted Chris Watts: "Swing on by the PD when you get a chance. We'll make a game plan for today."

A couple of minutes later Watts called back, saying he had just collected his father from the airport and was heading straight to the police station for the polygraph. On their way there, Chris and his father barely discussed that Shanann and the girls were missing.

"He just wanted to talk about sports," Chris later recalled. "He's always kind of distanced himself from a problem-type thing. He maybe asked just a few questions like, 'Do you know where they're at?' I just told him no."

At 11:00 A.M., Chris and Ronnie Watts walked into the Frederick Police Station and were met by Special Agent Coder in the lobby. Chris looked relaxed, wearing a North Carolina Tar Heels T-shirt, black athletic shorts, and flip-flops.

Ronnie Watts remained in the hallway while his son was taken into the same interview room as the night before. There waiting was CBI agent Tammy Lee, who would perform the polygraph test. The attractive blond agent was dressed casually in a white-and-black hooped top over a lilac blouse and slacks.

"Hey, Chris, how are you?" asked Coder as they walked in. "[Ready to] knock out a polygraph?"

"Yeah," Watts replied, as if he didn't have a care in the world.

"This is Tammy," said Coder, introducing them. "Did you meet Tammy yesterday?"

"No, you're the only one."

"Hi, Chris, how are you?" asked Agent Lee as they shook hands.

Then Coder said he would talk to Chris's father, telling him when he could go back to the house to wait, as the polygraph might take some time.

"I'm not sure if I'm going to be here for an hour or, like, four hours," said Watts.

"Between him and me," said Coder, "we'll figure out how to get him where he needs to go."

Chris Watts's biggest concern was that the interview room had no cell phone signal. He explained he'd been receiving a lot of interview requests from the *Today* show, *Morning Joe,* and *Good Morning America.*

Agent Coder told him not to worry and that he could do the interviews after his polygraph test was over. "While you're doing this, it's going to be completely okay to ignore your phone and the media and everyone. Right?"

"Right," answered Watts.

"So let's get this outta the way. Why don't we put a halt on the phone. On texting people. On *Good Morning America.* All those thoughts. Let's focus on this. Let's knock this out and then let's talk."

Coder left the interview room and shut the door, which automatically locked from the inside. Agent Lee had Watts sit down opposite her at the table, which had a laptop computer and polygraph equipment.

"So, how are you feeling today?" she asked.

"Sick to my stomach, honestly. The first day I thought, 'Okay, she's just somewhere,' but after all the activity at my house . . . it went to the other extreme. That either somebody has her or she's in trouble. And the kids are not safe."

Agent Lee started by telling him that it was "totally awesome" he had agreed to a polygraph. She explained how she had worked on the 2012 Jessica Ridgeway murder case, the ten-year-old Westminster, Colorado, girl who had been found strangled and dismembered. Lee had given seventeen-year-old Austin Sigg his polygraph test, resulting in his confessing to kidnapping and murder, for which he was now serving a life sentence.

"So they asked me if I would be willing to come here and chat with you," she said pointedly, "and hopefully get you cleared up and on your way . . .'cause then we don't have to keep focusing on Chris."

She said that polygraphs could be "nerve-racking," even if somebody didn't have anything to hide. But there were only two ways to fail.

"The first way would be if you fail to follow my instructions. The second way would be if you chose to lie to me today. As long as you tell me what the truth is today, you will have no problem with passing. Okay?"

"Okay."

"I hope that you know if you did have something to do with their disappearance, it would be really stupid for you to come in and take a polygraph today."

"Exactly."

She then read him his Miranda rights, reminding him that he did not have to talk to her. Watts said he understood and signed an Advisement of Rights and a polygraph permission form.

Agent Lee began by asking about his childhood, his relationship with his parents, and how he met Shanann. He was unusually talkative, spending more than fifteen minutes outlining their relationship, marriage, and the births of Bella and Celeste.

She then asked him to describe what had happened after Shanann and the girls had left at the end of June to spend six weeks in North Carolina.

"I was here just going to work and workin' out and going running and just keeping the house up."

He then described the week he spent with Shanann and the girls in North Carolina as idyllic, making no mention of Nutgate or any problems with Shanann.

"It was an awesome trip. Just seeing them react to the ocean . . . and Bella and Celeste just loved that."

Once again he ran through the events of early Monday morning and telling Shanann he wanted a separation.

"It was an emotional conversation. Obviously we were both crying, and after we talked, she said she was gonna take the kids to a friend's house, and that she'd be back later."

Watts nervously described what had happened since Shanann and the girls had gone missing. Once again, his account lacked any emotion and seemed rehearsed and self-pitying.

"I didn't want to be alone and my friends are supporting me. I just want to find them. Wherever they are, I hope they are safe. 'Cause just being in that house and not being able to tuck them in is just heart-wrenching. It's earth-shattering because those are my kids. It's a nightmare right now."

Then Lee, who knew all about Nikki Kessinger, asked if Shanann had accused him of having a girlfriend after he had asked for a separation.

"I think it would be a normal wife's reaction," Lee said. "Who is it?"

"That kinda came up. I was like, 'No, I'm not having an affair. That is the last thing that should be on your mind.'"

"Solid guy?"

"Yeah. I'm not the type of guy that's just going to say, 'All right, my wife's gone . . . who's the girl I can find for five weeks?' No, that's not me. I respect my wife and she respects me."

While Chris Watts was preparing for his polygraph, his father, Ronnie, was being interviewed next door by FBI special agent Marc Lehrer. Unlike his son, Ronnie told the agent how Shanann had had a "blowout" with his wife over Nutgate, the last time he'd seen her.

He described his daughter-in-law as "controlling, narcissistic, and possibly bipolar," saying she caused most of the issues with his son.

"Watts does not know where Shanann or her children may have gone," noted Agent Lehrer in his report. "Watts was very cooperative and amenable to future contact."

At 1:50 P.M., as they approached the fourth hour of the interview, Agent Tammy Lee began preparing Watts for the polygraph test.

"Obviously," she told him, "you've had a lot of time to think about this stuff and just talking to me. What are your thoughts . . . what are you thinking right now as far as what's happened?"

"The first day I thought she was with somebody. She's at a friend's house and she's just decompressing. Now I feel she's not safe . . . either she's in trouble or somebody has hurt her and the kids and we can't find them."

"So if I ask you on the polygraph test if you physically caused Shanann's disappearance, can you pass that question?"

"Yes," he replied resolutely.

"What do you think I mean . . . when I'm asking you if you physically caused Shanann's disappearance?"

"I feel you're asking me, did I have anything to do with it myself, or did I help somebody do it? And I had no part in any of that."

Then she asked how you could make somebody disappear, and Watts suggested hiring a hit man.

"That's what I want," she told him. "I want you to go through all of these scenarios in your head, because I want you to know for sure what I'm talking about when asking you if you physically caused her disappearance. So what different physical ways could you cause someone's disappearance through murder? You could stab someone, right?"

"Mmmm. Stab someone, shoot someone, hit 'em with a blunt object . . . use a weapon like a gun or a knife."

"You could smother someone."

"You *could* smother someone," Watts nervously agreed.

"You could strangle someone," said Agent Lee, fixing him in the eyes.

"I mean, yeah, you can. It's hard to even think about that kinda stuff right now."

Agent Lee asked if he would have any issues when she questioned whether he had caused his wife and daughters' disappearance.

"I can definitely pass."

"When I ask you if you physically caused Shanann's disappearance . . . your answer should be what?"

"No."

Agent Lee then told him the three questions he had to answer in the polygraph:

> Did you cause Shanann's disappearance?
> When was the last time you saw her?
> Do you know where she is now?

"I'm going to ask you about Shanann," said Lee. "I think we can all assume that wherever Shanann is, the little girls are."

"Yeah."

"So we just went through every single question on the test. How would you answer them on the test, okay?"

"Okay."

"We kinda have to expect the worst and hope for the best. If we do end up finding your wife and your two girls murdered, what do you think should happen to that person who would have done that?"

"The worst possible thing. Either life in prison or the

death penalty, isn't it? That's the only two things you can really do."

Then Agent Lee took a bathroom break, to give him time alone to contemplate before the polygraph began.

Around 2:00 P.M., CBI agents Matt Sailor and Greg Zentner met Chris Watts's boss, Luke Epple, at the Love's Travel Stop in Hudson, Colorado. They followed him down several dirt roads surrounded by sagebrush and cacti to the Cervi Ranch and the remote 319 well site.

The Anadarko supervisor explained the layout of the site. It had a well head, a separator, and three storage tanks mounted on a gravel pad. He told them that after the oil, gas, and water were separated, the gas is pumped to another location, while the mixture of oil and water is stored in the two giant holding tanks, each with a capacity of four hundred barrels. After separating inside the barrels, the water is fed into a third, smaller holding tank, leaving just the oil in the two big ones.

A drone was launched to take aerial photographs of the whole area, before a systematic search of the south side of the well site, as officers watched on a video feed. They soon zeroed in on what appeared to be a sheet lying on the ground, tucked in the brush to the south of the pad. CBI agent Matthew Sailor and another officer went to take a closer look, spotting a rectangular patch of ground that looked as if it had recently been dug up.

They walked over to the fitted sheet, which had the same distinctive pattern as the flat one found in Chris Watts's kitchen garbage a few hours earlier. It was covered in dirt stains as if it had been dragged along the ground. Also, two black garbage bags with red drawstrings were lying in the brush nearby.

Agent Sailor then had photos of the sheet found in the

Wattses' garbage emailed to him. The two sheets were a perfect match.

At 2:23 P.M., Agent Tammy Lee started hooking Chris Watts up to the polygraph machine. First she had him sit on a motion-sensor mat, instructing him to keep completely still during the test. Next, she attached pneumograph tubes to his belly and underneath his armpits, to measure his respiratory rate, wrapping a blood-pressure cuff around his right calf to measure the rate of blood flow through his body. Finally, she attached electrodermal activity (EDA) plates to two of his fingers to measure his body's electrical activity.

The polygraph began with a directed-lie practice test, where she wanted him to deliberately lie. She held up a large piece of paper with the numbers one, two, four, and five on it and asked him to write in the number three.

She told him she was going to ask if he had written down all the numbers. But he should lie when she asked if he had only written down the number three. "'Cause you really did write the number three, but I want you to say no, that you did not. I want you to lie to me, okay?"

She made him practice several times, lying about writing the number three but not about the others. Then she repeated it under test conditions.

"You do have to remain completely still. There is no coughing, belching, sneezing, sniffling, anything like that, during the test."

"Just breathing," Watts quipped nervously.

She then inflated the blood-pressure cuff around his calf and started the directed-lie test, which he passed with flying colors.

"That was awesome," Agent Lee told him. "So you obviously are a really bad liar."

She explained that when he had lied about writing the number three, the reaction on her laptop had been off the charts.

"I don't know if you heard me clicking," she told him, "but I had to turn down the sensitivity, because you were starting to go off the page. So that is what I need to see as a polygrapher, because that tells me that you know it's wrong to tell a lie."

"Okay, I didn't . . . ," he mumbled defensively, looking increasingly uncomfortable.

"No, that's a good thing. We don't wanna be good liars. So thank you for being a horrible liar."

She said it showed that when she asked him "significant" questions about his wife and daughters, it was "going to be even ten times more amplified" if he was not telling the truth.

"And the coolest thing about this right now," she told him, "there's only one person in this room that knows what the truth is. And in about five minutes, there's gonna be two of us."

At 2:52 P.M. she began the polygraph test, saying she was going to ask him the same questions three times.

"Stay still. Stay still. The test is about to begin. Do you understand I will only ask you the questions we have discussed?"

"Yes. Let's do it."

"Regarding Shanann's disappearance, do you intend to answer all the questions truthfully?"

"Yes."

"Did you physically cause Shanann's disappearance?"

"No."

"Are you lying about the last time you saw Shanann?"

"No."

"Do you know where Shanann is now?"

"No."

Agent Lee told him that this part of the test had been completed, and she was taking the polygraph instruments out of operation.

"You can relax. How do you feel?"

"Horrible. Nervous."

She repeated the same questions twice more, before detaching the instruments from Watts's body. Then, to grade his results, she left him alone in the interview room.

Half an hour later, Agent Lee returned briefly to collect her equipment, saying she would soon be back with Grahm Coder for a chat. She asked if Watts needed any crackers, water, or Mountain Dew.

"No, I'm fine right now," he replied nervously.

Watts then asked if he could turn on his cell phone, and Lee said that was fine.

"[Shanann's] mom has tried calling me probably at least five or six times," he explained.

"I think she's called the detective quite a few times, too."

Suddenly he held up his phone to show Lee his favorite picture of Bella and Celeste.

"Oh my God, they're adorable," said Lee, who is a mother of three. "They're way bigger than I thought. I think I saw a picture of them on the news when they were much tinier."

"That was *this* year," he said proudly.

While Chris Watts was being polygraphed, Sergeant Ian Albert held a press conference outside on Fifth Street.

"After visiting the home," he said, "our agency began the investigation of the following missing persons:

Shanann Watts, aged thirty-four; Bella Marie, aged four; Celeste, who also goes by CeCe, aged three; Shanann's two daughters."

Sergeant Albert told reporters that the help of the FBI and CBI had been enlisted, as the Frederick PD was not equipped to handle a case of this magnitude. "There's a lot at stake here. And we are exploring all avenues in order to not rule anything out."

He also appealed to the public to help find Shanann and her daughters, saying officers would be handing out more flyers and setting up additional checkpoints in the area.

"The hearts of our men and women of this agency go out to the family and friends of Shanann, Bella Marie, and Celeste. We are working around the clock on this case and will not rest until we have the answers that we are looking for."

34

"A LIFELINE"

At 4:00 P.M. Agent Tammy Lee returned to the interview room with Special Agent Coder. She had now graded Watts's polygraph test, and he had failed it by a mile.

"For someone who was a truth-teller," said Agent Lee, "we would consider them to be a grade two or higher. And we would consider someone to be deceptive if they were a negative four or below. Chris Watts scored a negative eighteen."

They walked in to find him watching his iPhone videos of Bella and Celeste playing and giggling together.

"So I brought Grahm in here," said Lee, "because we want to talk to you about your results, okay?"

"Okay," replied Watts. Coder pushed a large photograph of Bella and Celeste across the table in front of Watts. The two agents then sat down on the other side of the table, facing Watts, who had his arms tightly folded.

"So, it was completely clear that you were not honest during the testing," Agent Lee began, "and I think you already knew that. You did not pass the polygraph test."

"Okay," he replied matter-of-factly.

"So now we need to talk to you about what actually happened," she continued, "and I feel like you're probably ready to do that."

"I didn't lie to you on that polygraph," stammered Watts. "I promise."

"Chris, stop," said Agent Coder, looking him in the eye. "It's time."

"I—I'm not . . . ," mumbled Watts.

"Just stop for a minute," Coder told him. "I want you to take a deep breath right now."

Agent Lee said Watts was feeling sick to his stomach because he was not telling them the truth, and that he'd feel better when he did.

"We're not here to play games," she said. "We just want to know what happened. So you can start from the beginning and tell us."

Desperately, Watts swore that he was telling the truth and had not lied.

"It's not even an option right now," Agent Lee replied. "You did not pass the polygraph."

"I know," he feebly acquiesced.

"So I know you were being deceptive," Lee continued. "The issue right now is, what happened to Shanann, Bella, and Celeste? I know you want to tell us. I can see it in your face. This is where the rubber meets the road, Chris."

"I'm not trying to cover things up," he protested. "And I don't know they're not coming back home."

Agent Coder took over the interview, telling Watts that they now knew far more than he thought they did.

"Here's where I'm confused," Coder told him. "You're this great guy, and I'm not just telling you that. Everyone tells us that, okay? We can't find anyone to say anything bad about you. 'Chris is a great guy. He's a good father. He's a good man.' We're confused as to why you're not taking care of your beautiful children."

"I don't know where they're at. If I could have my babies

back home right now, I would. I want everybody back and it's the God-honest truth."

The two agents didn't reply, just staring at the fidgeting Watts for the next couple of minutes as the overhead clock ticked.

Agent Coder finally broke the silence. "We just can't figure out why there are [the] two Chrises we talked about last night."

"Yes," he responded weakly.

Coder observed that one Chris was the perfect father, who could pack a bag for his children and know exactly what to put in there, including diapers for accidents. That Chris read to his daughters at night, before tucking them into bed with a nighttime snack.

"It warms my heart that you're [that] type of dad," Coder told him. "I know you love them and you're not faking that, are you? It's real. There's a lot of guys that come in here and try to tell me that and I know they're lying. But you're in here today lying about something else. So we need to talk about that, okay."

"I cheated on her," Watts suddenly burst out.

"I know," said Coder. "And this is very good . . . keep going."

"I'm not proud of it." Watts shook his head. "I didn't think anything like that could happen. . . . I didn't think I'd ever do it, but I did."

He said when Shanann had accused him of cheating, he'd admitted it. "I feel horrible for it. She was pregnant and it was . . . I didn't hurt her. I cheated on her. I hurt her emotionally . . . but that's what I've been holding [back]."

Then he admitted having dinner with "her" last Saturday night, and being with "her" most of the time Shanann and the girls were in North Carolina.

"Keep going," said Agent Coder. "You're doin' a good

job. This is the Chris that I knew would come out today. This is the Chris who tells the truth 'cause you're a truth-teller."

"I fell out of love just 'cause I fell in love with *her*. I mean, that's the God's-honest truth."

"Who is *her*?" asked Coder.

"I don't want to get her involved in this," Watts pleaded. "I don't want to ruin her life [with] something like this."

Coder then told him that they knew all about his relationship with Nikki Kessinger.

"She's a wonderful person," said Watts. "I saw her [and she] took my breath away. I never felt that way about anybody in my lifetime."

"Chris, that's not your fault, man," Agent Coder reassured him. "That's something that happens."

Coder then changed tack, trying another approach to get at the truth. This time he would flatter Watts by using Shanann as a foil.

"This should have been the happiest time in your marriage, where you guys were thriving and productive. And I believe that Shanann's the reason none of that happened. I believe that she's a controlling person. Maybe doesn't listen to you as much as she should. I think that she can do whatever she wants and you can't, okay?"

Coder reasoned that Shanann had already started to leave the marriage, so it was "ironic" they were talking about Chris seeing another woman.

"The other thing I think is interesting," Coder continued, "is even though she's that type of person that's controlling, doesn't listen, does what she wants, is walking away from her kids, here you are defending her. Because to your core you want to take care of the people you love."

"I'll do whatever I can to help," said Watts, picking up on this new bait. "But I don't know where they're at."

"Chris, right now your dad's outside. He flew across the country to help you."

"I know."

"You're lying to him."

"I'm not lying to him."

"You've lied to everyone you've talked to, and they all bought it. Will you please help us find your babies?"

Both agents continued to pepper Watts with questions about what had really happened when Shanann came home early Monday morning. He refused to give an inch.

"Can you understand that this just doesn't make sense?" said Coder. "How is it possible that a woman and two kids are just completely gone off the face of the earth?"

"I promise you," Watts replied desperately. "I did nothing to those kids or her to make them vanish."

Then Tammy Lee took over, trying another ruse to get at the truth. "Was it an accident?"

"There was no accident. If there was an accident in the house, I wasn't there for it."

She observed how he had claimed to have cried during his emotional conversation with Shanann, yet hadn't shed a tear in almost two days of interviews.

"Not once," said Lee. "And help me understand that, because I don't get it. These are *your* baby girls."

"I know," Watts replied weakly.

"I lose my four-year-old in the store for ten seconds and I start to panic. I have not seen that from you at all. It's weird [and] it doesn't make sense to me."

"Okay, I love those girls to death . . . just because I haven't shed a tear . . ."

"Then show us that. Show us *this* Chris."

"I am that . . ."

"Not this Chris."

"I'm not showing you *that* Chris. I'm showing you *the* Chris that cares about his girls and his wife. Just because I haven't shed a tear shouldn't make you feel . . . that the love isn't there for them."

"Chris"—Agent Lee stared him straight in the eye—"did Shanann do something to them?"

"I don't know."

"I'm serious."

"I have no clue."

"Did Shanann do something to them, and then did you feel like you had to do something to Shanann?"

"No, they were in the house when I left."

Agent Lee noted that they could only have left the house in his truck.

"Did Shanann do something?" asked Agent Coder.

"I don't think she did anything to those kids. We both loved them with all our hearts. There's no way."

Then Agent Lee pondered whether something had happened to Bella and Celeste, leaving him to deal with it.

"You had to clean it up for Shanann," Coder chimed in, picking up on Lee's new line of questioning.

"Chris, you gotta tell us." Lee pointed to their photograph. "There's something that happened to these baby girls. Look at them!"

"I know. Before you came in, I was watching videos."

Agent Lee told him that no one doubted that he loved his girls, but everyone makes mistakes. "It's what we do with those mistakes that makes us who we are."

At this point Chris Watts conceived the diabolical idea to accuse Shanann of murdering Bella and Celeste. The wheels began turning in his head as he saw a way out of his predicament.

"Chris, it seems like you're thinking of it right now," said Coder. "What are you thinking about?"

"She couldn't have," Watts replied in disbelief.

"I feel like you cleaned up for her," Lee told him. "I feel that's the type of guy that you are."

"Chris, this is a weight that's gonna be on you for the rest of your life," said Agent Coder. "This is going to follow you forever. I promise you when you start talking to us, you will feel better. I know you already feel better getting the Nikki thing off your chest."

"Please don't involve her in the news or anything like that," pleaded Watts. "She can't do that."

"Chris, we're giving you a lifeline right now," said Tammy Lee. "You need to take it. You need to reach out and take it."

Agent Lee said she believed Shanann had done something to the girls, and he had fixed it to protect her.

"I did not do anything," Watts replied, grasping the lifeline. "I did not do anything to those kids."

"What did Shanann do to them, Chris?" asked Lee. "Chicks are crazy."

"Can I just talk to my dad?" he begged. "He flew across the country."

Watts asked if he could go home with his father for a few hours and then come back to continue the interview. The agents said no, but they would bring Ronnie into the interview room and leave them alone.

"He's your best friend," said Agent Lee, seeing Ronnie Watts as the bridge to a confession.

"There's only one person you wanted here most and it's your dad," said Coder. "What would you tell him?"

"I love him [and] I just want him to be by my side."

"He knows more than we do that you're a good man," said Coder. "And he knows you want to protect your wife, Shanann. I think he would tell you to do the right thing."

At 4:43 P.M. Ronnie Watts entered the interview room, wearing a light blue polo shirt emblazoned with the words

PAPA RONNIE. He had been waiting outside in the lobby for almost six hours. Agents Coder and Lee left them alone.

"They've had me back here forever, boy," said Ronnie, sitting down next to his son. "You gonna tell [me] what's goin' on?"

Watts said he had failed the polygraph test. "So . . . they're not going to let me go."

"Is there any reason why they shouldn't?"

"They know I had an affair. I came clean about that."

Ronnie asked if Chris wanted to tell him anything about Shanann and the girls.

"We had that conversation that morning. You know it was emotional. [I] told her about the separation and everything like that."

"Well, what happened after that?"

"I went downstairs and . . . I don't want to protect her."

"What?"

"I don't want to protect her." Chris shook his head. "But I don't know what else to say."

"What happened?"

"She hurt them."

"She hurt them?"

"Yeah, and then I freaked out and hurt her."

"What now?"

"And I freaked out and hurt her."

"You hurt her? So she started hurting the kids? Talk to me, Chris. What happened?"

"She smothered them. They were smothered."

"They what?" asked Ronnie incredulously.

"She strangled them."

"She smothered them?"

"I didn't hear anything. When I was downstairs, I came back up and they were gone. I don't know . . . like me talking to her . . . about the separation and everything."

"And she lost it?"

"I freaked out, and I did the same thing to fuckin' her. Those were *my* kids."

"Oh, Lord have mercy," said Ronnie, becoming emotional. "She freaked out over the separation and everything."

Chris explained that after leaving Shanann in the bedroom he had gone downstairs to leave for work, when he heard "a little commotion" upstairs. Then he came upstairs to find Shanann on top of Celeste.

"What, choking her? Or did she kill her?"

"They were blue."

"Both of 'em?"

"Yes."

"She choked both of them to death?"

"I freaked out and did the same thing to fuckin' her."

"Oh my God."

"I don't know what to say . . . like, I didn't call the cops about it."

"So then what'd you do? Haul the bodies off or something?"

"Sorry. I didn't know what else to do."

Chris said that Shanann knew about his affair, and after he came clean, she'd "lost it," strangling Bella and Celeste.

"Why the hell would she have to hurt them babies?" said Ronnie tearfully. "Oh, Lord. Damn it, damn it, damn it. I'm—I'm so sorry."

"I know." His son started to weep, too.

"I'm so sorry . . . you know I love you no matter what."

"I know. But this is the last time I'm going to see the light of day again."

Ronnie asked if Agent Coder knew, and Chris said he had wanted to tell Ronnie first.

"She actually killed both her children," Ronnie rationalized, "and you snapped and did the same to her . . . [in a fit] of rage. We'll need to find a good lawyer and see what the hell they can do."

At that moment, Agents Lee and Coder, who had been watching the video feed in the command center, came back into the interview room. Lee started rubbing Chris's shoulder to comfort him.

"Are you okay?" she asked.

"Uh, no, he's not," said his father, gently putting his hand on his son's shoulder.

Then Agent Lee asked Chris to tell them what he had just told his father. After taking several seconds to compose himself, Chris told them he had caught Shanann killing the girls. Now adding new details, he said that after hearing the commotion he'd gone upstairs to check the baby monitor camera in Bella's bedroom.

"Both covers were pulled off, and she was just laying there. And I thought maybe she was just hot."

He told the agents that he had then cycled the monitor to CeCe's room, seeing Shanann choking her, and "freaked out" and ran in and jumped on top of Shanann.

"What did you do?" asked Agent Lee.

"CeCe was blue. That was my babies . . . those were my kids."

"What happened?"

"I did the same thing to her . . . right there in CeCe's room."

He said that after strangling Shanann he put her back in their bed.

"What happened next?"

"I didn't know what to do. . . . I was shaking. Like, both of my kids were blue and they were gone. I'm not that person. She hurt my kids. Fuck! I had to do the same thing to her."

He told them that after putting Shanann's body in their bed, he pulled the sheets over her because he couldn't bear to see her.

"I felt horrible for what I did. And then look at my kids and see what she did. I didn't know what to do."

"So where are they now, Chris?" Lee asked. "We need to find your babies. You did the hard part. All you have left is to tell us where they're at."

"We can help you get 'em out of the cold," added Agent Coder.

"They're gone," Chris replied. "There's no bringing them back."

35

"THEY'RE IN THE OIL TANK?"

Finally, Chris Watts broke down, admitting he'd loaded Shanann, Bella, and Celeste's bodies in his truck and taken them to Cervi 319, where he was working that morning. Then Agents Coder and Lee went out to arrange a full-scale search of the well site, leaving father and son in the interview room. They closely monitored the video feed, as Chris was far more likely to confide in his father than he was in them.

"Christopher, I'm so sorry," said Ronnie, after the agents locked the door behind them.

"I don't know what the fuck to do. Mom always said she was an unstable person, but I never thought in a million years that could happen."

"I'm so sorry. [We're] gonna get you a lawyer and see what they can do. Killed 'em both as they lay in their beds sleeping."

"Yeah. I emotionally drove her to do something stupid."

"Well, no, that shouldn't trigger that. Chris, I'm sorry. Don't blame yourself for that. Call it a crime of passion. . . . I don't know."

Ronnie then suggested they accompany the agents to Cervi 319, so he could show them where the bodies were.

"I pretty much have to go right up to it, and I can just point."

"Well, are they buried in something?"

"Shanann is."

"What about the babies?

"Well, that's what I feel horrible about. They're in a freakin' oil tank."

"They're in the oil tank?" gasped his father in astonishment.

"I didn't know what else to do. Please, God, forgive me."

Thirty miles away, in Majestic View Park, Arvada, Colorado, Nikki Kessinger was meeting with FBI special agents Marc Lehrer and Philip Jones. They sat around a table as mosquitoes buzzed overhead, Kessinger getting bitten several times during the seventy-minute taped interview.

"So I met Chris at work," she began. "He informed me that he did have two kids [and] that he was currently in the process of a separation from his wife . . . that was becoming pretty finalized."

On Monday afternoon he'd told her that his family was gone and he didn't know where they were. She didn't think anything was wrong until the next day, when they were still missing.

"And that's when I decided . . . to come and talk to you guys and just let you know that I've been spending time with Chris."

She then outlined how their friendship had fast turned intimate.

"He was looking for a relationship with me. And I told him, 'I'm not comfortable with considering you my significant other . . . while you are still in the midst of a divorce.'"

"Was he in love with you?" asked Agent Lehrer.

"Yes."

"Did he tell you?"

"Yes."

"Were you in love with him?"

"No. I think it could have gotten there, had things played out in a decent manner."

Agent Lehrer then asked if Chris had ever lost his temper with her.

"No. He is one of the most gentle and kind men I have ever met in my life. He was so excited to talk about his kids. It always made him so happy. It was cute."

Only yesterday, she told them, she had discovered that Shanann was fifteen weeks pregnant. When she confronted Chris about it, he denied being the father.

"I asked him to tell me the truth, and he kept denying. And I was like, 'Chris, I know this child is yours.' And he kept saying, 'I don't want to ruin anything we have.' I'm like, 'Chris, you need to worry about your family . . . all four of them.'"

Kessinger said the only other person who knew about the affair, and that she was talking to the FBI, was her father.

"And it's really hard for me to process this," she told them, getting emotional, "because I think he's a really good guy and I'm worried about his wife and kids. It's just freaking me out, because those little girls are so little and she's pregnant."

Agent Lehrer thanked her for coming forward, saying she was in a unique position and to call them immediately if she heard from him.

"Do you want me to call him?"

"Not yet," said Agent Lehrer. "We're not going to ask you to do that at this point. We have a lot of investigative avenues. I know this is difficult for you, and I don't want anything more stressful than it already is. So right now I would just say sit tight."

At 5:48 P.M., Agents Tammy Lee and Grahm Coder came back into the interview room with a large color drone photograph of the Cervi 319 well site taken earlier that day.

The photo showed two twenty-foot-high oil tanks standing at the end of a car pad and surrounding field. It also included the distinctive fitted bedsheet lying in the scrubland.

Agent Lee placed the photo in front of Chris, asking him to point out where he'd left Shanann's and his daughters' bodies.

Watts looked at the photo and pointed to a patch of dirt in the field, a few yards away from the car pad.

"That's Shanann right there," he told them without a hint of emotion.

Agent Lee then gave him a pen and asked him to write an *S* where he'd buried her. After he marked it, she asked where Bella and Celeste were.

"They're right here," he coldly replied, pointing to the large oil tanks surrounded by a barbed-wire fence.

Agent Lee asked if he knew which tank each of the girls were in, and he marked a *B* on the left one and a *C* on the right one.

"Are they in the tanks?" asked Coder. "Can somebody who doesn't know what they're doing open those?"

"What's in the tanks?" said Lee.

"It's a mixture of oil and water," Chris replied.

Then Coder asked about the sheet found there, and Watts said that was what he had wrapped Shanann's body in.

"What about the girlies?" asked Lee. "What were they wrapped in?"

"Just in their pajamas."

"Just in their pajamas?" repeated Lee. "Not with their blankets or anything? Where did their blankets and toys and stuff go?"

"Probably blew away in the wind," Watts suggested.

He said he had dug a shallow grave for Shanann, using the shovel he always kept in his truck.

"Can you do me a huge favor?" Agent Lee asked. "Can you just write your name on the bottom, just so I know we didn't make those marks? I'm just gonna write the date on it, okay?"

For the next few minutes, the two agents closely questioned Watts's account of Shanann killing Bella and Celeste before he'd murdered her. They accused him of lying, saying that his story didn't make sense.

"That kinda looks weird, Chris," Agent Lee told him. "I would hate for Shanann to get a bad rap if she didn't have anything to do [with it]."

"People in my family have always said she's unstable," he replied, "but I never would have thought in a million fuckin' years."

"So you're good with the public knowing that Shanann killed her daughters?" Lee asked.

"I did not hurt those girls," he replied emphatically.

"Chris," said Agent Coder, "I'm not sure I believe you."

"I did not hurt those girls. I promise you, Grahm."

"Chris, you can imagine we're pretty cynical in our jobs," Coder said, "and tonight we've had to talk about a lot of things. Don't get mad at me, but what it looks like is that you found a new life, and the only way to get that new life was to get rid of the old life."

"No."

"And I think you killed those girls before their mom came home."

"No, I did not."

"And then killed Shanann."

"My God. No. No. No."

Coder asked why he hadn't called an ambulance for his daughters after Shanann had killed them.

"It just doesn't add up," said Coder. "So either you're this monster who just wanted this young girlfriend, so

I'm going to kill everyone and hope it works out or something . . . so I think we're very close to the truth but not quite there yet."

"I'm not a monster," Watts replied emotionally. "I didn't kill my babies. Everything I've told you is the truth."

"I think as many problems as you have with Shanann," said Agent Lee, "at the end of the day she seemed like she was a pretty good mom, right?"

"I was a pretty good dad as well," retorted Watts.

Just after 6:00 P.M. CBI agent Matthew Sailor learned that Chris Watts had confessed and received the photo Watts had marked showing the placement of the bodies. An aerial drone was relaunched to shoot more video and photograph the storage tanks from various angles.

After obtaining a search warrant, CBI crime scene analysts Dave Yocum and Karen Schroeder began documenting the crime scene with digital photographs and measurements. A coroner was summoned. They collected the fitted sheet, two black garbage bags, and a broken rake head, logging them into evidence.

Luke Epple led Sailor and Yocum up the stairs of the two oil holding tanks, using a gas-monitoring device as it was so dangerous. They opened the eight-inch thief hatch and shone a flashlight into the tank. But it was too dark to see anything, except visible gas fumes.

They also found numerous strands of blond hair stuck to the rim of the left tank's hatch opening and collected it as evidence. Arrangements were made to drain both tanks in the morning for the gruesome task of recovering the girls' bodies.

At 9:52 P.M. Wednesday night, Denver 7 reported that Chris Watts had now confessed to killing his wife and daughters and was helping police recover their bodies.

All four Colorado networks led off their ten-o'clock news shows with the story, which would soon go national.

Back in North Carolina, Shanann's family heard about his confession from a breaking online news report.

"And I heard my dad scream on the back porch," recalled Frankie Rzucek. "And we're running out there and he's crying. There on the big screen was 'Husband admits to murdering mother and children.'"

After hearing the horrific news, Frankie went on Facebook.

"I just want 30 seconds alone with that heartless psychopath," he wrote. "May Satan have mercy on his soul. My blood is boiling and the pain and anger and sadness I have in my heart. Nothing absolutely nothing would get in my way of taking away his life like he did mine and my ENTIRE FAMILY."

At 10:45 P.M., Lead Detective Dave Baumhover and Officer Scott Coonrod arrived at Cervi 319. They collected evidence from the CBI crime scene analysts, including the fitted sheet, two garbage bags, the top of a rake, and strands of Bella's hair found on the oil tank hatch.

Then, under arc lights, they started excavating an area of scrubland about one hundred feet from the oil tanks, where Chris Watts had marked on the photo that he had buried Shanann.

"The dirt appeared to have been freshly dug," Officer Coonrod later reported. "We located the body of an adult female, which we believed to be Shanann."

Her body lay facedown about nine inches below the surface. The knees were pulled up to the chest in a fetal position, with the left arm up toward her head. The body was already decomposing. She was wearing a blue pair of underwear and a light-colored shirt, and an amniotic sac, containing a fetus, was visible.

Shanann Watts was pronounced dead by the Weld County coroner at 12:05 A.M. Thursday. Her body was photographed and placed in a body bag, to be taken to the medical examiner's office for autopsy.

Just after eleven o'clock, at the exact same time that Shanann's body was recovered, her husband was handcuffed and taken into custody—twelve hours after he had arrived at the Frederick PD with his father. Watts was being held on three counts of first-degree murder and three counts of tampering with physical evidence.

He was photographed with his shirt off in the interview room. On the left side of his neck were red marks, which he claimed were mosquito bites. Similar ones were found on the front of his neck.

He was driven thirty-five miles north to Weld County Jail in Greeley. After being booked, he was allowed to phone his father, but the call did not go through, as Ronnie did not have a prepaid prison calling card.

Chris Watts was then placed on a suicide watch and went straight to bed, where he fell asleep immediately.

At 12:08 A.M. the Frederick Police Department officially announced Chris Watts's arrest for the murder of his family.

"In the evening hours of August 15th," read the police statement, "the Frederick Police Department, in conjunction with the FBI and the Colorado Bureau of Investigation, has made an arrest in connection to the missing persons case involving Shanann Watts and her two daughters, Bella and Celeste.

"Chris Watts, the husband of Shanann, has been placed into custody and is awaiting charges at this time. He will be held at the Weld County Jail."

The statement announced that a news conference,

which would be streamed live on Facebook, would be held Thursday at 10:30 A.M. at the Frederick courthouse.

Soon afterward, Lu Valentino released a statement on behalf of the Rzucek family:

"It is with deep hurt, confusion and anger to confirm our beautiful cousin Shanann Watts, her unborn child, and two angelic daughters, Bella (4), Celeste (3) were viciously murdered by husband Chris Watts; who confessed to the killings. Please keep Shanann's parents and brother in your prayers."

Shanann's devastated brother, Frankie, made his feelings clear in a post on Facebook early Thursday morning:

"That piece of shit may he rot in hell. He killed my pregnant sister and my two nieces. Her husband Chris Watts admitted to murdering my family. We just found out she was pregnant with a baby boy and his name was going to be Nico."

Frankie asked Shanann's friends and family not to give any interviews to the media.

36

RECOVERY

On Thursday morning, Chris Watts's confession and arrest was front-page news from coast to coast, as dozens of television stations replayed his sham appeal for his wife and daughters. *The New York Times* carried the story with the headline "He Begged on TV for His Family's Return. Then He Was Accused of Killing Them."

The story read, "Chris Watts stood on his porch in Frederick, Colo., on Tuesday and pleaded in an interview with a television reporter for his missing wife and two young children to come home. But there would be no reunion. On Wednesday night, Mr. Watts, 33, was arrested and accused of killing his wife, Shanann, 34, who was 15 weeks pregnant, and his two daughters, Bella, 4, and Celeste, 3. The police declined to discuss any motives for the killings."

The Denver Post reported that Chris and Shanann Watts had filed for Chapter 7 bankruptcy in June 2015, owing almost $450,000, and were at present being taken to court by the Wyndham Hill Master Association for nonpayment of dues.

The story also quoted from Shanann's numerous Facebook posts, extolling Chris as her rock and the love of her life.

At 7:30 A.M., Chris Watts's Anadarko team arrived at

work to find a counselor waiting to help them cope with the shocking news. The human resources department had already fired Watts with a hand-delivered letter to Weld County Jail.

"When they broke the news that he confessed at ten o'clock," said Anthony Brown, "I didn't even go to bed because I was crying and couldn't sleep."

Troy McCoy said he was devastated. "I'd been crying most of the night once I found out the news. [The counselor] was an older gentleman and he talked to us for about an hour."

Later that day, Anadarko released a statement to the press: "We are heartbroken by this, and our thoughts and prayers are with the loved ones and friends of the Watts family."

Le-Vel also released a statement on its Facebook page, alongside a photo of Shanann, Bella, and Celeste:

"Our hearts are broken for the loss of our dear friend Shanann Watts and her children. Shanann was an amazing woman, mother, friend, and overall person. She lit up every room and was a joy to be around. Our love, prayers, and support go out during this devastating time to her family, friends, and to all Thrivers who had the great fortune of knowing Shanann and her two beautiful daughters. We honor them on this sorrowful day."

At around 8:30 A.M., CBI agent Tammy Lee arrived at Cervi 319 to assist in the recovery of Bella's and Celeste's bodies. A three-member hazardous-materials team of Colorado state troopers was already on-site, preparing to manually drain the pair of four-hundred-barrel crude-oil tanks, which were each twenty feet tall and twelve feet in diameter.

Before the draining of the tanks, an Anadarko employee gave a safety briefing. The east tank battery, believed to contain Celeste's body, contained 9 feet of crude oil, and the west one with Bella's had 1.4 feet. The tanks would be drained through a metal strainer into a large vacuum truck to preserve any evidence.

As the hazmat team prepared to start draining the first tank, Agent Lee walked over to the shallow grave where Shanann's body had been found. An orange traffic cone now marked it. She then helped search for Bella's and Celeste's blankets and toys that Watts claimed he had left there, but nothing was found.

At 10:00 A.M. the hazmat team started off-loading the oil crude from the east tank into the holding truck. It would take six hours to empty.

Half an hour later, scores of reporters crowded into the tiny Frederick courthouse for a press conference. On the podium stood Frederick Police Department chief Todd Norris, Weld County district attorney Michael Rourke, CBI director John Camper, and the FBI's special agent in charge of the Denver office, Calvin Shivers.

"This is absolutely the worst possible outcome that any of us could imagine," said Director Camper. "And I think our hearts are broken for the town of Frederick as much as anybody's."

Then DA Rourke stepped up to the lectern, announcing that Chris Watts would appear in Weld County Court on a bond hearing that afternoon.

"I hope you all understand this investigation is still ongoing," the DA told reporters. "We are at the very preliminary stages . . . and so as a result of that we're going to be constrained in the types of questions we can answer."

He said formal charges against Watts would be filed Monday afternoon.

FBI agent Shivers said that Chris Watts's arrest was a perfect example of law enforcement agencies working together. "Unfortunately, it was not the outcome that we were looking for."

Sergeant Albert then took questions from the floor.

"Have you been able to recover the bodies?" asked a reporter.

"At this point," said Director Camper, "we have been able to recover a body that we're quite certain is Shanann Watts's body. We have strong reason to believe that we know where the bodies of the children are and recovery efforts are in process."

A reporter then asked why Chris Watts had killed his family.

"We can't get into [that]," replied Camper. "As horrible as this outcome is, our role now is to do everything we can to determine exactly what occurred."

Finally, Sergeant Albert was asked about the toll the investigation had taken on the Frederick Police Department.

"It's been earth-shattering," he said. "Our small department of twenty-plus officers have been working around the clock on this. It's been nonstop."

That morning, Lauren Arnold launched a fund-raiser on Facebook to raise $100,000 for the Rzucek family.

"I can't imagine being so far away in this situation," wrote Arnold. "Help me ease the financial burdens they may face and get them to Colorado to get their beloved girls."

Throughout the day, tearful well-wishers arrived at 2825 Saratoga Trail to pay their respects and light candles. A makeshift memorial on the front lawn had a cross, stuffed toys, flowers, and balloons.

TV news crews broadcast live from outside the Wattses' house, and helicopters circled overhead as reporters vied for interviews with neighbors.

"Everyone was talking about it," said Don Watt, who lives a couple of doors away. "It was very, very shocking for the neighborhood."

Among the grievers on the sidewalk outside the house were Emilie Baney and her son Cameron, a friend of Bella's.

"[We're] explaining to him what's going on and that he'll never see Bella again," Emilie told WRAL-TV News. "I just told him, 'We're going to make a card and give her a teddy bear and we're going to say goodbye.'"

At 2:30 P.M., Chris Watts appeared at the Weld County courthouse for a bail hearing. Several hours earlier, he had met Deputy State Public Defender James Merson in Weld County Jail to discuss defense strategy.

Watts was brought into the courtroom in handcuffs and shackles, wearing a regulation orange jail jumpsuit. During the twenty-minute hearing he displayed no emotion but was attentive, answering the judge's questions in a clear voice.

"This matter comes on for a first appearance," said District Court judge Marcello Kopcow. "Correct me if I'm wrong, but formal charges have not been filed yet?"

"That's correct, Your Honor," replied Weld County DA Michael Rourke, who said they would be filed by 3:30 P.M. Monday.

Judge Kopcow said he had reviewed the affidavit supporting the warrantless arrest and found probable cause. "Specifically, I see that Mr. Watts was arrested for three counts of first-degree murder and three counts of tampering with a deceased human body."

The judge told Watts he was denying bail and would officially inform him of the charges against him when they were filed by the DA's office.

"I believe your lawyer has filed about sixteen or so motions on your behalf," the judge told Watts, "including a request for a preliminary hearing."

One of the defense motions was for preserving trace DNA evidence at the Wattses' home and on the three bodies. Deputy DA Steve Wrenn questioned how he could guarantee the preservation, as only Shanann's body had so far been recovered.

"At this point there is not an autopsy scheduled," said Wrenn. "I don't know when that might happen."

Then Public Defender Merson asked the judge to seal the warrantless arrest affidavit because of the intense media coverage of the case.

"It's an ongoing investigation at this point," he told the judge. "I have concerns about . . . Mr. Watts's right to a fair trial and his due process rights."

Judge Kopcow agreed to seal the affidavit, saying he expected to unseal it after charges were filed on Monday. He set the next hearing for the following Tuesday morning, so Shanann's family could fly in from North Carolina.

While Chris Watts appeared in Weld County Court, the hazmat team were preparing to enter the east tank to recover Celeste's body. After removing the rear manhole and pumping off the remaining crude oil, one of the team walked up the stairway to the top of the tank and peered through the thief hatch.

"Sgt. Armstrong told me," wrote Trooper O. L. Wilson in his report, "he could see what looked like a body face down on the south side of the tank."

After photos were taken, the troopers, wearing hazmat suits and breathing apparatus, began the complicated process of removing the body. It was highly dangerous because of the level of oil sludge and the toxic fumes. The men could only remain in the tank a few minutes at a time. Trooper Darrin Reeder went in first, closely followed by Wilson.

"There was a body face down [and] it appeared to be a small female child," Wilson later reported. "Trooper Reeder grasped the upper portion of her right arm to turn her over [and] then lifted her by both arms as I held her right leg . . . as we moved the body towards the manway."

As Celeste's body was brought out of the tank, her hand was "degloved" of its skin, which was handed to Detective Dave Baumhover as evidence. Agent Tammy Lee watched with forensic pathologist Dr. Michael Burson as Celeste was placed in a white decontamination box with rope handles.

"Celeste was covered in oil," Lee observed, "[and] wearing a pink nightgown and I could see she was also wearing a [diaper]. Once outside the tank, Dr. Burson patted her stomach area down with oil absorbing pads. Celeste appeared to have skin slippage and was wrapped in a white sheet and then laid inside of an open body bag."

Celeste Watts was officially pronounced dead by Dr. Burson at 3:40 P.M.

The hazmat team now moved over to the west tank to recover Bella's body. It took far less time to drain, as it only contained about 1.4 feet of crude oil. Once it was empty, the two troopers entered the tank and saw Bella's oil-soaked body, still dressed in pink pajamas with images of hearts and butterflies.

"I grabbed her right arm near the wrist area," wrote Trooper Wilson, "and moved her towards the manway. At this point, Trooper Reeder was able to secure her left arm and left leg. [We] then passed the body through the manway. During this extraction there was some skin slippage where we had to touch the victim's body."

Then the troopers walked around the tank, which still

had about four inches of crude sludge in it, looking for evidence, but none was found.

As a safety precaution, Bella's body was tested for any buildup of combustibles by a four-gas monitor, while Dr. Burson patted her down with absorbent pads. Bella was officially declared dead at 5:50 P.M.

As Bella's and Celeste's bodies were driven away to the morgue at the McKee Medical Center for autopsy, the hazmat team had to be thoroughly decontaminated.

At 6:30 P.M., the Frederick Police Department issued a press release, announcing they had now recovered the remains of Bella and Celeste Watts. It did not mention that they had been recovered from two oil tanks.

"Evidence technicians from both the Colorado Bureau of Investigation and the Frederick Police Department located two bodies whom police have strong reason to believe are Bella and Celeste Watts, the daughters of Shanann Watts. While we will not disclose the location as to where the bodies were located, police can say that they were found in close proximity to the other body whom officers strongly believe is Shanann's."

But several hours later, Denver 7 broke the story that their bodies had been recovered from two oil tanks. Citing several reliable sources, it reported that Chris Watts had placed his two little daughters in the Anadarko-owned oil tanks "in order to hide the bodies and conceal the smell."

Late Thursday afternoon, CBI agents Kevin Koback and Tim Martinez arrived at Nikki Kessinger's home in Northglenn, Colorado, to bring her to the Thornton Police Department for a second interview. She was accompanied by her father, Duane.

Before it began, Nikki handed over some of Chris Watts's clothing, love letters, and a birthday card he had given her. She also handed them her iPhone to copy photos and messages, explaining some were "kind of raunchy."

"You're not being interrogated as a criminal," Agent Koback assured her. "We're here to understand your relationship with Chris and what you know about Chris and his family."

She said when she had first met Chris at work, he wasn't wearing a wedding ring and hadn't mentioned being married. "Then one day he told me that he had two kids. I was like, 'That's pretty cool.'"

"That sounded like a sarcastic comment," said Koback.

She said he told her he was living in his basement until his divorce came through.

Koback asked if Watts had ever discussed his financial situation, as he and Shanann appeared to have rebounded well after declaring bankruptcy.

"I think he was really frustrated with the situation. He told me, 'I feel like my paycheck goes into my bank account and [she] makes it go like this.' From the vibe I got [she] had really bad spending habits."

Kessinger said he often complained that his family lived paycheck to paycheck and could not afford their lavish lifestyle.

Then Agent Koback asked her to describe her relationship with Chris Watts.

"We got along really well. And I enjoyed it."

"Six to eight weeks . . . whatever it was. You guys have an intimate relationship during that time?"

"Yes."

"Did he ever tell you that he loved you?"

"Yes, he did."

"Did you ever tell him the same?"

"Couple of times."

Kessinger said she was trying to come to terms with her horrific situation, wondering about its long-term effects. "My name is about to be slandered. I don't know how long it's going to take to heal."

She said she wouldn't be able to go out in public for a couple of years, as people would point fingers at her. "This is a horrible, horrible thing. They're going to say, 'You're the woman that had an affair with the man who took out his whole family.'"

Agent Koback asked what she thought was the catalyst for Watts's killing his family.

"I've thought about this, and sometimes I think to myself, 'If I wasn't in this man's life, would his family still be alive?'"

37

"THE MANNER OF DEATH IS HOMICIDE"

At 9:55 A.M. Friday, Public Defender James Merson filed an emergency motion for DNA swabs to be taken from Bella's and Celeste's necks, to bolster Chris Watts's claim that their mother had strangled them.

"The autopsies for this case are scheduled to begin in 20 minutes," the motion read. "Defense counsel had an opportunity to speak with a DNA expert this morning [who] advised that even though the bodies of two of the decedents have been in an oil well filled with crude oil for several days, DNA would still be present."

Thirty-five minutes later, Dr. Michael Burson and his assistant Joey Weiner began Shanann's autopsy at McKee Medical Center in Loveland, Colorado. Also present were Deputy DAs Steve Wrenn and Patrick Roche, Weld County coroner Carl Blesch, Detective Dave Baumhover, and Agents Grahm Coder and Tammy Lee.

Before the autopsies began, Wrenn read out the defense motion requesting neck swabs, X-rays, and fingernail scrapings from Bella's and Celeste's bodies. A few minutes later came the news that Judge Kopcow had denied the requests.

Dr. Burson then performed the first autopsy, on Shanann Watts. After her clothing was removed, placed on a clean sheet, and photographed, it was logged into evidence by

Baumhover. Then the body was opened with a thoraco-abdominal incision.

"Shanann appeared to have a large amount of skin slippage," Agent Lee later wrote in her report, "and her amniotic sac protruding from her vaginal area. Dr. Burson examined the amniotic sac and removed Shanann's fetus."

The fetus was then collected as evidence and transported directly to the CBI's forensic laboratory for genetic analysis.

"During Shanann's autopsy," wrote Lee, "Dr. Burson pointed out several important findings. [Her] hyoid bone (in the middle of the neck) was not broken, although he pointed out bruising to the soft tissue on the right side of the hyoid bone. Dr. Burson also noted bruising to the muscles and tissue in Shanann's neck."

The pathologist found no other trauma to the body or evidence of any disease.

"Based on the history provided and the autopsy findings," read Dr. Burson's autopsy report, "the cause of death is asphyxiation due to manual strangulation by another individual. The manner of death is homicide."

At 1:30 P.M., Dr. Burson began his autopsy on Bella Watts, who was wearing an oil-soaked pink nightgown with hearts and butterflies and underwear. Her clothing was removed, photographed, and handed to Detective Baumhover.

"Bella also had a large amount of skin slippage," reported Agent Lee. "It appeared Bella had some scrapes to her buttocks and the tops of both shoulders."

The pathologist observed that Bella's frenulum (the skin connecting the top lip to the gum) was torn, and her gums and inner lip were bruised. Bella's injuries had been caused by hard downward pressure on her nose and mouth, and she had bitten into her tongue.

"Dr. Burson indicated Bella's death was violent," wrote Lee, "as it appeared she struggled to get away."

The pathologist found her cause of death was asphyxiation due to smothering.

"The toxicology results," he later reported, "likely represent decomposition and an artifact of being submerged in an oil tank for several days. The manner of death is homicide."

Celeste Watts's autopsy began at 5:30 P.M. She was dressed in a pink nightgown, Minnie Mouse underwear, and a diaper. These, like previous items, were laid out on a white sheet, photographed, and given to Detective Baumhover as evidence.

Like the other bodies, Celeste's had a lot of skin slippage but no sign of injury or bruising to her neck area.

"I did not observe any injury to Celeste's mouth or face," wrote Lee. "Dr. Burson also measured the hip and shoulder width of Bella and Celeste and advised the smallest width was 9½ inches. The opening to the hatch of the oil tank was only 8 inches in diameter."

Dr. Burson found the likely cause of death was asphyxiation due to smothering, and the manner of death was homicide.

Late Friday morning, CBI agent Kevin Koback telephoned Nikki Kessinger, after receiving an anguished text from her.

"I read the news this morning," she told him. "I found out where they found those little girls. It's so disgusting. That's so scary."

Once again she offered to assist the investigation in any way she could, saying she needed something in return. "I'm really trying to help you guys. I just need you to help me with my employer and try to just help me brace for this media thing. It might become a kind of media frenzy . . .

and I don't think the media is going to portray a very nice picture of me."

Agent Koback agreed that her mental health was most important, promising to have a victims' advocate call her.

At midday, Chris Watts's five-member defense team descended on 2825 Saratoga Trail, looking for anything to help his case. They walked through the encampment of TV news crews and scores of well-wishers, let themselves in, and started taking photographs. Neighbors called the police, who, after checking with the Weld County DA's office, allowed them to stay.

The Watts family murders were now national and international news, with all TV networks sending their top reporters to cover the grisly story. With hundreds of Shanann's Facebook videos and posts still freely available online, the story exploded.

"It did get really big, really fast," said Madeline St. Amour, who covered the story for the *Longmont Times-Call*. "At first I didn't think this was going to turn into anything, and then all of a sudden the national newspapers and TV stations are flying in."

Nathaniel Trinastich put a sign on his door saying NO COMMENT. DON'T KNOCK. DON'T BOTHER ME.

"The media were everywhere," he said. "They besieged us and stayed here for nearly a week. One reporter even asked if he could use my restroom. It was terrible."

Trinastich had put his home up for sale a few days before the murders and had now taken it off the market until things calmed down.

Later that day, Rzucek family spokesperson Lu Valentino posted an update on Facebook:

"NOTE: Whatever you are reading in print, seeing on TV about the Shanann Watts case as far as so-called friends, co-workers are concerned . . . take it with a grain of salt if it didn't come directly from authorities or family. Period."

That afternoon about a dozen Wyndham community members gathered at their clubhouse to mourn. The media were asked to leave before they closed the clubhouse doors and prayed. They voted to honor Shanann's memory by placing purple ribbons for lupus awareness all over the estate.

At 8:30 P.M. several hundred people gathered outside 2825 Saratoga Trail for a community candlelight vigil. They brought flowers, candles, and gifts to add to the memorial, lining the yard from the sidewalk to the steps of the porch. Colored balloons floated in the breeze. Bouquets of roses and stuffed teddy bears, unicorns, mermaids, and lambs were strewn all over the front lawn. Someone put up a sign reading CHOOSE LOVE, decorated with a purple ribbon.

"This is to celebrate, mourn, and get closure for a family that didn't deserve this," said Kelley Trippy, who organized the vigil for the estate's social committee. "This is a horrible, horrible, horrible story. It's affected us all whether you do know them or don't know them."

Among the mourners were Jeanna Dietz and her daughter, Eva.

"It's been awful to have to explain to my kids," said Jeanna. "I mean Chris is someone that they love and trust. It's been horrible to try and explain the unexplainable."

Since his arrest, Chris Watts had been on suicide watch alone in his cell in Unit 07 at the Weld County Jail. He was respectful and polite to the warders, spending hours blankly staring at the wall. Every day he was allowed an hour out of his cell for exercise.

The other inmates soon found out what he was there

for and started threatening him. Day and night they pounded on the walls of his cell and screamed obscenities. They told him to kill himself before one of them did.

Whenever he left his cell for exercise or to meet his lawyers in the visitors' room, the entire jail block was put on lockdown to protect him.

"The housing unit was very upset," wrote a prison deputy in his report, "about having their sliders shut indefinitely . . . and made their collective feelings clear by booing Watts when he came out of his room."

On Friday night another deputy became so concerned about Watts that he came in to see if Watts was all right.

"I asked him if he was feeling suicidal and he told me he was not," the deputy later wrote in his report. "He is just thinking about things and he's trying to excersize [sic] to keep busy."

On Saturday afternoon, Nikki Kessinger texted Agent Koback that Anadarko had placed her on an extended leave, and she had remembered more. Koback said he was out of town until Tuesday and would then be in contact.

"I am with my family tonight," she texted back, "and it's a safe and positive environment for me right now."

"You doing okay?"

"I'm alright. Informed my employer of the situation. Getting ready to head to a safe spot tonight in case my name is released tomorrow. Trying to be proactive and positive."

She asked if "his motive" would be revealed in the warrantless affidavit.

"Motive is never released," Koback replied. "That is media speculation."

That night, Kessinger searched the internet for Amber Frey, the mistress of Scott Peterson, who murdered his pregnant wife, Laci, in 2002. Two years later he was convicted of Laci's first-degree murder and their unborn son's second-degree murder and sentenced to death. He remains on death row in San Quentin Prison.

Kessinger googled to see how much money Frey had received for her bestselling book about the case, entitled *Witness: For the Prosecution of Scott Peterson,* and whether people hated her afterward.

38

"THEY SEEMED LIKE THE PICTURE OF SUBURBAN BLISS"

Late Monday afternoon, DA Michael Rourke held a press conference at Weld County District Court to announce nine felony charges against Chris Watts. But first Frank Rzucek, who had flown in with his son the day before, read out a prepared statement.

"Good afternoon, everybody," he began, voice choking with emotion. "I am Shanann's dad, this is her brother. We would like to thank everyone in the Frederick Police Department and all the agencies involved for working so hard to find my daughter, granddaughters, and Nico.

"Thank you, everyone, for coming out for the candlelight vigil and saying all your prayers. They are greatly appreciated. And keep the prayers coming for our family. Thank you very much."

Then DA Rourke solemnly walked up to the lectern to address reporters and read out the formal charges his office had now filed against Chris Watts:

- Three counts of first-degree murder after deliberation,
- Two counts of first-degree murder of a victim under twelve by a person in a position of trust,
- Three counts of tampering with a deceased human body,
- One count of first-degree unlawful termination of a pregnancy.

"Please keep in mind at this point," said Rourke, "the defendant is presumed innocent until proven guilty in a court of law."

DA Rourke said that the warrantless affidavit had now been unsealed and would be available at the end of the press conference. Then he invited questions, explaining that he couldn't discuss the ongoing investigation.

"At any point did you consider the death penalty?" a reporter asked.

"Way too early to have that conversation because we don't have to make a determination on that until sixty-three days after arraignment."

"Is that something you are considering?" asked another.

"I'm not going to answer questions about that at this point."

The arrest affidavit made headlines around the world with Watts's claim that he had seen Shanann strangling his daughters on their baby monitor and then, "in a rage," strangled Shanann.

It also revealed Watts had been having an affair with an Anadarko coworker, whose name had been redacted at the request of the defense.

At 10:30 A.M. Tuesday, Chris Watts was back in Weld County District Court for an advisement hearing. In the front row of the public gallery sat Shanann's father and brother.

As Judge Marcello Kopcow read out each charge, Frank Rzucek wept, his hands covering his eyes. His son, Frankie, put his arm around him for comfort as Frankie coldly stared at his brother-in-law, sitting at the defense table, shackled and wearing an orange jumpsuit.

Watts sighed as each of the nine felony charges was read out, answering, "Yes, sir," when the judge asked if he understood them. He was told that if convicted for the five counts of murder, the minimum sentence would be life imprisonment, and the maximum would be death.

"Do you have any questions?" asked the judge.

"No, sir." Watts bit his lip.

At the end of the seventeen-minute hearing, Watts's new defense lawyer, John Walsh, said his client waived his right to have a preliminary hearing within thirty-five days. Then the judge set the date of the next status conference for November 19.

At 2:35 P.M. Frank Rzucek was interviewed by CBI agent Matthew Sailor at the DoubleTree Hotel in Greeley, where he was staying.

"First of all, I just want to say I'm very sorry for your loss," said Agent Sailor. "These are terrible circumstances to have to meet you, and I'm sorry I have to do this."

He began by asking about Chris's relationship with Shanann and his daughters.

"He was a great father," Frank replied without hesitation. "I mean, I couldn't ask for a better father for the kids. Honestly. He did everything for them. Played with them. Bathed them. Husband-wise the same way."

Frank said he had never seen any problems in the marriage, until the summer, when Shanann had spent six weeks in North Carolina. "There was a little bit of difference in them. He was getting a little sterner with the girls, and I just took it as being a father."

Frank noted that his son-in-law had recently lost a lot of weight and started working out. "They were going through this new Thrive stuff that she was selling. And he started getting himself all built up. But he was always a body-type person."

Frank said that while Shanann was in North Carolina,

she never mentioned any marital problems. "Shanann never said anything to us about a separation, fights. I don't know if she just wanted to keep it from us and not get us involved."

He said the last time he had talked to Chris and his granddaughters was on FaceTime, the night before they went missing. "I believe Bella was eating cold pizza, and some kind of Jolly Rancher taffy."

The morning they disappeared, Sandi had spoken to Watts, who told her Shanann was "in one of her moods" and had taken the girls to a girlfriend's house.

"I just can't understand for him to do [this] to these two little children," said Frank, becoming emotional, "or saying my daughter did it. I don't believe that at all. She would never, ever hurt those kids. Those were her life and they have another baby. . . ."

"It's hard to wrap your head around," agreed Agent Sailor.

"You know I can't lie; he was a good dad and he was a good father from what we know."

Next, Agent Sailor interviewed Frankie Rzucek, who said he had loved Chris as a brother. But he, too, had noticed how coldly distant Chris was when he stayed with the couple in Aberdeen. Until this happened, said Frankie, he had considered Chris the perfect man for his sister and couldn't fathom why he had done it.

"It's like the devil got into him," Frankie said, "and turned him into a whole different person."

Later that day, a prison deputy came into Chris Watts's cell and handed him *Murder at the Kennedy Center,* by Margaret Truman, to read to try to occupy his mind. He loved the book and would from then on spend his time reading instead of staring blankly at the cell wall.

"Having a book to read," wrote Deputy Dobson in his inmate report that day, "seems to have significantly improved inmate Watts' demeanor."

Over the next few weeks, Watts became a voracious reader of murder books by authors such as Margaret Truman and Brad Thor.

While the Rzuceks were in Colorado, they arranged to bring Shanann's, Bella's, and Celeste's bodies back to North Carolina for burial. This expensive and highly complicated process was largely funded by the Facebook fund-raiser.

"The hardest thing was flying them here because they were in crude oil for four days," said Sandi Rzucek, "so they were flammable. We couldn't cremate them . . . they would have blown up a building."

As a safety measure, the girls had to have specially made sealed coffins, so the dangerous gases wouldn't leak out.

"So we never got to say goodbye to our family," said Sandi, "or see them or hug them or to tell them we loved them."

Back in Spring Lake, North Carolina, Ronnie and Cindy Watts were receiving hate mail and threats, although they had loved their granddaughters and were devastated.

"It's a nightmare," said Cindy. "We're just two ordinary working-class people, and [being] thrown into the spotlight has been overwhelming."

She said she supported her son and his claim that Shanann had murdered the girls. "I believe him one hundred percent. My whole family believes him."

Cindy said that since his arrest they had not been allowed to communicate with Chris, only receiving secondhand information from his attorneys. "Right now they say he's holding up the best he can. He's reading whatever books he's able to get ahold of."

On Wednesday, August 22, Nikki Kessinger was officially fired by Anadarko. After learning the news, she met with a Colorado Bureau of Investigation victims' advocate, before seeing Agent Koback.

"She inquired how to change her name," Koback later noted in his report. "I gave her cursory information on how to do so."

They also discussed her entering a witness protection program and moving to another state with a new identity.

Five days later, Bella and Celeste's obituary appeared in the Rzuceks' local newspaper, *The Pilot*. It announced that a funeral mass would be held the following Saturday at Sacred Heart Roman Catholic Church in Pinehurst, North Carolina.

"Shan'ann Cathryn Watts, 34; daughters Bella Marie Watts, 4, and Celeste Cathryn Watts, 3, and unborn son Nico Lee of Frederick Colo., died Thursday, Aug. 16, 2018.

"Shan'ann was born Jan 10, 1984 in New Jersey to Frank Rzucek and Sandra Onorati Rzucek. She was our pride and joy, a true gift from God. We were so blessed to have such a joyful and wonderful daughter whose beauty was that of a doll.

"Bella was born Dec. 17, 2013 in Colorado. Shan'ann was so excited to have her first baby girl. She spent every minute thanking God and taking care of her precious gift that the Lord had blessed her with. How she loved and cherished her.

"Celeste was born July 17, 2015 in Colorado. Oh how Shan'ann was so excited to have another child because of her battle with Lupus. She was determined to stay healthy and with her love for her Celeste. Every movement with her was a blessing.

"Shan'ann wanted one more child, praying for a baby boy. She named him Nico Lee. She had anticipated her son's arrival and knew he would be loved by his sisters and family."

A few hours before the obituary appeared, Trent Bolte, a twenty-eight-year-old makeup artist from Casper, Wyoming, went on Facebook claiming to be Chris Watts's gay lover.

"So let's talk about it," he wrote. "I've gotten multiple messages on fb, calls on my phone. Yes I knew #ChrisWatts, we did have relations last summer off and on thru April. NONE of the women or men that he slept with are guilty of anything except trusting a stranger."

A few hours later came a second post.

"And speaking from experience, NONE of us knew he was a murderer and a sociopath."

And then a third.

"And for the people trying to blackmail me and threatening to 'expose' me and Chris' relations, just do it cuz there's nothing I can change about the past."

On Tuesday night, Trent Bolte did an anonymous telephone interview with Ashleigh Banfield on the HLN cable show *Crime & Justice*.

"Breaking news," Banfield breathlessly told her viewers. "We are talking with a man from Chris Watts's past. A man who claims to be Chris Watts's former lover."

She said the show's producers had tracked him down, but they were not naming him for his own protection.

"How was it that you first met Chris Watts?" she asked.

"I met him on an app called MeetMe," replied Bolte. "He reached out to me and messaged me."

Bolte claimed that Watts had told him that he had two daughters. When Bolte had asked why Watts's profile said "straight," he'd replied that he was not out yet sexually. Soon afterward they had agreed to meet.

"When you first met him," asked Banfield, "how soon did your relationship turn sexual?"

"That night."

Banfield asked if he thought that Chris Watts had discovered he was gay and could no longer live with his life.

"Yes, I did," said Bolte, "but we had many conversations. I asked him if he's sure he's not bisexual, because obviously he had two children. He told me that he didn't know, but as of that moment he was attracted to me and only me as a male."

Bolte claimed they had multiple hookups over the next nine months, breaking up after Watts had arrived for a date with his two daughters in the back of his truck.

"He told me he had children, but he had portrayed that he was single. I met up with him . . . and he had his daughters with him. And the oldest pretty much spilled the beans that he was still married . . . when she asked if she could sleep with him and Mommy tonight."

Bolte claimed that when he had confronted him, Watts said he was a victim of "emotional and verbal abuse" and "trapped in a loveless marriage."

"It's an incredible story," Banfield told him, "and I appreciate you coming forward."

The next morning the sensational story of Chris Watts's purported gay lover made headlines all over the world. Within hours, Bolte was summoned to the Larimer County Sheriff's Office in Fort Collins for an interview with Agents Grahm Coder and Tammy Lee.

Bolte arrived at 4:00 P.M., and over the next two and a half hours the agents pumped him with questions about his alleged affair with Chris Watts. Although he provided several texts, Bolte had no proof that they had even met, let alone had a relationship.

"Bolte stated that he was less than 100 percent truthful," Agent Coder wrote in his report. "He stated that he did in fact meet Watts [who] paid for sex on multiple occasions."

At the end of the interview Bolte was asked if he would take a polygraph test, but said he would need to consult with his lawyer first. After further interviews with Bolte's mother and a boyfriend, Coder and Lee decided that Bolte was not credible.

39

THE FUNERAL

At 11:00 A.M. on Saturday, September 1, a funeral mass for Shanann, Bella, and Celeste Watts was held at the Sacred Heart Roman Catholic Church in Pinehurst. Notably absent were Chris Watts's family, who had decided to have their own memorial service at a later time.

"I called [Frank] before the funeral," said Ronnie Watts. "I said, 'Frank, with all the media and the way everybody's looking down on us, I don't think it's a good idea for us to be there.' And he said, 'Yeah, you're probably right.'"

Two hundred people attended the mass, and an estimated 150,000 people watched it on Facebook. Shanann's wooden casket, bearing her and her unborn son, Nico, lay in the center of the church in front of the pews. Two smaller silver-colored caskets, containing Bella and Celeste, were on either side of it.

The Reverend John Forbes officiated, overlaying each casket with a white pall, signifying the resurrection of the body and soul. He blessed each casket with holy water and the smoke of scented pines.

"We gather together today," the reverend told the congregation, "to offer praise and thanksgiving to God for the lives of Shanann, Bella Marie, Celeste, and Nico.

"When Jesus returns, we believe that we will be given

our resurrected bodies. Nico will have a full-grown body, as will his sisters. They will be able to stand with their mother before the very throne of God and see God face-to-face.

"Did God want them to die? God does not will evil. When God created us, he gave us free will so that we might love him. With free will comes the ability to sin, to defy the will of God that is always good. Sin affects not only the sinner but those around the one who sins. It is the nature of sin that we cannot control its evil effects even if we wish to do so."

He said it is impossible to see God's overall plan for us, although there was a sacred pattern to everything.

"Shanann was a woman of determination," he told the congregation. "Sandra, her mother, describes her as 'a fireball.' She had dreams to be fulfilled and she worked towards those dreams. She wanted to be an exceptional wife and mother. She wanted to support research into the disease that she had, lupus. She wanted to make a difference.

"Bella Marie, also called Bella B, and Celeste Cathryn, CeCe, were light for all around them, especially for their PopPop, Nona, and Uncle Frankie. They were filled with life and joy and shared it with all those they encountered."

The family would like to see some good come from this tragedy, he said, and wanted a law to recognize the lives of unborn children such as their grandson, Nico.

"They want to see justice done," he said, "knowing that God is the ultimate judge. They do not desire vengeance and death but justice and life."

He then read out a moving message from Shanann's father:

"Dear Shan, I have so much to say, but I will make it short. Daddy loves you. You are a wonderful daughter and great mother. You will always be Daddy's little girl. Till we meet again, I love you with all my heart."

The reverend also read out a letter from Frankie Rzucek, saying his sister was born to be a mother:

"Boy, was she ready. Closets were full even before she knew she was pregnant. She couldn't wait. She was very successful and independent before any man came along, and that's just the way she wanted it. I always worried about her and the girls being so far because I couldn't protect them."

After the hour-long mass, the ten pallbearers, including her father and brother, placed Shanann's casket in a white hearse, between the two smaller ones bearing her daughters.

Then they were driven to their final resting place at Bethesda Cemetery in Aberdeen.

40

A PLEA DEAL

Almost a month after the Wattses' murders, the story continued to make national headlines. It made the cover of *People* magazine three weeks running, with new revelations on its website daily. Ashleigh Banfield's *Crime & Justice* show now only covered the case.

As the world awaited new developments, thousands became obsessed with Shanann's voluminous Facebook postings and videos, which remained online as a tribute. Scores of public and private online groups had now sprung up, obsessed with the murders. A private group called Watts Family Murders: Analysis and Discussion had seventeen thousand members, and a public one, Prayers for Shanann, Bella, Celeste and Nico, boasted thirty thousand.

True-crime fanatics all over the world played detective, posting their elaborate theories of why Chris Watts had annihilated his family. They sifted through all of Shanann's Facebook videos searching for clues.

The September 3 edition of *People* magazine ran a cover story with the headline "Married to a Monster." The following week it ran another: "The Watts Family Murders: Secrets & Lies."

"Shanann and Chris Watts seemed to have it all," the

article read. "A happy marriage, two beautiful daughters and a baby on the way. But with Chris now being charged with killing them all, darker truths emerge."

The story included new details from an anonymous police source, who was not authorized to talk to the press. Watts's defense team immediately demanded an investigation into the leak.

"These extrajudicial statements have the effect of irretrievably tainting the potential jury pool," read the motion, "violating Mr. Watts' rights to a fair and impartial jury."

On September 17, Judge Kopcow denied the motion, finding that the defense had not produced any evidence that potential jurors had been prejudiced by the stories.

"The court is mindful that it must be ever vigilant to ensure the defendant receives a fair trial," wrote the judge in his ruling.

On Thursday, September 26, Dr. Micháel Burson finally signed the autopsy reports for Shanann, Bella, and Celeste. Toxicology tests had found that Shanann's blood alcohol level was 0.128, well above the legal limit. After handing over a copy of the autopsies to the defense, DA Rourke immediately filed a motion to seal them, citing concern about "tainting witnesses that have not yet been interviewed."

Then he ordered an investigation into why Shanann's blood alcohol level was elevated, and if she had been drinking prior to her murder.

The first week of October, CBI field agent Greg Zentner interviewed several of Shanann's friends about her alcohol consumption. Cindy Derossett, Cassie Rosenberg, and Karen Epps, who'd all been with Shanann in Arizona, said she had not drunk any alcohol. Nickole Atkinson told

Detective Baumhover that Shanann had only drunk water with lemon during the trip because she was pregnant.

On October 12, Judge Kopcow denied the prosecution's request to seal the autopsies, citing the Weld County coroner's office as the custodian of the records.

Three days later, Coroner Carl Blesch filed a petition to seal the autopsy reports, pending a court hearing at a later date to discuss the matter.

On October 18, Chris Watts was ordered to pay $37,000 toward the cost of burying his family. The Crime Victim Compensation Program also ordered him to pay Frank and Sandi Rzucek $5,400 in lost wages.

A week earlier, at a probate court hearing over Shanann's estate, Watts, via a telephone linkup from jail, had waived any claim he might have and appointed his father-in-law as executor.

In early October, Chris Watts's defense team had secretly approached the District Attorney's Office about a possible plea deal. DA Rourke was open to a deal but refused to dismiss any of the charges.

"I was not willing to entertain any further concessions above and beyond removing the death penalty," he said later.

When Frank and Sandi Rzucek found out, they told Rourke that they wanted to pursue a plea deal, in return for taking the death penalty off the table. DA Rourke and Deputy DA Steve Wrenn flew to Aberdeen to talk to Shanann's family. The two spent several days in the Rzucek kitchen, discussing how the case could drag on for years with appeals if Watts was convicted and sentenced to the death penalty.

Rourke cited the case of nineteen-year-old Nathan

Dunlap, who in 1993 had shot and killed four employees and seriously injured another at a Chuck E. Cheese restaurant in Aurora, Colorado. Dunlap had been found guilty of four counts of first-degree murder and attempted murder in 1996 and sentenced to death. He is still alive on death row.

"We spent quite a bit of time with the Rzucek family talking about . . . the realities of the death penalty," recalled Rourke. "We explained to them the extraordinary delays that currently exist in the state of Colorado. We discussed all the possible consequences, delays, penalties . . . and they were very strongly in favor of a resolution in this case short of the death penalty."

Finally the Rzuceks agreed to a plea deal, so they could have closure and move on with their lives.

"Sandi said it very, very poignantly to me," said Rourke, "She said, 'He made the choice to take those lives, but I don't want to be in the position to take his.'"

They also discussed forcing Watts to confess what had really happened as part of the plea deal, but decided he would probably lie.

"The Rzuceks were of the opinion," said Rourke, "that he would never be able to give us a full version—just because of who he is. He would never tell us the truth."

On Saturday, October 27, Chris Watts's family held their own memorial service by the graves of Shanann, Bella, and Celeste in Bethesda Cemetery in Aberdeen. Ronnie Watts had first secured Frank Rzucek's permission to do so.

"We had a bunch of my family," said Ronnie, "and we brought three wreaths out there for the girls and a little statue of a dog that looked just like Dieter. It was beautiful."

A Pentecostal preacher officiated at the service, and a female member of the congregation sang some of their favorite hymns by the graves, where the family had put up photographs of their granddaughters.

Cindy had bought a digital recorder from Walmart to record the service so her son could hear it later, but it malfunctioned.

"We just figured it was CeCe messing around," said Cindy.

Late Friday afternoon, November 2, Ronnie Watts received a call from the Weld County DA's Office, asking him to fly out to Colorado as soon as possible.

"They said Chris was taking a plea deal," recalled Ronnie. "I said, 'What kind of plea deal?' And they said Chris would answer all our questions when we get there."

The DA's Office also issued a media alert that Chris Watts would be in court on Tuesday afternoon, November 6, for a thirty-minute status conference. When reporters called to find out why the conference had been brought forward from the originally scheduled November 19, there was no further comment.

The following Monday morning, Ronnie, Cindy, and their daughter, Jamie, flew to Denver, feeling uneasy about the plea deal. They still believed that Shanann had killed her children and could not understand why Chris was taking the blame.

They arrived at Weld County Jail in late evening. They were told they could talk to him one at a time for thirty minutes, through a handheld telephone and a monitor. With him were his attorneys, John Walsh and Kathryn Herold. According to Cindy, who had not seen her son since his arrest, the family were told not to discuss the plea deal with him.

Ronnie went in first and made small talk, without mentioning Chris's pleading guilty. Then Cindy went in and immediately asked why he had accepted the plea deal if he had not killed Bella and Celeste.

"And he looked at his lawyers and then looked at me," said Cindy. "You could tell by the way he was moving his mouth that he just wanted to cry. He said, 'Mom, this was my decision.'"

Then a member of his defense team told Cindy to change the subject or the visit would end.

"I wasn't able to say anything else to him about it," she said. "So I talked to him about Bella and CeCe's memorial service that we had for them. He wasn't crying. He asked what pictures did we use and what songs, and you could see how he was trying to hold back tears."

At 2:00 P.M. on Tuesday, November 6, Chris Watts was led into Weld County Court in handcuffs and shackles, wearing a bulletproof vest. Shanann's family sat on one side of the courtroom and Chris Watts's family on the other. It was the first time they had been under one roof in many years. Frankie and Jamie, who had once been close, made eye contact, but the two sets of parents did not look at each other.

Judge Marcello Kopcow then read out each of the nine charges against Chris: three charges of first-degree murder after deliberation, two counts of first-degree murder of a child under the age of twelve in a position of trust, an unlawful termination of a pregnancy, and three counts of tampering with a deceased human body. Watts wept as he said, "Guilty," to each one.

In a shaky voice, Watts told the judge that he accepted the plea deal, to serve life in prison without parole, and was satisfied with his defense representation.

Judge Kopcow then set sentencing for 10:00 A.M. on November 19.

After the hearing, DA Rourke held a press conference, with the Rzucek family sitting in the front row.

"I hope there will be a sense of closure," he said. "I know that will never be fully realized because obviously the tragedy that sits before us today is a loss of four beautiful lives. No matter what happens . . . we can't get them back."

A reporter asked if Watts had now revealed what really happened.

"I don't know the answer to that question," said Rourke. "We've talked a lot about whether we would require him to come forward and give us what we believe to be a complete, accurate, and truthful statement. But I think all of those who were involved never truly believed that he would give us an accurate statement.

"What I can tell you most affirmatively today by what happened in the courtroom is, the spotlight that he tried to shine on Shanann falsely, incorrectly, and frankly a flat-out lie, has been corrected. The spotlight shines directly where it belongs . . . on him."

That night Frankie Rzucek posted on Facebook, "Guilty on all charges. Now the disgusting people of this world can leave my family and I the f*** alone."

Chris Watts's family were devastated, believing he had been "railroaded" into accepting the plea deal and that they should have been consulted. They also questioned why their son had never been psychiatrically evaluated after such a horrendous crime.

"They never did any kind of evaluations," said his father, "and said they had no reason to. It was a triple homicide [so] he should have had some type of mental test or evaluation."

When the family got back to North Carolina, Cindy started calling TV stations to plead their case.

"He's not a monster," she told ABC affiliate WTVD. "There's not one person that you can talk to that will say anything bad about this kid. He was normal."

Ronnie said he was supporting his son one hundred percent. "It's hard for me to believe he would hurt them girls. I just want the truth of what really happened. If he did it all, I can live with it, and if he didn't, I want him to fight."

Cindy said that Shanann was "more capable" of killing the two girls than her son. "Christopher, I don't see him capable at all, but if something happened that night and that did happen, God forbid if it did happen, what was the trigger? Why? What happened? I just want the truth, because he's not the sociopath next door."

After seeing the interview, Frank and Sandi Rzucek leaped to their daughter's defense, saying she was a faithful wife and a loving mother.

"Their false statements," they said, "however hurtful and inaccurate, will never alter the truth about Shanann and will never alter the truth about the crimes committed by their son, Chris Watts."

On Friday, November 16—three days before Chris Watts's sentencing—Nikki Kessinger finally broke her silence. She gave an exclusive interview to *Denver Post* reporter Elise Schmelzer in Kessinger's attorney's office and posed for a photograph.

"I don't think there is a logical explanation for what he did," she said. "It's a senseless act, and it's horrific."

Kessinger said their brief affair had ruined her life, and that she was being hounded by internet strangers after being named on social media.

"We had just met. I barely knew him." She said she had thought he was going through a divorce and played down their relationship, saying they only saw each other four or five times a week and had never discussed long-term plans.

41

"YOU HEARTLESS MONSTER"

Early Monday morning, November 19, a line of people gathered outside the Weld County District courthouse for Chris Watts's sentencing. A dusting of snow covered the sidewalks, and a line of news trucks were ready to broadcast the sentencing live.

The sentencing—exactly ninety-eight days after the murders—had been moved to the larger Division 16 courtroom, to accommodate all the journalists and members of the public who wished to see the final act in this high-profile case.

Ronnie and Cindy Watts had flown in on Saturday, and Judge Kopcow was allowing them to address the court under the Victims' Rights Act. It was also agreed that the Rzuceks would go in first and take their seats, before the Watts family entered. After sentencing the Rzuceks would leave first so there would be no contact between the families.

Wearing orange prison garb and in shackles, Chris Watts sat between his public defenders, John Walsh and Kathryn Herold. Across from them sat DA Michael Rourke, Deputy DA Steve Wrenn, and Lead Detective Dave Baumhover.

At 10:00 A.M. Judge Kopcow brought the court to order. "Let me first say that I realize the sentencing hearing is emotional for many of us. And I expect your behavior [to be] appropriate."

The district attorney then entered twenty-one photographs of Shanann, Bella, and Celeste as sentencing exhibits.

"And do you have individuals that would like to make a statement?" the judge asked him.

"I do, Your Honor. If I could first call upon Frank Rzucek."

Shanann's father, dressed in a black shirt, solemnly walked to the lectern.

"What I'd like to say to the court," he began in a voice shaking with emotion, "is that Shanann, Bella, [Celeste], and Nico were loving, caring people that loved life, that loved being around people who loved them."

Then he addressed his son-in-law, who sat behind him, with his head bowed and eyes closed. "How dare you take the lives of my daughter, Shanann, Bella, Celeste, and Nico. I trusted you to take care of them, not kill them. And they trusted you, the heartless monster, and then you take them out like trash. You disgust me.

"You carried them out of the house like trash. You bury my daughter, Shanann, and Nico in a shallow grave, and then you put Bella and Celeste in huge containers of crude oil. You heartless monster."

Fighting back tears, Frank told Watts that prison was too good for him, and that Shanann was "super-excited for justice today."

Then DA Rourke read out a statement from an ashen-faced Frankie Rzucek, who stood next to him:

"Your Honor, the past three months I've barely slept, because I've been going through a lot of different emotions. Because I did not see this coming. You went from being my brother, my sister's protector, and one of the most loved people in my family, to someone I will spend the rest of my life trying to understand.

"You don't deserve to be called a man," read Rourke, as Frankie turned to look at Watts, who was cowering at the defense table. "What kind of person slaughters the people that love them the most? I pray that you never have a moment's peace or a good night's rest in the cage you'll spend every day of your life in. A cage you are privileged to live in because my family isn't evil like you."

Finally, Shanann's mother, wearing a purple lupus ribbon, addressed the court, thanking everyone for their prayers, gifts, and cards.

"God makes no mistakes on who he puts in your life," she told the defendant. "Marriage is about love, trust, and friendship and unity. We marry for sickness and health to death do us part. Our daughter, Shanann, loved you with all of her heart. Your children loved you to the moon and back. Shanann put a crown on your head, but unfortunately, the day you took their life, God removed that crown."

Then, choking with emotion, she asked if he had seen the Father's Day video of Bella singing, "Daddy, you're my hero."

"I have no idea who gave you the right to take their lives," Sandi told him, "but I know God and his mighty angels were there at that moment to bring them home to paradise. God gives us free will, so not only did you take your family of four, you took your own life."

She told him that she had not wanted the death penalty because it was not her right to take his life. "Your life is between you and God right now, and I pray that he has mercy for you."

As she walked past her son-in-law, his lawyer John Walsh tried to comfort him.

Then Cindy and Ronnie Watts walked up to the lectern with victims' rights advocate Jean Powers, who would speak on their behalf. Later, Ronnie would say they had only met her that morning in their hotel room and thought she would only thank the judge for them.

Advocate Powers told Judge Kopcow that her clients now accepted that their son had done this, and that he was pleading guilty to all charges in return for a life sentence.

"It is his responsibility," she said. "We join the family in that we have questions. We don't know how such a thing could possibly happen or that a man that was responsible for raising his children and protecting his wife would take the steps that he did. We cannot begin to think that an explanation will ever justify it."

She said his parents had encouraged Chris to give a full confession, to try to ease the pain and suffering.

Then the defendant's mother addressed the court.

"My name is Cindy Watts. I am the grandmother of two beautiful granddaughters, Bella Marie, Celeste Cathryn Watts. I am also the mother of Christopher Watts, who I will be directing most of my statements to.

"First I'd like to begin by recognizing the absolute horror of this crime and acknowledging the devastating loss that both the Rzucek family, as well as our family, have faced."

She told the judge she still struggled to understand how and why this tragedy had occurred and stood united with the Rzuceks in their grief.

"And now to my son, Christopher. I have known you since the day you were born into this world. I have watched you grow from a quiet and sweet, curious child, who Bella reminded me so much of, into a young man who worked hard in sports and later mechanics to achieve your goals."

She told her son that she could not imagine what had

led up to this day, but would always love him uncondition-ally.

"As your mother, Chris," she said as he wept at the de-fense table, "I have always loved you and I still do. I hate what has happened. Your father and sister and I are strug-gling to understand why, but we will remain faithful as your family."

Turning around to look at him, she said, "We love you and we forgive you, Son."

Then Powers read out a statement from Ronnie Watts:

"Chris, I want to talk to you as a father and son. You are here today accepting responsibility. I want you to find peace, and today is your first step. The Bible says if we confess our sins, God is faithful and just and will forgive us. Chris, I forgive you and your sister forgives you and we will never abandon you. We love you, Dad."

Then the district attorney stood up to address Judge Kopcow. "Your Honor, there are no words to adequately describe the unimaginable tragedy that brings us before this court today. I'm not even going to try and express the horror, the pain, or the suffering that the defendant has caused to these families, to this community, and to all who are a part of this investigation."

Rourke said he now wanted to provide some new de-tails of the crime that were not in the affidavit.

"The questions that have screamed out to anyone who will listen are, Why did this have to happen? How could a seemingly normal husband and father annihilate his en-tire family? For what?"

Rourke said he didn't expect the defendant to ever re-veal what really happened, but wanted to piece together the evidence for some kind of understanding.

"And the evidence tells us this: The defendant coldly and deliberately ended four lives. Not in a fit of rage. Not by way of accident. But in a calculated and sickening manner."

Rourke told the judge that it would have taken Watts two to four minutes to strangle Shanann with his bare hands.

"The horror that she felt as the man that she loved wrapped his hands around her throat and choked the life out of her must have been unimaginable."

Then moving on to Bella and Celeste, Rourke ruminated on what they must have felt as their own father "was snuffing out their lives.

"They both died from smothering. The man seated to my right smothered his daughters. Why? Imagine the horror in Bella's mind as her father took her last breaths away."

Rourke then revealed how Bella had desperately fought for her life, rupturing her frenulum and biting her tongue multiple times.

"The defendant then methodically and calmly loaded their bodies into his work truck. Not in a hasty or disorganized way. He was seen from the neighbor's doorbell camera backing his truck into the driveway, going back and forth into the house three different times. One time for each of the bodies."

He told the judge how the defendant had driven the bodies of his wife and daughters to the remote Cervi 319 oil well, where he hoped they would never be found.

"In one final measure of disrespect for the family he once had, he insured they would not be together even in death. He disposed of them in different locations. He buried Shanann and Nico in a shallow grave away from the oil tanks. Bella and Celeste were thrown away in the oil tanks . . . different tanks so these little girls wouldn't be together in death."

He described how Watts had forcibly pushed Bella's

and Celeste's bodies feetfirst through a hatch just eight inches in diameter into the tanks.

"Bella had scratches on her left buttocks from being shoved through this hole. A tuft of blond hair was found on the edge of one of these hatches. The defendant told investigators that Bella's tank seemed emptier than CeCe's, because of the sound that the splashes made. These were his daughters."

Once his family were reported missing, the defendant started spinning a web of deception, appearing on television to ask for help in locating them.

"What is striking about this case, Your Honor, beyond the horrors of what I've already described to you, is the number of collateral victims that he created by his actions. While he stood in front of TV cameras asking for the safe return of his family, scores of law enforcement officers, neighbors, friends, and family scoured the area. They fretted for their safe return. They texted him begging for any information and sending him their best wishes. All the while he hid what he had done."

The defendant's motive was simple, said Rourke. He wanted a fresh start with his new girlfriend, although that hardly justified what he had done.

"Get a divorce. You don't annihilate your family and throw them away like garbage."

Rourke then demanded the maximum sentence under the plea agreement, asking for the life sentences for all the murders and the termination of a pregnancy to run consecutively.

"Four lives were lost at the hands of the defendant on August thirteenth. Prison for the remainder of his life is exactly where he belongs for murdering his entire family."

Next, public defender Kathryn Herold briefly addressed the judge on behalf of her client:

"Your Honor, Mr. Watts has asked us to share this morning that he is devastated by all of this. And although he understands that words are hollow at this point, he is sincerely sorry for all of this."

Finally, Judge Kopcow asked the defendant if he wished to make a statement.

"No, sir," replied Watts, shaking his head.

"So the court has considered the arguments made by the attorney," said the judge. "The court's going to find that the plea agreement is fair and reasonable under the circumstances."

He described the case as a "senseless crime," and the most "inhumane and vicious" one he had seen in his seventeen years as a judge.

"Nothing less than the maximum sentence would be appropriate," he told the defendant. "And anything less than the maximum sentence would depreciate the seriousness of this offense."

Chris Watts was sentenced to life in prison with no possibility of parole and ordered to pay court costs and restitution. The nine counts would run consecutively, meaning Watts would serve a total of three life sentences plus eighty-four years.

Straight after the sentencing, the Weld County coroner finally released the autopsy reports, showing that Shanann's blood alcohol level was 0.128. Later that afternoon at a press conference, DA Rourke explained that was the reason the autopsy had been sealed.

"I want to be abundantly and very, very clear about this," he told reporters. "This does not mean that she consumed alcohol, nor that she was intoxicated. That blood alcohol level is very, very consistent with normal human decomposition, based upon the location and the manner that Shanann and Nico's bodies were buried."

Taking questions, he was asked whether Nikki Kessinger had ever been a suspect.

"She originally came forward and spoke to investigators on her own volition," he said. "We don't have any reason to believe that she had any prior knowledge or involvement in the death of Shanann, Bella, Celeste, and Nico."

That same morning, attorneys for the Rzucek family filed a civil action against Chris Watts for punitive damages under Colorado's Wrongful Death statute, to ensure he wouldn't receive anything from Shanann's estate.

"Defendant is a felonious killer," it read. "As a consequence of his actions, he is prohibited from maintaining any estate action or otherwise profiting from his crimes."

A week later, Ronnie Watts claimed he had been intimidated at the sentencing, and the statement read out on his behalf by the victims' advocate did not reflect his views.

"I wasn't actually paying much attention to what she was saying," he said, "until I went back and watched the video. We didn't agree to any of that at all."

Ronnie said he still believed his son was innocent of killing Bella and Celeste. "I don't think he'd ever do anything to hurt them girls. Until he tells me something different, I ain't going to believe it."

At the end of November, the first of three large caches of discovery was released by the Weld County DA's Office. Tucked away in the two thousand pages of evidence were Nikki Kessinger's phone records, revealing she had searched the internet for Chris and Shanann Watts nine months before the affair started.

When a Crime Online reporter checked with DA Rourke, he confirmed it was true.

"It is not a typographical error in the report," said Rourke. "[The detectives] are reporting what was contained in the data from her phone. I don't know the answer to the question of why or how those dates ended up in her phone."

42

A CONFESSION

The first week of December, after ten days of evaluation in the Denver Reception and Diagnostic Center, Chris Watts was secretly moved to the Dodge Correctional Institution in Waupun, Wisconsin, for his own safety. He was driven one thousand miles east in an unmarked van, stopping only at sheriff's offices in Nebraska and Iowa to use the bathroom.

Over the next few weeks he settled into a routine. He was placed in the maximum-security prison's evaluation unit, with a cell to himself, a shower, and access to a TV room. He worked out in the gym three days a week and played basketball with the other inmates.

In the next cell to his was Jake Thomas Patterson, who had abducted thirteen-year-old Jayme Closs from her family home in October 2018, after killing her parents. Twenty-one-year-old Patterson then held Jayme captive for eighty-eight days in a cabin in rural Wisconsin before she escaped and summoned help.

Like Watts, Patterson, who had been sentenced to two life sentences plus an additional forty years, was also being kept away from other inmates for his own protection. Soon the two convicted murderers became friends. Every night Chris would read him verses from the Bible and then discuss them.

"When they'd go out for rec, the other prisoners would start yelling at them," said Cindy Watts, "and [Patterson would] start yelling things back. Christopher told him, 'Don't do that. Just calm down.'"

After Patterson was transferred to another prison, Ronnie Watts began a correspondence with his parents, as they were both in the same situation.

"They were devastated," said Cindy, "just like we were devastated, because we don't understand what happened to our kids."

Every night, Chris Watts spoke to his parents for an hour, mainly talking about finding God and helping the other inmates with religious instruction.

"He knows the Bible inside and out," said Cindy. "He gives me four scriptures every night and I read them in the morning."

He put up photographs of Shanann, Bella, and Celeste on the wall of his cell, which he would talk to every night. He also wrote them letters, which he sent to his parents.

"We go to the gravesite and read them out," said Cindy. "They're beautiful letters that brought tears to my eyes. I never knew my son [because] he never expressed emotions. It was hard for him to verbalize, but he can write it down on paper."

The notorious inmate was also receiving letters from female admirers from all over the world, sending him sexy photographs.

"I know I'm a stranger but I care about you and your situation," wrote one young woman. "I can't help it. Is there anything that you need? Please let me know and don't be shy."

Another told him she was going to write him a letter a day until he responded.

"I just want to be your friend and talk every now and

then," she told him. "If you do write me back I'd be the happiest girl alive."

On February 18, 2019, at 7:45 A.M., Chris Watts was brought into the computer room at Dodge Correctional Institution, where Agents Grahm Coder and Tammy Lee and Detective Dave Baumhover were waiting. They had secretly arranged to come to Wisconsin to try to get Watts to tell them what really happened, and give the Rzuceks some closure.

"Hey, Chris, do you remember us?" they asked.

"Errr . . . yes." He looked puzzled. "I just didn't for a moment there."

"Good to see you," said Agent Coder, as if greeting an old friend.

"How are you doing?" asked Lee.

"I'm okay, how about you?" said Watts.

Agent Coder assured Watts that his case was now closed, and there would be no further charges. Coder explained that they all worked for different law enforcement agencies and had met during the investigation, staying in touch after it concluded.

"We keep talking to each other," said Coder, "and we've separately said, 'Did Chris seem unique to you?' And we keep having that conversation and we can't quite put our finger on it. Right?"

Coder told Watts that his life leading up to the murders was interesting.

"And for me personally," said Coder, "one of the last things you told me was, 'Grahm, I'm sorry that I started lying to you.' And that's stuck with me. I've never, ever worked a case like this where someone told me that. You know, as I walked away, I thought, 'Chris is different. Chris is a little bit unique.'"

Coder said they never got to ask a "thousand questions," which was why they'd decided to visit him in Wisconsin.

"I think you'll like it," Coder told him. "I think it will give you some closure. Are you available to talk to us?"

"I am." Watts perked up. "Definitely."

"We're going to talk about some hard issues today," Coder continued, "but I don't intend to take you to a dark place. I hope when we're done, you'll feel better. I hope it will be therapeutic."

Over the next five hours, the three law enforcement officers were friendly and chatty, first asking how Watts was coping in prison. He told them it was far better here than Colorado.

They also asked about Trent Bolte, who had claimed to have had a sexual relationship with him.

"No," said Watts, "I've never met the guy."

"Grahm and I interviewed him," said Lee.

"A waste of our lives," Coder chimed in.

Then Coder brought up the "hardest subject," asking what had really happened after Shanann arrived home from Arizona.

"So nothing really happened that night," Watts replied. "She got home at two and I felt her get into bed."

He said he felt her "stirring around" and had a feeling she knew he was cheating because of the high restaurant credit-card charge.

"And she started rubbing her hand on me, and we ended up having sex. But I guess that was more like a test."

He said that during sex something had gone off in his head. "It was maybe like a trigger point. You have to push a button on a bomb and it just blows up."

They had then gone to sleep for a couple of hours, and after getting dressed for work, he came back into the bedroom to tell her he wanted a separation. Shanann accused him of seeing somebody else, but he wouldn't admit it.

"I just felt guilty. More guilty than ever before."

He said they had spoken for about half an hour and he asked her to cancel their trip to Aspen the next weekend.

Then he got back in bed and climbed on top of her, straddling her waist. She told him to get off, so he didn't hurt the baby. She then told him she was leaving and he'd never see her or the kids again.

Upon hearing this, he put his hands around her neck and strangled her.

"It's like the whole . . . everything that happened that morning, I just don't know. Like, I try to go back in my head and I'm just like . . . I didn't want to do this, but I did it. And everything kind of like . . ."

"Did you feel like you had to?" asked Coder.

"I just felt like it was . . . I don't even want to say I felt like I had to. I just felt like there was already something in my mind that was implanted that I was going to do it . . . and I had no control over it."

"You'd never thought about it before?"

"Like in the sentencing hearing, that prosecutor said it takes two to four minutes for something like that to happen. Why couldn't I just let go? I didn't."

"Was it like feeling like it was in motion and you just couldn't stop it?" asked Detective Baumhover.

"Yeah. It's like, I don't even want to know what she saw when she looked back at me. Honestly."

"Did you look at her?" Lee questioned. "What was she doing?"

"She wasn't fighting. Maybe she was praying."

He said that Bella had then walked in and asked what was wrong with her mother. He told her that she wasn't feeling well.

"I put Shanann in that sheet that you found at the site and carried her downstairs and backed the truck up."

As he had carried her downstairs, her foot had hit each

step, waking up Celeste, who came out to see what was going on. Then, as Bella trailed behind asking what he was doing to Mommy, he had loaded Shanann's body in the back of the truck.

"Was Bella alive when you guys get in the truck?" asked Coder.

"Yeah."

"Oh, okay, what happened?"

"We went back up," Watts said, becoming emotional. "I don't really want to talk about this part. Those were my kids. I don't want to talk about that night. Every time I see pictures of them I don't know how this could have happened. Being a dad was the best part of my life. I took it all away."

"That's the hardest part for us, Chris," said Tammy Lee, "is that we see those videos . . . and that love that you had for your girls. And it's hard to understand how a dad who's given piggyback rides and making snacks, and watching princess movies and those kinds of things . . . how you get to that point."

"Something else was controlling me that day. And I had no control over it to fight back."

Agent Lee asked what had happened after the girls got in his truck, with their blankets and stuffed toys.

"It's like forty-five minutes to an hour ride out there. I'm just kind of nervous, shaking . . . not knowing what's going to happen."

During the drive, he said, the girls lay next to each other, falling asleep. Bella said that it smelled.

"So what happened when you got out there?" asked Lee.

"I took Shanann out to a place off to the side." He said he had left the girls in the back of the truck.

"And then what happened after that?" said Lee.

"CeCe was first. She had a blue blanket. A Yankee

blanket. I put the blanket over her head. . . . I strangled her right there in the back seat."

"What was Bella doing?" asked Lee.

"She was sitting beside her. She didn't say anything."

Then Coder asked what he was thinking when he was smothering Celeste.

"I wasn't. If I was thinking, this wouldn't have happened."

He said he had then "pulled" Celeste's body out of the truck, while Bella helplessly watched from inside.

"What did you do with her?" asked Coder.

"I put her in the tank."

"So she went into the tank," Coder asked, "and Bella was still in the back of the truck alive?"

"Yeah."

"With regard to that tank. Did you bring up CeCe, put her down, open the hatch?"

"Brought her up . . . opened the hatch."

"And you put her in?"

"Yeah."

"And so she went in feetfirst?" asked Coder.

"Yeah."

"Did you have to move her around a bit to get her in there?"

"I think so. I didn't have to hit her or anything like that."

"And then close the hatch?"

"Yeah."

Watts said he had then returned to his truck for Bella.

"She said, 'What happened to CeCe?' She asked, 'Will the same thing happen to me as CeCe?'"

"Okay, so Bella's pretty smart," said Coder. "How did she sound when she asked you that, Chris?"

"She had that soft voice she always has," he sobbed.

"And what exactly did she say?"

"She said, '[Will] exactly the same thing happen to me

as CeCe?' And then I said, 'Yes.' She said, 'No, Daddy!'
And that's the last thing she said. I put that blanket over
her, too, and did the same thing."

Agent Coder then asked why Watts had put the girls in
separate tanks, and he said there was no reason.

"Bella was a little bit bigger," observed Coder, "was she
harder to get in?"

"It felt like it a little bit."

Watts said that after disposing of his daughters, he buried Shanann's body.

"I cleared away some weeds. [I] had a shovel, a rake,
and a Weedwacker, as far as our tools in the truck."

"And so once she's buried, then what?" asked Baumhover.

"That's when people start showing up."

They finished in late afternoon, chatting about the heavy
snowfall that day. Watts told the detectives he hoped to
get a job in the kitchen, saying his newfound relationship
with God had helped him adapt to his new life behind bars.

"It was good to see you guys," he told them, when a
warden arrived to take him back to his cell.

"It was good to see you, too," said Agent Lee. "Take
care of yourself."

"Thank you, much appreciated," Coder told him.

"Have a safe flight," said Watts.

EPILOGUE

A year after the Watts murders, many investigators who worked on the case were still trying to come to terms with it. Soon after returning from the Dodge Correctional Institution, Lead Detective Dave Baumhover began suffering from post-traumatic stress disorder (PTSD). One day he was eating in a Phoenix restaurant when two little girls came in, and he had to walk out, as they reminded him of Bella and Celeste.

In March he was diagnosed with PTSD and hasn't been back to the Frederick Police Department since. He may never be able to return to duty.

The detective, who had worked the Watts case from the very beginning, had gone to Wisconsin for closure. After learning the terrible truth, he lay on his hotel bed, unable to pick up his wife's phone calls. Back in Frederick, he started having panic attacks, and when he went back to work, the flashbacks became more frequent and he couldn't sleep. After his PTSD diagnosis, he entered counseling and is now on workers' compensation.

CBI agent Tammy Lee is also in therapy. A couple of days after seeing Bella's body recovered from the oil tank, the experienced investigator broke down at a hair salon sobbing. Every time she saw mothers with kids, she would start crying, as it reminded her of all the Facebook videos of Bella and Celeste.

"I felt like I knew them," she told *The Denver Post*. "I've been to many homicides of children. This one was different. I felt like I knew what they sounded like. I knew what they looked like when they played and how they sounded when they giggled. I felt like I was mourning their deaths."

Weld County DA Michael Rourke also has recurring nightmares about oil tanks. Every time he drives past an oil field, the memories come flooding back.

"I see those little girls," he explained. "Their faces. And their names. And then every time I think about them, the next thought in my mind is about my own daughter. This changed all of us."

On July 17, 2019, Celeste Watts would have celebrated her fourth birthday. Her father wrote her a birthday letter from prison, which his parents read over her grave.

"Hey Super girl," it began. "Happy Birthday. Four years old today. I have a picture of you at Bella's second birthday party and you were so tiny. I could tell by your expression you wanted to be splashing around like your sister. Ironically, I have another picture of you the next summer in the neighborhood pool flying into my arms with the biggest smile on your face. You were always flying around so the nickname Super Girl seemed to fit nicely."

He told his youngest daughter that she was "Daddy's Girl" because she was stuck to him like glue and he loved it. "Every picture I have you are in my arms or on my lap or holding my hand," he wrote.

"It doesn't matter what you were doing or what you were playing with, you would drop everything and dart across the room and tackle my leg. I would pick you up and your head would instantly go on my shoulder. I was your safe haven."

Writing from his cell, he appeared detached from reality and oblivious to what had happened, as he described lovingly preparing her for bed by reading her favorite book, *That's Not My Lion.*

"You loved all your blankies in the right order, and you couldn't go to sleep without at least two books. If it were up to you I would be reading your whole collection in a room. I would read every book in your room a million times over if it meant being able to see you again."

He finished by writing that he knew she was now in the everlasting arms of Jesus Christ and would never trade that to come to Earth.

"You're in a place of pure joy and pure love that brings me comfort," he told her.

"I miss you so much CeCe. Tell Bella, Nico and Mommy that I love them and miss them so much. I know you hear me talk to all of you everyday and that brings a smile to my face. I love you all to the moon and back, always and forever.

"Love, Daddy."

In the last week of September 2019, Ronnie and Cindy Watts visited their son in the Dodge Correctional Institution. Over two days they spent ten hours with him in the visitors' room, seeking answers to what had happened in hopes of getting some closure.

"We had so many questions," said his mother. "But when I left, I was more confused than I was before."

Over the past few months, Watts had been befriended by a sixty-five-year-old Christian Center worker called

Cheryln Cadle. They first became pen pals before she started visiting him to talk about the Bible and his recent conversion to God. Then he began writing her letters, giving a totally new account of the murders, which she turned into a book called *Letters from Christopher.*

He wrote that he had already decided to murder his family when he put Bella and Celeste to bed that Sunday night before Shanann came home. He now claimed to have first smothered Bella and then Celeste with a pillow, before killing Shanann.

"After Shanann had passed," he wrote, "Bella and Celeste woke back up. I'm not sure how they woke back up. Bella's eyes were bruised and both girls looked like they had been through trauma."

He had then taken them to Cervi 319 and smothered them again, before dropping their bodies in the oil tanks to make sure they were dead.

"This is a third confession," said his mother. "He's told us so many different stories now, and I don't know what to believe anymore. But one time he told us that he would take [what really happened] to the grave with him."

A month later, Chris Watts agreed to pay the Rzucek family $6 million, although it is unlikely that they will ever receive the money. A civil court judge had previously ordered him to pay $1 million each for the deaths of Shanann, Bella, and Celeste, as well as $3 million for the Rzuceks' emotional pain.

"The Rzucek family has not been the same since August 13, 2018," stated a motion filed by the Rzuceks' attorney. "They have suffered with anger, loneliness, sadness, and depression. Following the discovery of their daughter and grandchildren's murders, they were unable to work, leave the house, or even eat."

The filing also revealed how the family had endured

online attacks and death threats from conspiracy theorists, who falsely claim that Shanann was responsible for the killings.

"They have lost nearly all trust in people and humanity," wrote their attorney.